THE COURT COMEDIES OF
JOHN LYLY
A Study in Allegorical Dramaturgy

THE COURT
COMEDIES OF

John Lyly

*A STUDY
IN ALLEGORICAL
DRAMATURGY*

BY PETER SACCIO

PRINCETON, NEW JERSEY
PRINCETON UNIVERSITY PRESS
1969

Publication of this book has been aided
by the Whitney Darrow Publication Reserve Fund
of Princeton University Press

This book has been composed in Caslon Old Face.

Printed in the United States of America

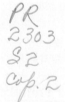

ACKNOWLEDGMENTS

I wish to thank the Woodrow Wilson Foundation for their generous dissertation fellowship, which supported me when I was writing much of the first version of this book. I am grateful to the staffs of the Firestone, Marquand, and Speer Libraries at Princeton University, and the Baker Library at Dartmouth College, for their helpfulness. The Research Committee at Dartmouth provided me with funds for clerical assistance.

I am heavily indebted to my teachers and colleagues at various universities. Charles Prouty introduced me to Lyly. James Cox, Robert Hill, Scott Morgan, and Michael Rewa have read and commented on portions of the manuscript or discussed with me the problems that it raises. It has been particularly valuable and enjoyable to have Robert Hunter's assistance, not only on this book, but also in our common endeavor to teach Shakespeare and the Elizabethan drama.

My largest debts are to Alan Downer and Thomas Roche. No pupil of Professor Downer can fail to learn from the penetration, clarity, and wit of his courses and published writings on drama of all periods. No pupil of Professor Roche can fail to benefit from his brilliant teaching of Spenser, to be grateful for his "vision" and for his unfailing readiness to assist and advise. To them, my warmest thanks.

PETER SACCIO

Sanborn House
Dartmouth College
August, 1968

v

CONTENTS

I didn't know whether I was looking
at a noisy farce, a spook show, or
another damned allegory, which indeed
it turned out to be.

—Theater review in *The New Yorker*

THE COURT COMEDIES OF
JOHN LYLY

A Study in Allegorical Dramaturgy

INTRODUCTION

You that with allegorie's curious frame,
Of other's children changelings use to make,
With me those paines for God's sake do not take:
I list not dig so deepe for brasen fame.
                                —*Astrophil and Stella*

THIS BOOK does not attempt to replace any children with changelings. It does, however, deal with allegory and takes some pains to recognize the nature and function of several highly curious frames devised by a playwright who sought, if not brazen fame, at least the practical rewards of royal pleasure. The frames in question are the dramatic structures of five comedies that John Lyly wrote for the entertainment of Queen Elizabeth and her Court in the 1580's: *Campaspe, Sapho and Phao, Gallathea, Endimion,* and *Love's Metamorphosis.* Aside from the fact that these plays were written by the same man for production under the same circumstances by the same or similar actors (the Children of the Chapel Royal and the Children of Paul's), there are three distinguishing characteristics that bind them into a group susceptible of critical treatment.

First, all but one employ the classical gods as major characters. In this respect they are quite unlike the public Elizabethan drama, in which the gods rarely, and then only briefly, appear. The exception in the group is *Campaspe*: no god appears, but the classical characters, especially the half-historical, half-legendary Alexander, provide some of the same associations.

Secondly, these are plays of slight plot. They do not exploit the narrative potential of the stories that are their sources. Here lies the real curiosity, in the modern sense of the word, of these comedies. We ordinarily expect to find a narrative in a play, to witness a conflict leading through a variety of causally related episodes to a resolution. This is a deliberately loose definition of dramatic narrative; it allows for the Greek practice of focus on the final moments of a myth, for the Elizabethan use of romantic plot followed from beginning to end, and for the tightly worked cause-effect articulation and the retrospective action of Ibsen and his disciples. The Court comedies, however, are almost completely static. Each revolves around one or more situations that are not developed in any way deserving the name of plot. Little takes place, and the events that do occur have the limited dimension of anecdotes. Such a kind of dramaturgy might be called "situational."

The dramaturgical techniques used in these comedies have not been adequately described. The treatment of Lyly in the standard histories of Elizabethan drama is largely confined to lists of elements recurring in his plays and to discussion of his influence on Shakespeare. The two extended treatments of Lyly's dramaturgy, those of T. W. Baldwin and G. K. Hunter, also leave something to be desired. Baldwin's attempt, in *Shakspere's Five-Act Structure* (Urbana, Ill., 1947), to demonstrate Lyly's adherence to a Terentian scheme is misguided. Except in *Mother Bombie*, Lyly did not write anything like a Roman comedy. Baldwin is obliged to invent narrative lines, causal connections, and motivations in order to make Lyly fit the Roman scheme, and even then Lyly appears a very dim shadow of Roman comedy with a completely un-Roman effect. For example, Baldwin isolates Alexander's conflict between love and war in *Campaspe* to provide a narrative line with the usual Roman cruces. This conflict actually occurs in only three scenes of the play, and a great deal else happens that bears no causal relation to it. In discussing *Gallathea* Baldwin invents an episode in order to find a narrative: he says that in I.ii Diana's nymph insults Cupid, thereby motivating Cupid's depredations among other chaste nymphs. There is really no action at all in this scene, merely a statement of position by the adherents of love and chastity.[1]

G. K. Hunter's *John Lyly: The Humanist as Courtier* (Cambridge, Mass., 1962) is an excellent book and one to which I shall make many references. With welcome briskness, Hunter discards the older classifications of Lyly's plays, those inept and confusing categories of "historical," "allegorical," "pastoral," and "realistic" made current by R. Warwick Bond in *The Complete Works of John Lyly* (Oxford, 1902). He replaces these labels with division into two groups, "unification round debate" and "harmonious variety." Unfortunately, his treatment of the plays, in spite of many shrewd remarks and much apt appreciative comment, is marked by a peculiar distance from them. He has little to say about their content except as it relates to the Court in which they were presented. This distance is reflected in his two categories. "Debate" does not very closely describe *Endimion*, for example; the debate between love and friendship occupies one important scene, but only that scene. The label "harmonious variety" applies to almost any good Elizabethan play, given Elizabethan panoramic scope and multiple plotting. It is necessary to go beyond Hunter and grapple more directly with

---

[1] My disagreement with Baldwin is elaborated, with full references, in the chapters devoted to *Campaspe* and *Gallathea*. The actionless quality of Lyly's plays has been well stressed in an article coming to hand after this book went to press, Michael Best, "Lyly's Static Drama," *Renaissance Drama*, n.s. I (1968), 75–86.

the elements of the plays themselves, with acts, scenes, speeches, props, images, themes.

Thirdly, all these plays have strong overtones of allegory. In a sense this follows naturally from their plotlessness. In the broadest possible definition, allegory is a form of literature in which thematic interest predominates over mimetic interest.[2] Materials for plot, the arrangement and relationships of characters, are not exploited to the end of presenting a causally connected chain of events that imitates the actions of real men. Rather, our attention is directed to the significance of events and characters as they suggest concepts and are relatable in the world of ideas.

This definition of allegory, however, satisfactory as it may be for grouping large quantities of literature, is too blunt a tool for close examination of literary works. This book aims at descriptions of allegory suitable for Lyly's comedies. Obviously, such descriptions cannot be given in an Introduction: they will appear as we go along. Certain principles, however, may be noted here.

In the morality plays, allegory may be called a form. A morality operates by personifying and setting into dramatic motion certain abstractions that belong to a schematic description of life. Virtues and vices strive for the allegiance of everyman. For all the human feeling, the touches of characterization, the realistic localization in that wonderfully vital drama that flourished well into the sixteenth century, the moralities are thoroughly and radically allegorical. They are practically meaningless without the moral names of the characters.[3] The allegorical meaning, in other

---

[2] This is essentially the definition given in the packed, provocative discussion by Northrop Frye, *Anatomy of Criticism* (Princeton, 1957), pp. 89–92, and expanded by Angus Fletcher, *Allegory: The Theory of a Symbolic Mode* (Ithaca, 1964), Introduction and pp. 304ff.

[3] This is a descriptive statement, not an evaluative one. I am not

words, is the rationale for the play from its very inception. It can be said that a morality play *is* an allegory.

It cannot be said that a Lyly play *is* an allegory in the same sense. Allegory in the Court drama is a mode of meaning, not a form. The fable does not arise from a prior intellectual scheme. The situations in Lyly are not abstract: they are tales from history and myth. As Lyly develops them into plays with highly wrought artistry ("curious" in the Elizabethan sense), they take on allegorical dimension. That is, the reader or spectator receives a series of suggestions from patterns in the action, from details in the language, from manipulation and modification of well-known Renaissance symbols, and these suggestions may constitute an allegorical meaning. We have no direct evidence as to how soon in the process of composition ideas began to influence the nature of the play. Lyly's highly artificial construction suggests that he worked rather abstractly.[4] Nonetheless, *we* must begin with the literal situation. Thus allegory here is not a form but a mode of literary operation, a stimulation of larger senses of meaning from the literal sense of the play, an interaction between the play and its audience.

I am heeding here the lessons taught us by recent investigations of non-dramatic allegory in the Renaissance, particularly allegory in Spenser. Rosemond Tuve and Thomas P. Roche have eloquently stressed the primacy of the literal sense of the narrative in *The Faerie Queene* and the necessity of respect for the fiction, warning against the distortion wrought by casually constructing equational re-

---

trying to say that morality characters are unreal: to the medieval mind they had a greater reality than particular embodiments would have had.

[4] M. C. Bradbrook compares Lyly's supposed procedure with Shakespeare's on this point in *Shakespeare and Elizabethan Poetry* (London, 1951), pp. 46–47.

lationships between single elements in the poem and external ideas.[5] As Roche remarks, "The heresy of the paraphrase applies as much to allegory as to other forms of poetic expression."[6] I am particularly anxious to distinguish my kind of allegorical reading from two sorts of allegorizing that have been popular in Lyly studies. From N. J. Halpin's *Oberon's Vision in the Midsummer-Night's Dream* (London, 1843) to Josephine Waters Bennett's "Oxford and *Endimion*" (*PMLA*, LVII [1942], 354–369), criticism has pointed out a variety of historical or topical allegories in Lyly's plays. These interpretations are never very satisfactory, although some allusions may be correctly identified. Occasionally Lyly has been said to intend meanings that would have been tactless in a courtier-playwright seeking favor; frequently we know too little of the minutiae of the Court intrigues supposedly transcribed. Such allegories are usually merely passing glances at analogous situations, and thus provide poor interpretations of whole plays. There is a further problem involved. Representation of real events or persons in literary works requires an analogy between the literary and the historical elements. Analogies are intellectual, requiring abstractions as middle terms. The literary element figures a general or universal; the historical element is another example or particular under the aegis of that general. From this point

[5] Rosemond Tuve, *Allegorical Imagery: Some Medieval Books and Their Posterity* (Princeton, 1966), especially the chapter "Imposed Allegory." Concerning the integrity of the fiction, Miss Tuve points out (p. 222n.) that acceptance of the story as such is the equivalent in secular allegory of the claim made for the historical truth of Old Testament narrative in the primary form of Christian allegory, Biblical typology. Thomas P. Roche, Jr., *The Kindly Flame: A Study of the Third and Fourth Books of Spenser's Faerie Queene* (Princeton, 1964), especially pp. 3–31, where Roche explains in detail the ontological basis for Renaissance allegory.

[6] Roche, p. 31.

of view the historical parallel is less important than the intervening general that is thematically invoked. The fact (if it is establishable) that an historical event or person is alluded to by a literary one may thus increase our knowledge of the context of the play, but it does not increase our understanding of the play itself, since we must first understand the play in order to perceive the analogy.

The plays have also been seen as allegorical expositions of particular philosophical doctrines: for example, P. W. Long's Neoplatonic reading in "The Purport of Lyly's *Endimion*" (*PMLA*, XXIV [1909], 164–184) and Bernard F. Huppé's psychological reading in "Allegory of Love in Lyly's Court Comedies" (*ELH*, XIV [1947], 93–113). These interpretations put the cart before the horse. The playwright is seen as starting with the allegorical sense and then devising local habitation for his abstract ideas. He is a preacher and his play resembles an Aesopian fable in being designed to convey unambiguously a single point or series of points. Renaissance allegory is here robbed of its suggestiveness, its vigorous richness, and becomes an instrument for expository discourse. We are quite certain, in the main, what the author of *Everyman* meant to "say"; there is no doubt about the things we should do in order to prepare for death. We do not have this certitude about a Lyly play, and we seldom have the feeling that we are being told to believe or do specified things. The literal sense, the literary invention is primary. The allegory is a device for exploring implications and ideas, a "method of reading in which we are made to think about things we already know." [7]

[7] Rosemond Tuve, in a Christian Gauss seminar, Princeton University, May, 1959, as quoted by Roche, p. 30. The two kinds of Lyly interpretation rejected here have been grouped to be set aside with similar arguments in an all-too-brief article, J. A. Bryant, Jr., "The

Introduction

In summary, I am concerned with three major aspects of the Court comedies: their materials (mythology), their technique (situational dramaturgy), and their mode of meaning (allegory). I am not limiting, however, the term "Court comedy" to the five Lyly plays mentioned, although they are the center of the group. In varying degrees six other plays deserve the title, and they also receive attention. All of them resemble the Lyly plays in having major Olympians in the cast. In other respects they manifest modifications of the Lylian peculiarities.

Lyly's late plays *Midas* and *The Woman in the Moon* were both performed at Court, the former by Paul's and the latter apparently by an adult company. In both Lyly is abandoning what I have called situational form. Each in its own way is a blend of situational drama and narrative drama with developed plot. They are Lyly's modulation, late in his career, from his established mode of Court comedy to something nearer popular Elizabethan form.[8] George Peele's *The Arraignment of Paris* was performed at Court by the Children of the Chapel at or slightly before the time that Lyly was writing *Campaspe*. Peele, of course, went on to become a public theater dramatist; in this play, however, he constructs a combination of situa-

Nature of the Allegory in Lyly's *Endymion*," *Renaissance Papers*, Southeastern Renaissance Conference (1956), pp. 4–11. Bryant finds at the root of the doctrine-hunting approach the definition of allegory offered by C. S. Lewis in *The Allegory of Love* (Oxford, 1936), pp. 44–45. G. Wilson Knight, in his article "Lyly," *RES*, XV (1939), 146–163, has stressed the primacy of the literal situation and has demonstrated how particular passages flower with implications. Knight tends to ignore context, however, and does not discuss whole plays. He sees in Lyly, moreover, a Romantic communion with Nature and an exaltation of Hellenism over Christianity that are quite unimaginable in Renaissance Court literature.

[8] I have excluded one Lyly play from this study: *Mother Bombie*. The title-page does not mention Court performance; there are no gods in the cast; and the play is an experiment in regular Roman intrigue comedy.

8

tional and narrative dramaturgy not unlike that of the late Lyly plays.

The anonymous *Rare Triumphs of Love and Fortune* was performed at Court in 1582. It was acted, however, by the Earl of Derby's Men; it may thus have been in the public theater repertory. If the term "Court comedy" is restricted to plays composed with an eye on Court performance, this play stands only on the margin of deserving such a title. Robert Wilson's *The Cobbler's Prophecy* is an unusual work in which mortals, gods, and Muses are joined by moral personifications from the popular tradition of earlier Tudor times. It is difficult to believe that so crude a play entertained nobility, but internal evidence persuasively argues private performance. In both *The Rare Triumphs of Love and Fortune* and *The Cobbler's Prophecy* a romantic narrative is surrounded by and intermingled with the situational device of a debate between rival divinities.

Finally, there is the anonymous *Maid's Metamorphosis*. This play was performed by the revived Paul's company in 1600, possibly at a noble wedding attended by the Queen. For my purposes, the significance of this play lies in the fact that it marks the end of situational drama. Into a god-inhabited pastoral world such as we find in *Gallathea* and *Love's Metamorphosis* is thrust a romantic narrative concerning a hermit who is really a deposed king and a beautiful maiden who rejects the amorous onslaught of Apollo and eventually marries a wandering prince, the wedding taking place in the Edenic garden of the Muses. The Lylian setting and devices (e.g. metamorphosis, foresters and shepherds competing for the heroine) have been orchestrated into the plot of a narrative comedy.[9]

[9] Certain scholarly problems surround many of the eleven plays treated in this book: problems of authorship, exact date and place of first performance, conflicting statements on the title-pages of different quarto editions of the same play, and the like. Although these problems

Introduction

My method is a close critical examination of the plays in the context of the mythographical tradition and of Renaissance notions about allegory. Lyly's relations with the Court and the working conditions of his art have been so lucidly expounded by G. K. Hunter that there is no reason to go over his ground. My aim is to find out how the plays operate as plays. Chapter I discusses Court staging and its contribution to meaning. Chapter II concerns Lyly's first play, *Campaspe*; the discussion concentrates on dramaturgy, on his conduct of a relatively plotless situation. The absence of mythology from this play frees attention more fully for matters of technique and its relation to meaning. Chapter III will deal with the effects of the introduction of mythology and with a concomitant alteration of dramaturgy. *Gallathea* will be the focus of the discussion, and the conclusions reached on the basis of that play will be applied in Chapter IV to *Sapho and Phao*, *Love's Metamorphosis*, and *Endimion*. The fifth and final chapter will concern the six ancillary plays in which the situational form is giving way to Elizabethan romantic plot. I shall conclude with an attempt to estimate the role, I think an important one, that the Court comedies, with their allegorical mode of meaning, played in the development of Elizabethan drama as a whole.

have been investigated in the last forty years, no new facts or arguments have displaced the summary of our knowledge and reasonable conjecture given in E. K. Chambers, *The Elizabethan Stage*, and H. N. Hillebrand, *The Child Actors*. Consequently, I have not rehearsed these problems here, and, for easy reference, I give a brief account of what is known in the Appendix. I have excluded from this book two plays that may occur to the reader as requiring attention here. Marlowe's *Dido, Queen of Carthage* is a Chapel play (although its date is uncertain) and involves the gods to a slightly greater extent than does its Virgilian source. It is, however, a tragedy (or perhaps a satire on tragic themes) with a fully developed plot. Nashe's *Summer's Last Will and Testament*, performed for Archbishop Whitgift at Croydon in 1592, is too much of a pageant to be illuminating in connection with Lyly's dramaturgy.

I. A STAGE FOR ALLEGORY

THE FIVE plays forming the central body of Court comedy in the 1580's were, with the possible exception of *Love's Metamorphosis*, performed at Court.[1] *Campaspe* and *Sapho and Phao* were also performed at the first Blackfriars theater, under the official pretense of rehearsal for the Court performance. The rest of Lyly's comedies were performed, with the same excuse, at the private theater in the Paul's boys' own quarters. We know nothing about the physical arrangements in the Paul's theater. There have been two recent attempts to throw light on the first Blackfriars stage, both of which will be discussed below. In the main, our information about the staging of Court comedy comes from the Revels Accounts of Court productions and from the stage directions of the printed texts.

Certain scholarly errors concerning Court staging have

---

[1] The title-page of the quarto of *Love's Metamorphosis* does not definitely assert Court performance; it merely describes the play as "A Wittie and Courtly Pastorall." This piece of hedging causes one to suspect that the play had not received such august patronage: publishers are aware of the advertising value of definite statements, and certainly definite statements are made about Court performance on the title-pages of Lyly's other comedies (except *Mother Bombie*). There may, however, be another explanation for the caution. The quarto appeared in 1601, after the play had been transferred from Paul's to the Chapel, and some dozen years after a putative Court performance (see Appendix). Memories grow dim. In any case, such is the likeness between *Love's Metamorphosis* and Lyly's other plays, especially *Gallathea*, that I will treat it as a Court comedy without further qualm or qualification.

been successfully combatted. The chief misapprehension in R. Warwick Bond's edition of Lyly is his belief that the plays were staged in the manner of the popular Elizabethan theater.[2] Bond's belief led to his insertion of stage directions such as "(DIOGENES' *tub is thrust on*)."[3] Researches in the Revels Accounts permitted E. K. Chambers firmly to reject Bond's theory in favor of a variation of medieval multiple staging.[4] Chambers' view has been endorsed by subsequent investigators. An attempt to posit the influence of Italian stagecraft, in particular to argue that Tudor multiple staging was organized by the principles of perspective laid down in Serlio's *Architettura*, has failed for lack of evidence. We have no information showing the use of perspective in English stagecraft before Inigo Jones.[5]

Multiple staging consists of a number of "mansions" or "houses" placed independently on the stage with a neutral acting area in between. The houses were painted constructions of wood and canvas, representing palaces, shops, caves, battlements, cities, and the like. The Revels Accounts record many of these constructions, referring to them sometimes by the name of the thing represented, as "cittie," "battlement," "Cuntrey howse," "Senate howse,"[6] and

[2] R. Warwick Bond, *The Complete Works of John Lyly* (Oxford, 1902), II.266.

[3] *Campaspe*, I.iii.109, in Bond's *Complete Works*, vol. II.

[4] Chambers, *The Elizabethan Stage* (Oxford, 1923), III.32. See also Allardyce Nicoll's summary article, "Studies in the Elizabethan Stage since 1900," *Shakespeare Survey*, I (1948), 11.

[5] Lily B. Campbell argues for the use of Serlian perspective in *Scenes and Machines on the English Stage during the Renaissance* (Cambridge, England, 1923), pp. 95–115. J. H. McDowell replies effectively in "Tudor Court Staging: A Study in Perspective," *JEGP*, XLIV (1945), 194–207.

[6] Albert Feuillerat, *Documents Relating to the Office of the Revels in the Time of Queen Elizabeth* (Louvain, 1908), pp. 328, 336, 349, 350.

sometimes merely by the term "howse." [7] Large numbers
of these constructions were built. For example, the records
of the Christmas-to-Lent season of 1580–1580/1 note the
employment, in seven different plays, of four cities, one
"great citty," one senate house, and one house—all of
which are described as "new." Also employed, but not
described as new, were a great city (the same one?) and
a palace.[8] The employment of numerous new cities in one
short period suggests that the structures differed from
each other significantly and thus were designed for individual plays. Otherwise, minor alterations or a quick re-
painting would have sufficed to maintain variety at less
cost. There is strong evidence that natural greenery was
used for pastoral plays: payment is recorded for "cariage
of trees & other things to the Coorte for A wildernesse
in A playe." [9]

The most important principle of multiple staging is that
the houses were placed independently on the stage. They
were not organized into the unity of a street as in a
Roman comedy. The stage does not attempt to represent
any particular location containing houses. It merely presents
the houses relevant to a play, regardless of what might
be their naturalistic spatial relation. Such a design is
suggested by an inventory in the Revels Accounts for
the season of 1567–1567/8, which lists "diuers howses
[for several plays] . . . Stratoes howse, Gobbyns howse,
Orestioes howse Rome, the Pallace of prosperitie Scotlande
and a gret Castell one thothere side." [10] The capriciousness
of the commas and the ambiguity of the grammar in this
list make interpretation difficult, but the final phrases seem
to mean that, for one play, a house representing Scotland
stood on one side of the stage and a great castle on the
other. This sort of arrangement is certainly the case for

[7] Feuillerat, pp. 320, 365.   [9] Feuillerat, p. 180.
[8] Feuillerat, p. 336.   [10] Feuillerat, p. 119.

our plays. *Sapho and Phao* involves at least two houses, Sapho's chamber and Vulcan's forge. In Act V, Venus, who has announced that she will wait for Cupid at the forge, says, "I meruale Cupid commeth not all this while. How now, in Saphoes lappe?" [11] She simply crosses the stage to join the scene in Sapho's chamber, which would naturalistically be a remote distance from the forge. [12]

It is probable, Chambers concluded, that the Blackfriars theater merely reproduced the conditions of a Court hall. [13] Two recent investigations of the Blackfriars, however, must be considered here. Irwin Smith has recently published a major work, *Shakespeare's Blackfriars Playhouse* (New York, 1964), in which he traces the history of the Black-

[11] [John Lyly], *Sapho and Phao* (London, 1584), sig. F4ʳ. In Bond's text the line occurs at V.ii.45–46.

[12] Feuillerat, in *Le Bureau des Menus-Plaisirs et la Mise en Scène à la Cour d'Elizabeth* (Louvain, 1910), pp. 74–76 and notes, presents several other arguments for the multiple staging of these plays. An elaborate and convincing design has been worked out along these lines for Marlowe's *Dido* in Chambers, III.35–36. Lyly's Court staging derives, of course, from medieval practice. The ultimate origin is the techniques of liturgical drama, acted with various sites in the church as stage locations. Various kinds of multiple staging developed when the drama moved into the open air: scaffolds scattered about an area, enclosing or partially enclosing the audience (which may occasionally have moved from the vicinity of one scaffold to that of another in following the play), and, closer to Lyly's practice, the houses brought together in one place (the church steps, some kind of a stage) which the audience viewed as a unit. Multiple staging was actually less common in medieval England, where, of course, the mystery cycles adopted the pageant wagon technique, than in France, where, under the name of *decor simultané*, it flourished through the Renaissance. See Grace Frank, *The Medieval French Drama* (Oxford, 1954), pp. 69–73, 83–84, 90–91, 163–169, and Gustave Cohen, *Histoire de la Mise en Scène dans le Théâtre Religieux Français du Moyen Age* (Paris, rev. ed. 1926), Book I Chapter II, Book III Chapter II, and Plate I, which reproduces the miniature of the Valenciennes stage on which the *Mystère de la Passion* was performed in 1547.

[13] Chambers, III.47.

friars buildings from the foundation of the monastery, and attempts to reconstruct the stages of both the first Blackfriars theater (Lyly's) and the second (Shakespeare's). Smith has successfully established which rooms were used for the two theaters (not the same ones for both), but his reconstruction of the first Blackfriars breaks down when it comes to the stage itself. He points out that we can determine the design of the stage "only on the basis of what we know of Elizabethan playhouses and stages in general, together with what we can glean from the three extant plays known to have been acted there." [14] Smith, however, knows more about Elizabethan playhouses than is warranted by the evidence: his reconstruction hinges on an inner stage not mentioned in his list of initial assumptions but soon taken for granted in his discussion. [15] This is not just a matter of improper assumptions. An inner stage was not used at Court, where the plays were acted upon temporary platforms with the houses discussed above. It is difficult to see why a company that aimed at Court performance would execute their "rehearsals" under quite different conditions.

An even more fundamental problem vitiates Smith's reconstruction. He lists the "three extant plays known to have been acted" at the first Blackfriars as *Campaspe, Sapho and Phao,* and *The Arraignment of Paris.* For details about the stage he relies almost exclusively on the third, since its requirements are far more elaborate than those of the other two: thunder and lightning, a trap, a bower ("inner stage") capable of containing nine seated

[14] Smith, *Shakespeare's Blackfriars Playhouse,* p. 137.

[15] Smith, pp. 137–141. The same kind of methodological failure occurs in Smith's discussion of the second Blackfriars. T. J. King demonstrates, in his important review article in *Renaissance Drama,* IX (1966), 291–309, that many of the King's Men plays discussed by Smith could have been performed far more economically than he asserts.

Olympian deities.[16] Granted, however, that the Chapel boys who acted *The Arraignment of Paris* at Court were also acting at Blackfriars, there is no evidence that they performed this play there. Indeed, *The Arraignment of Paris* would be impossible at Blackfriars. The fifth act, in which the disputed apple is given to Elizabeth, requires the physical presence of the Queen. For all the Court plays, of course, the Queen must have appeared to the rest of the audience as practically part of the production; in Peele's play she is made the *sine qua non* of the denouement. The elaborate and specific blazon that occupies most of the act could not be transferred to any one else and depends upon her bodily presence. Smith has no evidence to go on.[17]

A more interesting contribution to the investigation of the first Blackfriars stage has been William Miller's recently presented evidence for the use of *periaktoi*.[18] In the marginalia to his translation of Virgil's third georgic,

[16] Smith (p. 140) actually says eleven gods, but see Peele's careful stage direction, *The Arraignment of Paris*, ed. Harold H. Child and W. W. Greg, Malone Society Reprints (Oxford, 1910), sig. D2ᵛ.

[17] It has been conjectured that *The Arraignment of Paris* existed in an alternative version suitable for Blackfriars performance. For example, Robert Mark Benbow, in his "Critical Edition of *The Araygnement of Paris* by George Peele" (Yale University Doctoral Dissertation, 1950), pp. 10–11, notes various loose ends in the play and observes that it is unprofitable to write a play for only one performance. It is not unprofitable, however, to do so if one may gain royal favor thereby. In any case, another version would have been a very different play. Once the original judgment of Paris is called into question, the only candidate really in the running is Eliza. The apple could hardly be given to Pallas or Juno, and to return it to Venus would be anticlimactic. To speculate on the staging of a non-existent play is fruitless.

[18] William E. Miller, "*Periaktoi* in the Old Blackfriars," *MLN*, LXXIV (1959), 1–3. Leslie Hotson, in *Shakespeare's Wooden O* (London, 1960), p. 154n., has raised objections to Miller's interpretation of the evidence, objections that Miller has successfully demolished in "*Periaktoi*: Around Again," *SQ*, XV (Winter, 1964), 61–65.

Abraham Fleming remarks that Virgil's word *scaena* must be a "kind of pagent, called *versilis, siue versatilis.*" Fleming then refers the reader to Vitruvius, and adds: "This deuise was not vnlike the motion of late yeares to be seene in the black friers." [19] The relevant passage in Vitruvius (V.vi.8) explains the *periaktos* as a revolvable three-sided prism painted with different scenes on its faces. The publication of Fleming's translation in 1589 pins the reference to the first Blackfriars. Fleming's note is the only known evidence of *periaktoi* in the English theater before Inigo Jones. Since it is so small and unspecific a piece of information, its helpfulness is problematic. I cannot see the use of *periaktoi* in the extant plays of the first Blackfriars, *Campaspe* and *Sapho and Phao*. *Periaktoi* are scene-changing devices, and scenes do not change in a multiple-staging arrangement. Rotating *periaktoi* might be merely distracting: they would accomplish, by means of one convention, a task already performed by other conventions, violating the capital theatrical rule of unity of effect. Conceivably *periaktoi* played a decorative or symbolic function; various possibilities exist, but on the present slender evidence no sturdy probabilities appear.[20]

It is now necessary to be more particular about the staging of the plays with which we are concerned. Both *Campaspe* and *Sapho and Phao* illustrate well the principles and possibilities of multiple staging. Unfortunately, with each play there is some doubt about the number of houses employed. Each requires at least two. In *Campaspe* the

[19] Quoted from Miller, *"Periaktoi* in the Old Blackfriars," p. 2.

[20] It has been suggested to me that the scene of Eumenides at the well in *Endimion* might employ *periaktoi*. It is an interesting suggestion: *Endimion* has so many imagined locales (one thinks also of Tellus' castle in the desert) that *periaktoi* could be quite useful, as they could be also for the "scene-change" to Delphi at the end of *Midas*. This is pure speculation, however, since *Endimion* and *Midas* are not Blackfriars plays.

heroine sits for her portrait by the painter Apelles within Apelles' shop, and during the sitting they talk about the paintings there displayed (III.iii). This shop has a practical door, curtain, or other device capable of screening the interior from view: when Campaspe arrives for the sitting Apelles directs his page to stay without and deny admittance to any visitors; the couple then *"Exeunt,"* the page has a scene with other pages, and then the aforementioned conversation between artist and model occurs (III.i–III.iii). Diogenes' tub is the second house. The philosophers cross to it in I.iii, as does Alexander in II.ii and III.iv, the latter time saying, "But behold *Diogenes* talking with one at his tub." [21] Chambers and G. K. Hunter agree that a third house, representing Alexander's palace, was on stage.[22] There is no absolute requirement in the text for it: no action takes place inside the palace, and no stage business demands it. But it seems most likely that the palace was there. In II.ii reference is made to it giving it equal status with the tub, as if both were visible. If *Campaspe* were a public theater play, one could hardly conclude its presence. In a multiple-staging theater, with two houses already representing the homes of the two other major male characters, the presence of Alexander's palace is virtually a certainty. The action of the play flows freely back and forth among the houses, ignoring those temporarily irrelevant and in one scene (I.i) ignoring all three.

In *Campaspe* all three houses may be supposed to be near the marketplace of Athens. *Sapho and Phao* entails a bolder foreshortening of space. The houses represent Sapho's bedchamber, the cave of Sybilla at the entrance

---

[21] [John Lyly], *A Moste Excellent Comedie of Alexander, Campaspe, and Diogenes,* ed. W. W. Greg, Malone Society Reprints (Oxford, 1934), sig. D1ʳ. In Bond's text, the line occurs at III.iv.44–45.

[22] Chambers, III.32; Hunter, *John Lyly: The Humanist as Courtier* (Cambridge, Mass., 1962), p. 108.

to the underworld, and Vulcan's forge. Again the action flows freely, running indeed without time lapse from the middle of Act III to the end of the play. The opening scenes of the play occur near Phao's ferry, but no house for this location is required.[23] Hunter has suggested that the same house was used for Sybilla's cave and Vulcan's forge: the latter location is employed only once and there is no direct interplay between it and the cave.[24] Unlike the problem with Alexander's palace, one cannot here invoke the claims of symmetry as an argument for three independent houses. One can point out, however, that the Revels Accounts show no stinting in the building of houses; to make one construction unnecessarily do the work of two may be false economy when one is entertaining a queen.

Gallathea has a unified pastoral setting. The play takes place on the banks of the Humber, and the stage is dominated by a tree, under which characters sit (I.i) and to which a virgin is bound for sacrifice (V.ii). No other set properties are required. *Love's Metamorphosis* also requires a tree, upon which verses and garlands are hung (I.i,ii). It is a trick tree: it is cut down in the course of the action, a process entailing the death of a nymph therein.[25] The temple of Cupid appears on the opposite side of the stage (II.i), and the Siren of IV.ii may be sitting on a rock.

None of the central group of plays calls for action at a raised level. Two of the marginal plays do, and, interestingly enough, they are the ones probably acted by adult companies: *The Rare Triumphs of Love and Fortune* and *The Woman in the Moon*. In both these plays the human action is observed from above by the gods. Happily, *Love*

---

[23] See Chambers' analysis, III.33.

[24] Hunter, p. 109.

[25] As Hunter (p. 110) has pointed out, Lyly became fond of using this tree. Characters in both *Endimion* and *The Woman in the Moon* are arborified or de-arborified on stage.

and Fortune is recorded by name in the Revels Accounts: for it "newe provision was made of one Citty and one Battlement of Canvas iij Ells of sarcenet A [blank] of canvas, and viij. paire of gloves." [26] The action of the play passes freely between a court and a cave in the woods, which account for the "Citty" and the unnamed structure of canvas. The presiding gods were clearly upon the battlement, there being no other use in the play for it. "Battlement" is presumably a general term for a raised platform allowing for action at an upper level. Both plays also call for trap doors. In the first scene of *Love and Fortune* Tisiphone exits, crying "open thou earth, gape hollow hell belowe." [27] In III.ii of *The Woman in the Moon* a complicated farcical action requires Stesias to hide himself in a cave out of which he later "riseth." [28]

An enormous and ever-continuing quantity of scholarship has been devoted to the reconstruction of the Elizabethan stages. Concern with the physical objects thereon ought not to obscure the basic nature of those stages, on which physical objects played only a small role. Chambers was criticized by Harley Granville-Barker for excessive realism in his reconstruction, and the warning is still timely: "The *vision* of the audience comprised the speakers and actors of the play, and such material things, as by their use of them, they brought to a momentary life, an apparent reality. Further than this it did not stray. Apart from the use that inner, outer, and upper stage were momentarily put to they were nothing, they were ar-

[26] Feuillerat, *Revels*, p. 349.

[27] *The Rare Triumphs of Love and Fortune*, ed. W. W. Greg, Malone Society Reprints (Oxford, 1931), sig. A2^v.

[28] Iohn Lyllie, *The Woman in the Moone* (London, 1597), sig. D4^r. In Bond's text the stage direction occurs after III.ii.320. I am indebted in this paragraph to Chambers' extended argument on these two plays, III.45–46.

tistically non-existent. And scene after scene might pass with the actors moving to all intents merely in the ambit of the play's story." [29] Although the Court stage had more furniture than the public theaters of which Granville-Barker was writing, we are still concerned with what Richard Southern has so well called the "open stage." On this stage, a naturalistic effect in dialogue can be obtained when wanted, but only if it is wanted; figures may come forward, detaching themselves from the physical background and from other on-stage actors, with no suspension of illusion; gods and symbolic figures may enter and look on with no incongruity.[30] In particular, the claims of time and place that bind realistic theater may be broken at will. *Campaspe* brings together locations that might naturalistically be close; *Sapho and Phao* foreshortens more violently; *Midas* involves a "scene-change" from Phrygia to Delphi. In any play the action may occur before a specific house, but it may also occur in the "free-stage" area, that is, in no place in particular. Freedom of time follows naturally. It is impossible to reduce the time-scheme of *Endimion* to consistency: the hero sleeps for forty years, aging into an old man, yet no one else in the play grows old. The whole thrust of the method of performance obliterates from consciousness such anomalies. The references to the passing of time in *Endimion* are cast up, not to our realistic objections, but to our symbolic apprehension.

Yet, although there are placeless scenes, there are not

[29] Harley Granville-Barker, "A Note Upon Chapters XX. and XXI. of *The Elizabethan Stage*," *RES*, I (1925), 68. His italics.

[30] Some of these effects have been mentioned in Southern's *The Open Stage* (London, 1953), pp. 35–36, 71–72. See also the remarks on the medieval treatment of space in George R. Kernodle, *From Art to Theatre: Form and Convention in the Renaissance* (Chicago, 1944), p. 16.

as many placeless scenes as there are in the popular Elizabethan drama. There are no *long* stretches of action unidentified with any of the houses, and the houses are always there. The Court stage is an open stage, but not so open as the public stage. This situation contributes a unique element to the plays' effects. The Court plays are, in their own way, attached to place. This way is not the representative method of creating a particular setting in which the action realistically occurs, a street, a hall, or the like. It is the intellectual method of juxtaposition. The stage of *Campaspe,* for example, presents (probably) three houses, with a no-man's-land in the center. The three houses are those of the king, the artist who is his subject, and the iconoclastic philosopher. The action of the play sets the king and the artist into rivalry over a woman; they are in conflict on other matters as well; and all of the *dramatis personae* are subject to the scathing criticism of the iconoclast. The three houses thus come to represent three different points of view, three different ways of life in conflict with each other. Yet, as the three houses are juxtaposed on one stage, so the three ways of life go on in one kingdom. The setting is a dramatic symbol of the problem of the play. It is Alexander's task to arrange these houses in harmonious order with one other, and it is the duty of the other characters to join in the harmony, each making his unique contribution within the structure of the whole.[31]

Sapho and Phao makes a different use of its intellectual space. If, as seems most likely, there was no attempt at

[31] In the Middle Ages multiple staging similarly suggested the play's total meaning. Grace Frank observes, "Such staging kept a synthesis of the play's meaning constantly before the audience. In [the Anglo-Norman] *Resureccion,* for example, heaven and hell, the crucifix, the tomb, the mansions of Pilate and the high priests, Emmaus and the Sea of Galilee were continuously in sight, each with its overtones of significance" (*The Medieval French Drama,* p. 91).

physical representation of Phao's ferry, then Phao operates in the free-stage area at the beginning of the play. In the final speech of the play, he is back in the free-stage area, bidding farewell on the one hand to Sybilla, his counselor in love, and on the other hand to Syracuse, the city of his beloved. The houses of Sapho, who loved him, of Sybilla, who gave him lengthy and often contradictory advice on love, and of Vulcan, who made the arrows causing the onset and cessation of love, are left behind.[32] Phao's career has been circular, a point reinforced by the epilogue, which uses a long series of metaphors suggesting intricate circular movement in describing the play.[33] The houses are thus not only realistic representations of the settings of the action; they are also symbolic representations of the cruces of the action. They present the key elements of the love process whose coordination creates the play. Moreover, cross-cutting Phao's strand of the play is another, focussing on Cupid. This is also symbolically presented by the juxtaposition of houses. Cupid's power lies in his arrows, which originate in Vulcan's forge (a scene is devoted to making them). With these arrows he wreaks havoc on Sapho, Phao, and Venus herself. We last see him, however, transferred

[32] The point is unaffected by the question of whether Vulcan and Sybilla actually used the same house.

[33] "They that *treade in a maze*, walke oftentimes in one path, and *at the laste come out wher they enterd in*. We fear we haue *lead you all this while in a Labyrinth of conceites*, diuerse times hearing one deuice, & haue now *brought you to an end, where we first beganne*. Which wearisome trauaile you must impute to the necessitie of the hystorie, as *Theseus* did his labor to the arte of the Labyrinth. Ther is nothing causeth such giddines, as *going in a wheele*, neither can there any thing breede such tediousnesse, as hearing manie wordes vttered in a small compasse. But if you accept this *daunce of a Farie in a circle*, wee will hereafter at your your willes frame our fingers to all formes. . . ." ([John Lyly], *Sapho and Phao* (London, 1584), sig. G2ʳ. My italics except for "Theseus.")

23

from the Vulcan side of the stage to the Sapho side, sitting in the queen's lap. The transfer enables Sapho to rid herself of passion and enables Phao to convert his passion into respectful worship from afar. The metamorphosis of love uncontrolled to love controlled is presented in the removal of Cupid from the house on stage right, say, to the house on stage left.

In *Gallathea* Lyly temporarily abandons multiple staging for a pastoral setting unified around a single tree. Lyly's second pastoral, however, *Love's Metamorphosis*, returns to the multiple pattern: Cupid's temple confronts the sacred tree of Ceres. Since in this play Ceres is a patroness of chastity, and the tree is actually a nymph of hers arborified to elude rape, the tree may be taken as Ceres' "house." If the Siren has an on-stage rock, the stage picture presents a neat triangle physically enclosing characters who must choose among the alternatives of love, chastity, and lascivious indulgence.

The juxtaposition of contrasting places, each laden with distinct values, is of course frequent in Elizabethan drama. To use only Shakespearean examples, one recalls the famous oppositions between Edward's England and Macbeth's Scotland in Act IV of *Macbeth*, between Court and Tavern in *1 Henry IV*, between Rome and Egypt in *Antony and Cleopatra*. Elizabethan drama thrives on parallelism and contrast, and normally derives unity, if at all, out of wide variety. There is a major difference, however, between the methods used by the public theater and those used by the Court theater to achieve these pregnant confrontations. Shakespeare, working with a largely bare stage, creates oppositions in a temporal dimension; the juxtapositions occur in successive scenes, are constantly shifting, and are physical only in terms of the actors. Lyly has a stage giving him certain resources that Shakespeare lacks: he can embody patterns of action and idea in houses that are simultaneously and permanently present. He can work in a continuous symbolic framework designed especially for each play.[34]

The physical properties of the Court stage thus make a contribution to meaning in a way unlike those of the public stage. The properties of the public stage usually work by synecdoche, the part presenting the whole. A throne, for example, indicates a presence chamber. Lyly's stage properties are genuine dramatic symbols. That is, they are physical objects figuring forth themes and ideas crucial to the play's action and meaning. The several houses, present throughout the play, are juxtaposed in a pattern that suggests a corresponding pattern in the ideas they figure. Therefore, the Lylian stage picture precisely fulfills the conventional Elizabethan definition of allegory: the stage picture is a continued metaphor. Lyly's stage, with its juxtaposition of symbols in a pattern to be animated by the words and deeds of the characters, is a stage for allegory.

---

[34] The public Elizabethan stage, of course, has a continuous symbolic framework provided by the "stage as world" metaphor and embodied in the physical presence of the "heavens" above and the "hell" beneath the stage. This framework, however, is not designed for the individual play. It is a structure enclosing all plays and all of life. It may be used by the individual play (although it certainly is not used by all), but it exists on so general a level that the kind of universalization it provides might better be called "applicability" rather than "allegory."

II. THE WORLD OF *CAMPASPE*

A. PROBLEMS

T HE MOST striking overall quality of *Campaspe* is its
variety.[1] The play is set in classical Athens as conceived by the Renaissance imagination: a fine
combination of the imperial Athens of Alexander, the
scholarly Athens of philosophers, the creative Athens of
artists, and the luxurious Athens of wealthy citizens. Display is always a major element of Court drama, even more
so than of the splendid public theater of the Elizabethans;
but no extant play previous to *Campaspe* and none of
Lyly's subsequent comedies has a panorama quite as wide
as this one. There is physical spectacle: the spoils of Thebes
and the mythological paintings of Apelles. There is
spectacle in the variety of characters: philosophers debate
the *ens entium,* page-boys indulge in quips, and a courtesan
frolics and sings with her customers. Set speeches on a
variety of topics abound: Alexander and Hephestion deliver orations in praise and dispraise of love; Apelles delivers a blazon on Campaspe's beauty; Diogenes harangues
a crowd with forceful invective. There are two catechisms:
a scholarly one between Alexander and the philosophers,
and an erotic one between Apelles and Campaspe. We

[1] Quotations are drawn from the first quarto (1584) as reprinted by
W. W. Greg, ed., *A Moste Excellent Comedie of Alexander, Campaspe,
and Diogenes,* Malone Society Reprints (Oxford, 1933). They are
acknowledged in the text by the signature numbers of this quarto,
followed by the act, scene, and line numbers of R. Warwick Bond, ed.,
The Complete Works of John Lyly (Oxford, 1902), vol. II.

hear songs and see feats of dancing and acrobatics. The range of verbal and visual display yields entertainment in its most basic sense: the play is a showcase of different kinds of delightful performance.

To describe *Campaspe* thus, however, can make it appear merely a variety show. What builds these scenes into a dramatic unity? There is, of course, consistency in the euphuistic prose style and in the single location of the play. Setting and verbal style alone, however, although they assist unity of effect, do not create unity of action or meaning. It is the task of this chapter to describe the mode of integration by which Lyly creates a play out of this classical showcase, by which he gives meaning to the theatrical experience.

The spine of the play has often been found in the conflict within the hero. Alexander the Great falls in love with a beautiful captive, Campaspe, and therefore pauses in his career of conquest, to the distress of his lieutenants. The artist Apelles, ordered by the king to paint Campaspe's portrait, falls in love with her and she returns his love. When Alexander discovers this, he unites them and proceeds on his way. T. W. Baldwin observes that the play is built on a question: "Shall Alexander choose love or arms?" [2] That question is certainly important in the play, more important than any other particular issue. To say that the play is "about" this conflict, however, is vastly to overestimate its bulk. The conflict occurs significantly in only three of the nineteen scenes (II.ii, III.iv, and V.iv). The action of *Campaspe* is not like that of a Restoration heroic play, where the central conflict may be similarly formulated. Alexander exists in a state of suspension between the alternatives. Unlike Almanzor, the hero of *The Conquest of Granada,* he does not make a series of con-

[2] T. W. Baldwin, *Shakspere's Five-Act Structure* (Urbana, 1947), p. 512. See also Baldwin's plot summary on pp. 496–497.

trasting decisions contributing to the development of a definite sequence of events. Unlike Dryden, Lyly does not fill the play with the struggle in the hero's mind. Alexander is concerned with many other matters besides love and war.

G. K. Hunter has also seen a debate theme in the play: "Wherein lies true kingliness? Is it in the power to command others or in the power to command ourselves?" [3] This formulation is sufficiently general to encompass a greater number of the play's events than does Baldwin's. It includes the Campaspe affair, for Alexander's final gift of the girl to the artist is presented as an act of self-command. In other scenes Alexander is concerned to order his kingdom: he must deal not only with artists and captives but also with philosophers, lieutenants, and beggars. Hunter's debate-theme is an important element of the play, and I shall return to it. But even this theme does not unify the play. The scenes between Apelles and Campaspe, most of the Diogenes scenes, the scenes with the pages and with the courtesan Lais do not bear upon kingliness. Are we to understand that half the play is merely an entertainment?

The difficulties experienced in isolating a single question as a spine for the play arise from the peculiar way in which the story is handled. *Campaspe* does not present a developed plot about Alexander's experiences in Athens. He is the chief figure of the play, but he does not dominate the action as do the kings of history plays. The central love story has the dimensions of an anecdote, not of a dramatic narrative. It is, of course, only an anecdote in the play's sources, a tale first told by Pliny and repeated, among other places, in Castiglione.[4] Lyly does not develop it be-

[3] G. K. Hunter, *John Lyly: The Humanist as Courtier* (Cambridge, Mass., 1962), p. 161.

[4] Pliny, *Natural History*, XXXV.xxxvi.85–87 (tr. H. Rackham, Loeb

yond anecdotal dimensions. There are no love scenes between Alexander and Campaspe. Indeed, they appear on
stage together only twice before the final scene, and on
each of these occasions their dialogue is limited to a single
question-and-answer exchange. Hunter remarks that this
peculiar treatment of love results from Lyly's tact: "he
avoids seeming to know anything direct about the amatory
emotions of royal persons." [5] Tact may be the efficient
cause for Lyly's distant treatment of Alexander's passion
(although one is inclined to doubt it: Lyly gives Alexander
a love-soliloquy, and two months later produced a play in
which the royal Sapho tosses in her bed in an agony of
desire); but it does not explain the dramatic effect of this
treatment. The presentation of the love-affair, indeed,
drives toward dramatic disengagement. Alexander does
not confess his love to the beloved but to his lieutenant
Hephestion. Campaspe's feelings about Alexander are held
in reserve until her soliloquy in Act IV, and even then she
is brief. We can divine her position on the matter from an
earlier scene: when she sits for her portrait (III.iii), she
remarks unfavorably on Jupiter's affairs with mortal
women, and her comments can be understood to reflect
upon her own situation with Alexander. But placed as
they are, these comments do not constitute an event in the
personal relationship between lover and beloved. Lyly is
exploring the situation between them, but he is refusing to
make a narrative of it.

The love between Apelles and Campaspe is handled
with a similar absence of real action. This couple, at least,
do have two scenes together, but those scenes are curiously
uncommunicative. The second one (IV.iv) consists of the

Classical Library [London and Cambridge, Mass., 1952], IX.325);
Baldassare Castiglione, *The Book of the Courtier,* tr. Sir Thomas Hoby,
ed. Walter Raleigh (London, 1900), pp. 95–97.

[5] Hunter, p. 164.

artfully indirect dialogue that Lyly usually writes for love scenes: hints but no declarations. The first (III.iii) does not even get so far. Apelles' interest is obvious, but Campaspe gives no sign of her feelings. Thus, when Apelles soliloquizes two scenes later, his love, like Alexander's, exists in a curious state of suspension because neither he nor we know what the lady's feelings are until the next act. It is important, and perhaps difficult, for the reader to notice this suspension. Since we expect a narrative in a play, and since we know, of course, how the situation is going to turn out, we may think that things are happening before they really do. We may think, indeed, that things *are* happening when nothing is. A triangle is established, but only very slowly do we find out that it *is* a triangle. Once the triangle gets underway, only two events take place to alter the situation: Apelles blemishes the portrait in order to have Campaspe sit for him again, and Alexander devises a stratagem to make Apelles reveal his love. Lyly is avoiding the development of plot. Such events as he cannot avoid he plays down: Alexander forms his suspicions of Apelles' passion offstage.

The lack of plot is also evident in the scenes not concerned with the love-triangle. Two single characters, Timoclea and a begging Cynic, and four groups of characters, the philosophers (except Diogenes), the Athenian citizens, the boys who perform for Diogenes and their father, and Lais and her customers, put in appearances in only one scene and then vanish from the play, leaving the general state of affairs completely unaffected. Hephestion and the courtiers protest and grumble about Alexander's stay in Athens, but they do nothing. The deeds and sayings of Diogenes, who appears in eight scenes, neither contribute to the main action nor form a coherent underplot.

There is even an absence of preparation for scenes that are to follow. If we do not know the story, Alexander's

love for Campaspe is astonishing on the basis of their previous acquaintance: he has largely ignored her in I.i, and
then four scenes later (he has been busy with philosophers)
he declares passionate love. Diogenes delivers a jeremiad
against the citizens and we are apparently expected to find
the accusations just. Since, however, we have not previously seen the citizens, we know nothing of their vices.
This arrangement is particularly odd, because in the next
act there is a scene (with Lais) that would prepare for the
harangue.

Obviously it is foolish to seek the realistic plot of a
well-made play in Elizabethan drama. The point here is
that one will not find any kind of plot at all in *Campaspe*.
The main action is very slow and spaced out, and oppor-
tunities for joining the characters in conflict are sedulously
ignored. The other scenes are full of activity (the characters are quite busy when they appear) but their deeds are
not woven into any coherent line of action. These scenes
have only a unitary value. They are, like the main action,
anecdotes.

The curiously paratactic quality of action in *Campaspe*
appears in the characterization as well. Many characters,
as I have pointed out, make only one appearance: with
them Lyly obviates the necessity of sustained depiction of
character. In those characters who appear frequently (most
of the scenes have at least one of the four major persons,
Alexander, Apelles, Campaspe, or Diogenes, on stage),
there is no depth. Once one has said that Apelles is an
accomplished artist and a passionate lover and that Campaspe is a beautiful, low-born virgin who prefers to remain
in her own station in life, one has plumbed the depths of
their personalities. The peculiar quality of the action contributes to this flatness of character. Having so oddly disengaged the lovers, Lyly cannot display personality in action. It is, after all, by means of the deeds and the con-

flicts of persons that the dramatist usually reveals their inner natures. The separation of the lovers creates a kind of non-characterization of them.

Alexander, more centrally focussed on, is more complex. In him the parataxis approaches dual personality. In one scene (II.ii) he tells Hephestion of his overwhelming love for Campaspe; at his next appearance (III.iv) he calmly tells Hephestion that he prefers Bucephalus. Nothing has happened between the two occasions, he is not trying to deceive Hephestion, and he still loves Campaspe. The point about Bucephalus must be understood only in terms of the scene in which it occurs, within the frame of the particular anecdote. Lyly makes no attempt at psychological continuity. He even goes so far, at times, as to disrupt the non-psychological characterization of Alexander. We know of Alexander, at least, that he is merciful and respects truth. Yet two of his courtiers, brave, intelligent and honorable men of whom we know no wrong, are loath to tell Alexander the truth about the disorder of his unemployed army for fear he will wrathfully punish them (IV.iii). Their fear is totally inconsistent with what we and they know of Alexander.

To summarize, no central dramatic thrust or unity is to be found here in concatenated plot or developed characterization. Characters are not internally explored and are sometimes inconsistent; events are as discrete as the stage houses in and around which they take place. Elizabethan criticism gives us no specific key for understanding Lyly's dramaturgy. There is very little Elizabethan dramatic criticism in any case; when it discusses comedy, it is concerned with Roman comedy, and the series of peculiarities I have been describing do not occur in the Roman tradition. One must proceed empirically, by examination of the play itself. *Campaspe* is, I believe, unified; indeed, it possesses a remarkably thorough coherence. Lyly is in full control of his plotlessness. The rest of this section establishes an approach to Lyly's dramaturgy and exemplifies the operation of the play in one scene. The rest of the chapter attempts to demonstrate Lyly's dramaturgy by an examination of the whole play.

Hunter is on the right track in suggesting that *Campaspe* is unified around an idea, that the scenes present aspects of a complex notion in order to define it. His particular interpretation, however, that the idea is kingliness, is too narrow. Kingliness is important in *Campaspe,* but to isolate it as the "subject" is to focus too quickly on the leading character. We must begin with the various actions of the play, with the anecdotes that occupy the individual scenes. These anecdotes, I believe, cast up ideas, ideas that are relatable in a pattern corresponding to the pattern of the action. The anecdotes thus form vehicles for allegorical suggestion.

Let us begin with Lyly's sources. The characters and incidents of *Campaspe* are largely unoriginal. The love-story, as I have mentioned, comes from Pliny and Castiglione. Pliny also recounts Alexander's attempt to paint under the tutelage of Apelles.[6] Plutarch's life of Alexander has been rifled, notably for the episode of Timoclea and (almost verbatim from North's translation) for Alexander's cross-examination of the philosophers.[7] The scenes involving Diogenes, as Bond industriously demonstrated in his notes, are almost entirely dramatizations of the anecdotes told of the Cynic in the pages of that biographer of philosophers, Diogenes Laertius. The rejection of the begging Cynic is founded on two anecdotes in Seneca.

Much of this material has been altered. In Plutarch the

[6] Pliny, XXXV.xxxvi.85.

[7] Plutarch, *Lives of the Noble Grecians and Romans,* tr. Sir Thomas North, ed. George Wyndham (London, 1895), IV.310–312, 372–373.

story of Timoclea is more violent: raped by a Macedonian captain during the sack of Thebes, she revenges herself by pushing her ravisher into a well and hurling down rocks after him. In Lyly she merely makes a haughty speech to Alexander. Plutarch's version of Timoclea's revenge is quite stageable, and Lyly's episode makes the same point, that Timoclea is a high-spirited woman and Alexander respects her valor and treats her accordingly. But the change is necessary, not only because pushing rapists into wells is tonally out of keeping with the courtliness of Lyly's play, but also because the rape would destroy the concept of Alexander's mildness in conquest and the revenge would over-establish Timoclea's courage at the expense of Alexander's magnanimity in recognizing it.

Often, however, the point of an anecdote is changed, not only in Lyly, but in the medieval-Renaissance tradition of its use. An anecdote is relatively free-floating in literary tradition. It consists of a simple situation and a punch-line. The characters involved exist for the single quality they display in the episode, if indeed they exist for that much—many of the Alexander stories that come down from classical sources could be told as well of any other king or general. Consequently, an anecdote may be bent to many purposes. Whereas an alteration in a larger narrative may be of no particular import, a small change of any kind in an anecdote, whether of detail, context, or attitude, can easily change the point altogether. Since the anecdote exists for its point, the whole thing has then been transformed. An anecdote is in effect an independent unit of narrative or dramaturgical energy that can be put into a fairly wide variety of settings to serve a fairly large number of purposes. Although scholarship may establish a tradition of use for particular stories, it may be impossible to establish a concomitant tradition of significance.

To exemplify. In *Campaspe*, III.iv, Alexander and

Diogenes both refuse to give alms to a begging Cynic. The episode derives ultimately from Seneca's discussion of liberality in *De Beneficiis*, II.16–17.[8] As Seneca tells the tale, Alexander once gave a city to one of his soldiers. The soldier, not in the least wanting a city, attempted to refuse it on the grounds that it was not proper for him to accept so great a gift. Alexander overrode the refusal by maintaining that it was not proper for so great a king to give anything less. Seneca's next story concerns the refusal of a king named Antigonus to succor a begging Cynic. Antigonus declined to give him a talent on the grounds that beggars should not ask for so much, or a denarius on the grounds that kings cannot with dignity give so little. In his commentary on these paired anecdotes, Seneca accuses Alexander of ostentation and a lack of true generosity. He admits that Antigonus might be accused of uncharitable chop-logic, since he thought of the talent only in relation to beggars and the denarius only in relations to kings; but ultimately Seneca decides that Antigonus did rightly, since Cynics, having renounced money, should not be given it when they break their vows and take to begging. According to George Cary, who has traced in detail the history of this and other Alexander stories, the medieval recensionists found it easier to acquit Alexander than the obscure Antigonus, and, in repeating, splitting, recombining, and otherwise altering this pair of stories, they came up with a variety of judgments on the liberality displayed.[9] The stories were malleable material free to be adjusted to the demands of whatever moral point the repeater wished to make. Source-study can tell us that this anecdote has been available to fifteen centuries of writers wishing to make

[8] Seneca, *Moral Essays,* tr. John W. Basore, Loeb Classical Library (London and Cambridge, Mass., 1935), III.79–83.

[9] George Cary, *The Medieval Alexander,* ed. D. J. A. Ross (Cambridge, Eng., 1956), pp. 86, 90, 280, 348–349, 351, 361.

points about liberality (or about magnanimity, or about
the keeping of ascetic vows); it can help us *negatively* to
determine the meaning of the anecdote in any particular
case by providing a gallery of contrasting cases; but only
through the individual case can we *positively* determine
the meaning intended on that particular occasion.

Lyly's version of the story goes as follows:

ALEX. . . . But behold *Diogenes* talking with one at his
tub.

CRYSUS One pennie *Diogenes*, I am a Cynick.

DIOG. He made thee a begger, that first gaue thee any
thing.

CRYSUS Why, if thou wilte giue nothinge, no bodye wil
giue thee.

DIOG. I want nothing, till the springes dry, & the earth
perish.

CRYSUS I gather for the Gods.

DIOG. And I care not for those gods, which want money.

CRYSUS Thou art a right Cynicke, that wyll gyue nothing.

DIOG. Thou art not, that wil beg any thing.

CRYSUS *Alexander,* kinge *Alexander,* giue a poore Cynick
a groat.

ALEX. It is not for a king to giue a groat.

CRYSUS Then giue me a talent.

ALEX. It is not for a begger to aske a talent. Awaye.

(Dɪʳ; III.iv.44–57)

This is pure anecdote. It manifests the discontinuity of
action characteristic of *Campaspe*. It is quite unrelated to
anything before or after; the beggar appears at Diogenes'
tub out of nowhere, crosses to Alexander's palace halfway
through the passage, and then disappears after thirteen
lines, leaving no one influenced by him and no one concerned with what becomes of him. We never hear of him

again, and in a stage performance we would not even learn that his name was Crysus. The episode is so totally irrelevant to the action of the rest of the play that we immediately wonder why Lyly put it in.

Lyly has recast the Senecan anecdote. He uses the double form but eliminates the soldier and the city; transferring Alexander into the begging Cynic story, he gives him Antigonus' reason for rejecting the beggar, that kings should not give groats and beggars should not ask talents. Diogenes is given the view that Seneca himself advanced in the commentary, that money should not be given those who have forsworn it. This is a thoroughly decorous treatment. Diogenes' rebuke comes properly from a fellow member of the philosophical sect whose views are involved, and it is enriched with Cynical observations on desire and the gods. Alexander's argument stresses magnanimity (in an Aristotelian rather than a charitable Christian sense) and the keeping of one's place in the order of society, a most appropriate concern for a Renaissance king.

But decorum is not merely the *technique* of the scene. Decorum as technique is a set of conventions governing the method of portrayal and consistency of characters: kings in plays should be kingly, or, as is the case with Richard II, we should know why they are not. Since this episode is discrete, decorum is also the *content* of the scene. The decorousness of the arguments is the only reason for the presence of the episode. The scene exists to show Alexander as a king. It defines him. It exists to show Diogenes as a Cynic. It defines him. It exists to show both in relation to a third person, and they construct their relationships in accordance with the abstract positions that they hold. Diogenes' position is a matter of intellectual conviction, Alexander's one of social and political fact; neither's is a matter of individual emotion or personality. We are not seeing individual character in action: if we were, the speeches of Alexander, whom we are clearly meant to respect and admire, would be shocking. We see public, abstract characters, characters whose essence is a position in the structure of the world.[10] The very fact that Lyly uses the double form of the anecdote makes the significance of the scene clear. Rejection is the action in both cases, but the contrasting reasons proceed straight from the contrasting public characters of Alexander and Diogenes. Alexander's response to the beggar, juxtaposed to Diogenes' response, tells us that he is to be understood, not as a particular personality, but as a king. That is his essence. The scene is almost a diagram of proper relationships conceived on the basis of public character.

I cannot here, of course, deal with the episode of the begging Cynic in its context, with the manner in which it relates to other anecdotes within the structure of the play. But this scene, because of its brevity and isolation, provides

[10] The character of Crysus is conceived on similarly intellectual lines. He is a begging Cynic, that is, a self-contradiction. Concerning Diogenes, the vigor of his speeches (as illustrated in the quoted passage) may *look* like individual personality, but this appearance is deceptive. The vigor arises from intellectual, abstract roots: he advocates and carries out a philosophy that is itself individualistic to the point of anarchism: "I would haue none of *Diogenes* minde, but *Diogenes*," he has earlier remarked (C1ᵛ; II.ii.134–135). He is a grotesque, an embodiment of his Cynicism. His characterization is as external as is Alexander's, for it consists of his occupation and fulfillment of a particular place in a philosophical order as Alexander's consists of his occupation of a particular place in a political order. We are led to care neither how he came by his views nor where they will ultimately lead him. Compare him, for example, with that other Elizabethan misanthrope, Jacques. Diogenes is Jacques' intellectual superior, but his ideas and opinions create very nearly all of the man that there is, whereas Shakespeare is concerned with the tension between man and role, more interested in the kind of man who would cultivate an elaborate melancholy than in the melancholy as such. Diogenes' vigor is, in fact, comparable to the liveliness of a Vice in a morality play.

a peculiarly clear example of the kind of dramatic action that occurs in *Campaspe*. No other scene is quite so emblematic in effect, but the elements present here are the elements that operate, in a more complicated fashion, throughout the play. The characters in *Campaspe* are individuals, but their individuality lies not in personality but in their particularity of status in a number of external structures. They are, as it were, intersections in the orders of society, of philosophical views, of subjects of discussion. They are not as simple as the characters in morality plays who represent single abstractions; since they are particulars involved in a number of generals, they come closer to humanity than do Lechery and Good Deeds moving in their lively and eternal codified pattern. But they lack the welter of personal aspects that even the economical form of the drama can provide for the representation of humanity. They continually push toward the imaging of *the* king, *the* Cynic, *the* artist. They are not psychological personalities who express directly and indirectly the complex states of their souls, the sort of characters that the Elizabethan dramatists came very gradually to create; they are intellectual constructions who define and describe themselves. In acting them, one does not look for an emotional "subtext" to ride upon, but reads the speeches rhetorically. The original boy-actors, necessarily formal in their portrayal of adults, doubtless sustained this intellectual level of characterization; as Hunter remarks, there could be no question of the boys' living rather than acting their roles.[11] The thematic concern of *Campaspe* is the fit relationships of these characters, decorum, propriety. Hunter's kingliness is a large part of this, since kingliness is decorum for a king. But decorum, in the large cast of this play, must also be heeded by many persons who are not kings. The action of

[11] Hunter, p. 94.

Campaspe is to define and arrange. What a king or an artist should be, what lines of relationship should be drawn between them, is the constant concern of the scenes as, in their anecdotal form, they pose one suggested arrangement against another.

This description of the characterization, theme, and action of *Campaspe* does not automatically solve all the problems in the play that this section has pointed out. It contains, however, the seeds of solution. I hope, in the rest of the chapter, to substantiate this description by a discussion of the whole play and to arrive, on that basis, at a theory of meaning appropriate to *Campaspe*. I wish to start, however, not with the first scene, but with a more basic element of the play: its verbal style. Lyly's euphuism is a particularly appropriate tool for the kind of thematic concern that *Campaspe* presents.

B. THE EUPHUISM OF *CAMPASPE*

The standard definition of euphuism is that of Morris Croll.[12] The chief characteristic of the style, according to Croll, is the persistent employment of three rhetorical schemes understood solely as figures of sound, devices of vocal ornament. These three figures are isocolon (successive phrases or clauses of approximately the same length), parison (parallel placing of the corresponding grammatical members of such successive units), and paramoion (similarity of sound in the parallel members, in the form of alliteration, assonance, consonance, or rime). All three figures are illustrated in the sentence: "Heere, yea, heere *Euphues*, maiste thou see not the carued visarde of a lewde

[12] John Lyly, *Euphues: The Anatomy of Wit & Euphues and his England,* ed. Morris William Croll and Harry Clemons (London and New York, 1916). The introduction, which contains the discussion of euphuism, was the work of Croll alone.

woman, but the incarnate visage of a lasciuious wanton, not the shaddowe of loue, but the substaunce of luste." [13]

Croll was aiming at the most succinct definition possible, trying to isolate only the essence of the style. Thus he deliberately omitted various features of euphuism always noted by students. These are resupplied in Hunter's list: word-repetition and sound-echo outside the parisonic figure; proverbs and rhetorical questions, especially in series; and extended similes drawn from natural history, whether genuine, fantastic but traditional, or invented by Lyly himself. [14]

The older description of euphuism as a style distinguished by the pervasive use of antithesis [15] Croll regarded as "a prolific mother of errors,—if it is not itself an error." [16] Arguing that Lyly's antitheses are merely figures of words arranged for aural effect rather than figures of thought in which genuine distinctions are being propounded, he concluded that use of the term "antithesis" was unjustified. Upon this point, the only major modification of Croll's analysis has turned. In a brilliant article (later endorsed by Hunter), Jonas Barish has attacked Croll's view of antithesis as tendentious and normative rather than descriptive, and accused Croll of hardening the distinction between figures of sound and figures of thought to the point where Lyly's syntax is seen as com-

[13] John Lyly, *Euphues: The Anatomy of Wit*, in Bond, *Complete Works*, I.189.

[14] Hunter, p. 265. As Hunter points out, the natural history similes are the aspect of Lyly's style most frequently noted in the references of his contemporaries.

[15] See, for example, C. G. Child, *Johy Lyly and Euphuism* (Erlangen and Leipzig, 1894), pp. 44ff. and Albert Feuillerat, *John Lyly* (Cambridge, Eng., 1910), pp. 412ff.

[16] Croll, p. xvii.

pletely mechanical and unrelated to meaning.[17] Barish points out that "syntactic formulae are not the clothes of thought, they are of its essence; they are not mere schemes imposed on meaning, they are the determinants of meaning."[18] He reinstates antithesis as a primary mode of Lylian thought, and, beyond that, he argues that Lyly's style is distinguished by an all-pervasive logicality, a constant subdivision of topics into not only antitheses but also non-antithetic parallels, opposites that are not mutually exclusive, complements, composites, and so forth. The result is a universe minutely fragmented by a highly logical mind.

Croll's introduction and Barish's article are the two most considerable contributions to the study of euphuism since Child's summary of and improvement on the nineteenth-century (largely German) scholarship.[19] From the point of view of one interested in Lyly as dramatist, the major defect in all this work is the cursory consideration given to the place of euphuism in the plays. Definitions and descriptions of the style are invariably based upon its use in the two romances from which it takes its name; commentary on the style of the plays, however lengthy or laudatory,[20] is invariably in the simple form of remarks about

---

[17] Jonas Barish, "The Prose Style of John Lyly," *ELH*, XXIII (1956), 14–35.

[18] Barish, p. 16.

[19] The only other major contributions are William Ringler's demonstration (somewhat overstated) of the influence of the Latin lectures of John Rainolds, delivered at Oxford in the 1570's, on Lyly and his fellow euphuists ("The Immediate Source of Euphuism," *PMLA*, LIII [1938], 678–686), and the admirable review of the whole matter by Hunter, pp. 260ff.

[20] Both Feuillerat (p. 443) and, very enthusiastically, C. S. Lewis (*English Literature in the Sixteenth Century Excluding Drama* [Oxford, 1954], pp. 316–317), find euphuism more successful in the plays than in the romances.

the gradual abandonment of the more formal devices [21] or
the continuing operation of the analytical procedure.[22]

Such remarks do not go nearly deep enough. Even the
tight descriptions of Croll and Barish do not get to the
heart of the euphuism of the plays. In *Campaspe,*
supposedly Lyly's most euphuistic play,[23] the basic unit of
expression is neither Croll's isocolon-parison figure nor the
various grammatical patterns of antithesis and parallelism
that Barish suggests. It is rather a statement of identity or
attribution. The play abounds in remarks of the form, *"a
is b,"* where *b* is a noun or adjective in the nominative case
and the statement is intended to isolate a central aspect of
a; and of the form, *"a does b,"* where doing *b* is conceived
of as an action particularly characteristic of *a.* Both sorts
of statement make assertions about the major properties of
the subject; that is, they are forms of definition. It is an
error to think of euphuism only in terms of contrasting or
parallel units. Each unit must first be looked at independently. The basic element of dialogue in *Campaspe* is
the complete, usually short, declarative sentence that turns
on the verb "to be" or a verb of action characteristic to the
subject, the verb being in the present tense except in the
case of historical allusion. For example: "Thou art a right
Cynicke" (D1^r; III.iv.52); "Princes [are] to be yelded
vnto" (D3^r; III.v.37–38); "Greene grasse must turne to
dry hay" (D4^v; IV.i.48); "Loue falleth like dewe aswel
vpõ the low grasse" (F3^v; V.iv.129); "We see it incident
in artificers to be inamoured of their own workes" (F1^v;
V.iv.13–14: this line differs in grammatical form but has
the same definitional effect).

The resultant definitions are not logical definitions as
understood by the Renaissance—that is, they are not definitions by genus and species. They are rhetorical definitions,

---

[21] Child, pp. 84–100.   [22] Barish, pp. 27–35.   [23] Child, p. 91.

often moral commonplaces, generalized statements about the natures and activities and obligations peculiar to kings and to maidens, to philosophy and to art, to virtue and to conquest. Technically, such statements usually fall under the rubric *descriptio*, the third category in the following passage from Cicero's *Topica*: "When the question concerns what a thing is, one has to explain the concept, and the peculiar or proper quality of the thing [definition by genus and species], analyze it and enumerate its parts [definition by division into mutually exclusive parts that together constitute the whole]. For these are the essentials of definition. We also include description, which the Greeks call χαρακτήρ (character or hallmark)." [24] This sort of definition, definition by hallmark, appears in the pseudo-Ciceronian *Rhetorica ad Herennium* as that which "in brief and clear-cut fashion grasps the characteristic qualities of a thing." [25] Often this figure, especially when designated by the term "horismus," defines by stating both what the object is and what it is not.[26] That is, the definition expands into an antithesis.

Generalizations as they are, these definitions do not cover the field completely. They are local statements, and the verbal unfolding of the play proceeds by their juxtaposition. One form of juxtaposition is particularly important:

[24] *Topica*, tr. H. M. Hubbell, Loeb Classical Library (London and Cambridge, Mass., 1949), XXII.83.

[25] *Rhetorica ad Herennium* (*De Ratione Dicendi*), tr. Harry Caplan, Loeb Classical Library (London and Cambridge, Mass., 1954), IV.xxv. 35.

[26] Puttenham's illustrations for horismus are of this kind: see *The Arte of English Poetry*, ed. G. D. Willcock and A. Walker (Cambridge, Eng., 1936), p. 231. Some of the illustrations in the *Ad Herennium* passage cited above are also of this kind, as is (the most famous example) Shakespeare's definition of love in Sonnet 116, "Let me not to the marriage of true minds." Lyly, of course, frequently uses the full form of horismus.

the conjunction of two definitions in a single sentence to create either the characteristic euphuistic epigram or the proposition that initiates the characteristic euphuistic debate, to be swelled by a barrage of subsidiary antitheses and parallel examples. It is the constant pursuit of Lyly's dialogue to create such juxtapositions, to adumbrate the relationships between the individual items he has separately set up. But to discuss, as Barish does, the contrasts, parallels, and antitheses that Lyly produces, as if they were the *basic* units of the style, without emphasizing the original definitions, is to see only part of the picture. The contrasts are not always immediate, but often only partial, or indirect, or on another level from the initial statement, or involved in a curving or stepwise movement away from that statement. If one does not see from what direction the juxtapositions come, it becomes difficult to appreciate their quality or to see where they are driving. It becomes as impossible to appreciate the movement of the dialogue as it is impossible to reconstruct the movement of dancers from occasional still photographs of a ballet. Finally, if one misses the definitions and heeds only the contrasts, one misses half the value of Barish's own term for the essential quality of Lyly's style, logicality. It is the definitions that come first.

Analysis of several examples is advisable. Alexander's courtiers open the play:

CLYT. *Parmenio,* I cannot tel whether I should more commend in *Alexanders* victories, courage, or curtesie, in the one being a resolution without feare, in the other a liberalitie aboue custõe: *Thebes* is raysed, the people not racked, towers throwne down, bodies not thrust aside, a cõquest without conflict, and a cruell warre in a milde peace.

PARME. *Clytus,* it becommeth the sonne of *Phillip* to be

none other then *Alexander* is: therefore seeing in the
father a full perfection, who could haue doubted in the
sonne an excellencie. For as the moone can borrow nothing els of the sunne but light, so of a sire, in whome
nothing but vertue was, what coulde the childe receiue
but singuler? It is for Turkes [i.e. turquoises] to staine
each other, not for *Dyamondes*, in the one to bee made
a difference in goodnes, in the other no comparison.

(A1ʳ; I.i.1–13)

These speeches accomplish with notable economy the
task of revealing the historical period, particular situation,
and chief character of *Campaspe*. The exposition, however,
is conducted in terms of a specific inquiry: which of Alexander's qualities is best displayed in his conquest of Thebes?
Clitus suggests two, courage and courtesy, and immediately
defines them. These definitions are hardly complete:
Renaissance treatise-writers busied with these topics are
not content with the likes of "resolution without feare"
and "liberalitie aboue custoe." Lyly, however, is not writing a treatise. Salient qualities at least of the two abstractions are isolated and made more clear by the addition of
prepositional phrases. The two abstractions are set together
and illustrated by a series of contrasting examples. Parmenio then picks up the discussion, not with further remarks on courage and courtesy, but by comparing the
possessor of those two virtues to his father Philip. We are
moved to a higher level of terms, and the second juxtaposition depends partially on the definitions of Alexander
that have been established in the first.

Two points in the opening sentence of Parmenio's reply
deserve comment. First, the likeness he asserts between
Philip and Alexander has an ethical coloring: "it becommeth the sonne of *Phillip* to be none other then *Alexander* is." There is a latent sense in many of these state-

ments that Parmenio's present phrasing brings into promi-
nence: the predicate term of a definition can be proper to
the subject term both in the sense that the property in
question *is* characteristic and in the sense that it *should be*
characteristic. The Latin *proprietas* means both "property"
(in the sense of attribute) and "propriety." When anything
possesses one of its distinctive qualities, it is fulfilling its
proper function in the general scheme of things. The idea
of decorum, noted in the previous section as the basic concern of the action of *Campaspe,* penetrates to the verbal
roots of the play. The phrasing, "it becomes *x* to be *y*," is
central to theme.

Secondly, in the latter part of his sentence Parmenio
shifts slightly the relationships he is setting up. He starts
by observing very precisely that it is fitting for the son of
Philip to be "none other then *Alexander* is" (I say "very
precisely" because the possible phrasing, that it fits him
to be "as he is," would leave open the possibility that it also
might fit him to be otherwise). Then he moves, adjusting
the relationship, to an implied assertion of the *equality* of
the two distinguished men on the basis of respective
possession of synonymous qualities ("perfection" and
"excellencie"). The shift is slight, admittedly, but it
is well to notice that a Lylian speech can do this, in view
of the frequent critical comments on Lyly's repetitiveness.
Two subsequent similes reinforce the general statement,
but this is not a case of Lyly's pulling two items out of
his satchel where one (according to Sidney) [27] would do.
The rather slippery analogy of the sun and the moon is
meant to suggest the efficient cause of Alexander's virtue;
that of the turquoises and diamonds refines the notion of
their equality. Alexander receives his virtues from Philip,

[27] See "An Apologie for Poetrie," in *Elizabethan Critical Essays,* ed.
G. Gregory Smith (Oxford, 1904), I, 202–203.

and both men are so outstanding that like diamonds, the primates in the class of stones as kings are the primates in the class of men, neither can cast the other into shadow. Insufficient attention, a natural result of the supposition that Lyly's analogies merely repeat each other, might lead us to suppose Lyly so careless as to compare two men on the point of equality to two celestial bodies that are certainly not equal.

Lyly usually exerts his stylistic energy on particular points, leaving implicit the transitions between them. This aspect of his writing has been noticed with respect to the progress of the long argumentative discourses in *Euphues*,[28] and small instances of the habit are evident in the present passage. The fact that Alexander's treatment of towers and bodies exemplifies his courage and courtesy is left for the actor's voice to make clear. While Parmenio articulates a formal simile in the sun-moon illustration, his remarks on jewels stand merely as a parallel example. This is paratactic style, and it is analogous to the paratactic, anecdotal structure of scenes in *Campaspe*. The value of this consistency between verbal technique and dramatic technique will be explored in the final section of the chapter.

The speeches of Clitus and Parmenio, here and elsewhere in the play, demonstrate a full use of euphuistic devices in Croll's sense of the term. Isocolon and parison are conspicuous in Clitus' definitions, and they are supplemented with alliteration in his examples. Also notably euphuistic are the long speeches in the play: Hephestion's protest against Alexander's declaration of love, the love-soliloquies of Apelles and Campaspe, and Alexander's speech uniting the lovers. The vigorous emphasis that the

[28] Child, p. 46; W. N. King, "John Lyly and Elizabethan Rhetoric," *SP*, LII (1955), 161.

style achieves, its ability firmly to establish related points, make it suitable for moments of exposition and resolution and for speeches that draw lines of conflict. But definition followed by juxtaposition is the basis of all the dialogue in *Campaspe*, whether or not Croll's schemata are in use. To take an example freer of the Crollian devices, Clitus and Parmenio are talking with the noble Timoclea:

PARME. Madame, you neede not doubt, it is *Alexander*, that is, the conquerour.

TIMO. *Alexander* hath ouercome, not conquered.

PARME. To bring al vnder his subiection is to cōquer.

TIMO. He cannot subdue that which is diuine.

PARME. *Thebes* was not.

TIMO. Vertue is.

CLYTUS *Alexander* as hee tendreth vertue, so hee will you, he drinketh not bloud, but thirsteth after honor, he is greedy of victory, but neuer satisfied with mercie.[29] In fight terrible, as beecommeth a captaine, in conqueste milde, as beseemeth a king. In al things then which nothing can be greater he is *Alexander*.

CAMPAS. Then if it be such a thing to be *Alexander*, I hope it shalbe no miserable thing to be a virgin.

(A1ᵛ; I.i.41–54)

Lyly's vigor of expression is striking here. His verbal economy and his avoidance of periphrasis and of aureate

----

[29] Although none of Lyly's editors has seen fit to comment on this line, it seems to me that his pursuit of the eating metaphor has led him into a clause which, superficially at least, means the opposite of what is intended. It appears to mean that Alexander, dissatisfied with mercy, goes on to something else; whereas it is intended to mean that he is always trying for more. The difficulty lies in using an ingestion metaphor (appropriate to blood, honor, and victory) for mercy, which, from the king's point of view, is given out, not taken in.

vocabulary, everywhere bestowing energy on his style, achieve in this exchange between Timoclea and Parmenio a quality which C. S. Lewis justifiably calls "grandeur." [30] The tight balancing of clauses survives only in Clitus' more extended speech. In the lines preceding that speech, antithesis is achieved by stichomythic dialogue, each speaker picking up explicitly or implicitly a single word from his cue-line and performing a different, more-or-less contradictory turn upon it.

The passage is concerned wholly with the definition of Alexander. It is a set of statements concerning the position, power, and desires of the hero of the play. It establishes some of his qualities and sets up a context in which we can view him when he appears. There is no simile here, and the only metaphor is Clitus' commonplace eating imagery. We are concerned with ascertaining precisely what things are, not what they are like. The aim is to determine the properties of the king, by drawing or denying lines of relationship between him and other persons and circumstances in the immediate situation.

The word "property" has here, particularly in connection with Clitus' long speech, the double sense mentioned above. It is both factual and ethical, both what the man is, has, and does, and what it is fitting for him to be, have, and do. The two senses are intimately related: a man's obligations are here presented as arising out of the facts about him, particularly the fact of status. Because Alexander is a captain, he ought to be terrible in fight, and so he is. Because he is a king, he ought to be mild in conquest, and so he is. Lyly is presenting Alexander as the holder of a certain rank in the world, as a public character abstractly conceived, and Clitus' evaluation of him, here as before, depends upon his fulfillment of the duties enjoined by that

[30] Lewis, p. 316.

rank. Property decrees propriety here, and will do so throughout the play.

The passage illustrates particularly well another aspect of the definition process. A thing defined is defined in relation to other things, and therefore the related things must be defined also. Alexander is a conqueror: what is the nature of conquest and who is subject to it? Timoclea proposes a distinction between conquest and overcoming; Parmenio defines conquest in a manner which implies the suitability of the term to the present situation, but Timoclea disagrees. There emerges a statement that the term is appropriate to Thebes, a city, but not to virtue, a spiritual quality. So the process circles out from the initial statement and comes to a conclusion when the immediate area has been sketched in and we return to where we started: Parmenio has begun with a statement of Alexander's identity as conqueror, and, when the dialogue has arranged conquest, divinity, Thebes, virtue, and Alexander's desires in proper order, Clitus closes the flurry with the statement, "In al things . . . he is *Alexander*." Campaspe then sets Alexander next to a new entity, "a virgin"—we are given a hint of a set of definitional relationships yet to come, in this case a juxtaposition that contains one of the central issues of the play. How are we to define the relationship between a high-minded conqueror and a low-born virgin?

Lyly's dramatic euphuism, then, has three essential characteristics: it is founded on definitions, the definitions are placed in juxtaposition, and the dialogue moves through the pattern of juxtaposition setting it in order. It is a vigorous style; it is a factual and intellectual style. It is a tool superbly fitted for the intellectual exploration of a complex world. Euphuism here is analogous to the anecdotal structure that sets that world in motion, and to the multiple staging that contains that world. Let us turn to the world itself.

The World of Campaspe

C. ACT I: CONQUEST AND PHILOSOPHY

Since the quotations used in the previous section are drawn from the opening scene of *Campaspe,* I need not here dwell on it at length. The action and physical objects of the scene perform an expository function in a manner similar to that of the dialogue. Clitus and Parmenio introduce us verbally to Alexander's greatness. Visually the chief figure is introduced and set off by the presence of three groups of objects and people. First, as the references of Parmenio and Alexander indicate,[31] there are Theban spoils on the stage, treasure and whatnot, presumably brought on by the soldiers guarding the captives. Here are the physical acquisitions of conquest, the concretes of empire. Secondly, there are the captives, Timoclea and Campaspe, the former providing the test of Alexander's magnanimity.[32] Thirdly, there are the dutiful lieutenants, giving us the abstract terms in which we are to think of Alexander at this point. Booty, loyal lieutenants, and captives whose nobility and virtue he recognizes and respects: these define the successful and merciful captain.[33]

This much established, Alexander is left on stage to announce his intentions to his principal lieutenant and confidant, Hephestion. The captain, concerned with peace as well as war, wishes to foster philosophy and the arts. Future juxtapositions are thus prepared (the play is not

[31] A1^v; I.i.26 and A2^r; I.i.58.

[32] I have briefly discussed the function of the Timoclea interlude above, pp. 33–34.

[33] Alice S. Venezky remarks that "Lyly avoids the triumphal entry usually associated with his hero" and that the play begins "quietly" (*Pageantry on the Shakespearean Stage* [New York, 1951], p. 40). This is an under-estimate: Miss Venezky fails to note the praises of the lieutenants and the presence of the spoils. In contrast to some entries and triumphs that she describes, however, she is right in saying that this entry is not overwhelming: Lyly wants us to think and therefore does not dazzle us.

completely lacking in preparation), for, along with Campaspe, an artist and several philosophers will provide Alexander's major contacts in the play. Hephestion picks up the plan and forms with it another definition of Alexander: he extols the combination of philosopher and king.

The first scene is pervaded by the nobility of Timoclea and Alexander, and ends with the latter's resolution to seek wisdom. This lofty universe is immediately replaced by three pages whose desires are pungently expressed in the line, "I had rather fill my guttes, then my braines" ($A3^r$; I.ii.53–54). Manes and Psyllus complain and jest about their hunger; Granichus praises his master Plato for keeping as good a kitchen as a school. The scene concludes with a song in honor of wine, women, and especially food.

The comic pages are a staple element of Lylian drama; they are always concerned with their stomachs and always entertain us with chop-logic. Lyly's constant use of them, however, ought not to be taken as an indication that they have no particular relevance to the main events in any given play. In *Endimion*, it is generally agreed, the scenes with the pages and Sir Tophas constitute a parodic subplot; and, as I shall argue in Chapter III, the boys in *Gallathea* are involved in similarly related action. In *Campaspe*, they are not tightly integrated by analogous action; they do, however, provide a different point of view on the philosophy and art that Alexander has just resolved to foster and that will shortly appear embodied in the pages' masters. The tone is of course light: they do not writhe in the agony of starvation. The point is made, nonetheless, that the body has its claims as well as the mind. Pages have *their* status in the world too, with its own claims and relationships, with its own perspectives and possibilities. High-mindedness is not for every one.

There is also the chop-logic: Manes produces a syllogism to prove that the body when imprisoned is immortal. In an age as devoted to logic and rhetoric as the Elizabethan, the building of outrageously fallacious arguments by slight perversion of logical rules provides a notably pointed form of intellectual entertainment. In *Campaspe,* the practice has a particular significance. Logical argument, based on definition, constitutes the primary mode of dialogue in the play. The pages consciously pervert argument for their own amusement, and they eventually turn definition itself to humorous purposes, as when Manes tells Psyllus, "Cry hath diuerse significations, and may bee alluded to manye thinges, knaue but one, and can be applyed but to thee" (C2ᵛ; III.ii.23–25). Lyly is of course not questioning the seriousness or intelligence of his other characters. He is giving the kaleidoscope another whirl, this time for pure fun. In doing so, he is weaving a thread throughout the play that graciously appears to disclaim the importance of his own creation, a tactful gesture when one's audience is a queen.

Scene iii, Alexander's interview with the philosophers, is introduced by the monologue of Melippus. Like the opening dialogue of Clitus and Parmenio in the first scene, the necessary work of the monologue is the exposition of fact but its ultimate function is to present the terms in which we are to understand the following scene. Hence the unusual situation of an extraneous character delivering so long a speech. The issue at stake is the relationship between the philosophers and the king and his court. Melippus presents an absolute incompatibility between courtiers (he is one himself) and philosophers: "Seeing bookish men are so blockish, & so great clearkes such simple courtiers, I will neither be partaker of their comons nor their commēdations" (A4ʳ; I.iii.8–10). According to his account, one of the philosophers is so devoted to study that he must be spoonfed lest he not eat at all; he himself, on the other hand, is devoted to *his* job with all the passion of a fussy man ("I had neuer such adoe"!): the two are at opposite extremes. His account of Diogenes lifts the opposition a step, from the level of philosophers versus courtiers to the level of philosophers versus kings (Diogenes demands that Alexander come to him).

Alexander very quickly establishes the order he wants with the philosophers. They enter discussing metaphysics; he makes them functionaries of his court. He defines their precise role by alluding to the case of Calistenes, one of the famous classical examples of philosophers over-stepping their bounds in their relations with kings. Philosophy is not to intrude upon statecraft. The scholars' function is to instruct the young and to reassure the old, not to make policy and stand next to the throne: "Treasons againste [the] prince shall not bee borne out with the reasons of . . . Phylosophy. . . . In kinges causes I will not stande to schollers arguments" (B1ʳ; I.iii.70–76). Alexander then proceeds to test the philosophers with the catechism reported by Plutarch. He has no intention of joining personally in the professional pursuit of wisdom. He is king and judge, and only means "often to trye them" (B1ᵛ; I.iii.98).

It is apparent that Lyly's concern in the scene is solely with the establishment of the proper relationships among these men, for that is all that is done. Hephestion had expected that Alexander himself would turn philosopher, and comments, "Therefore would I leaue war, to studie wisdome, were I *Alexander.*" Alexander answers with an indirect assertion of his own identity: "So would I, were I *Hephestion*" (B1ᵛ; I.iii.100–102). What Alexander is, is settled and permanent. As king, he deals with philosophers to order his realm, not to become one of them.

Alexander leaves the stage, and the final thirty lines

of the scene introduce Diogenes in juxtaposition to the relationships established. His position is that of the thorough individualist, and consequently he accuses Plato and Aristotle of sycophancy. They in turn reproach him with neglect of king and duty, of breaking the laws and of general peevishness. We are left with a constellation: Alexander above because of his royalty, Diogenes outside because of his intellectual individualism, Plato and Aristotle in between because they have accommodated philosophy and courtiership in the interests of the total structure, Alexander's kingdom.

D. ACTS II, III, AND IV: LOVE AND THE REALM OF POWER

1. Alexander in Love

Alexander has been established as the merciful conqueror in war and the wise governor in peace. Some of the variety of Athens has been displayed. The second movement of the play begins. But in terms of total line-length, more than a quarter of the play has already passed, and only now does Lyly introduce the central conflict, the love affair and its relation to Alexander's career. The issues of the first act cannot be regarded as mere preliminaries to the "main action"—Alexander's relation to philosophy is no less a part of the subject of the play than his causally unrelated love for Campaspe. Indeed, his relationship with Diogenes is established and continued simultaneously with the love-affair.

Love, however, is the major irruptive force in this world. Its entry, in II.ii, is marked by an extraordinary outburst of pure euphuism in Lyly's earlier, *Euphues* manner: Hephestion's lengthy oration on the inappropriateness of Alexander's love for his captive. This speech halts the dialogue flow altogether to substitute for it a different rhythm, the rhythm of a monologue densely arguing one side of a case, a fanfaronnade of rhetorical questions (including all of the first five sentences), mythological references, and illustrations drawn from natural history. Alexander replies in kind. The effect of these speeches is to provide a clear introduction to the major issue in the offing, a firm driving of stakes into the ground to initiate the problem that will be of concern for much of the rest of the play. It is not that euphuism is particularly appropriate for love, but that it is a very useful style to draw strongly the lines of conflict on an important matter.[34]

The dialogue between Alexander and Hephestion, and Alexander's subsequent interview with Diogenes, introduce love in its relations to power and to reason. The character of love itself is pointedly *not* defined. The opening exchanges in which Alexander is leading up to his confession set a keynote for the scene by establishing the ambiguous value of the passion:

> ALEX. Is loue a vice?
> HEPH. It is no vertue.
> (B3ᵛ; II.ii.15–16)

The definition is avoided, and in its place we have, in these two sentences, a statement of the difficulties of classifying love. That statement will be supplemented later: before the play is over, all the major characters express ideas on love. Here the ambiguous value assigned to love is co-ordinate with the tangle it creates, for qualities previously associated with Alexander here slip from his grasp.

Rather than defining love, Alexander gives us in reply

---

[34] See the brief discussion of the dramatic value of Lyly's placing of certain other long speeches by Geoffrey Tillotson, "The Prose of Lyly's Comedies," *Essays in Criticism and Research* (Cambridge, England, 1943), pp. 25–26.

to Hephestion's long protest an outburst portraying the
effect of love upon him:

> My case were light *Hephestion,* and not worthy to be
> called loue, if reason were a remedie, or sentēses could
> salue, that sense cannot conceaue. Litle do you know,
> and therefore sleightly doe you regard the dead embers
> in a priuate persõ, or liue coles in a great prince, whose
> passions and thoughts do as farre exceede others in
> extremitie, as their callinges doe in Maiestie. An Eclipse
> in the Sunne is more then the fallinge of a starre, none
> can conceiue the tormentes of a king, vnlesse hee be a
> king, whose desires are not inferiour to their dignities.
> And then iudge *Hephestion* if the agonies of loue be
> dangerous in a subiect, whether they be not more then
> deadly vnto *Alexander,* whose deep and not to be con-
> ceiued sighes, cleaue the heart in shiuers, whose wounded
> thoughtes can neither be expressed nor endured.
>
> (B4ʳ–C1ʳ; II.ii.77–89)

Alexander is a volcano of desire. But for all the "ex-
tremetie" in this speech, it is curiously abstract and im-
personal. It does not mention the beloved object—indeed,
aside from Alexander's brief reference to the "sweete face
of *Campaspe"* at the beginning of the scene, only Hephestion speaks of her beauty. Neither is it charged with the
individual personality of Alexander as lover. The only
intrusion of the momentary and personal, the daily flux
of things, on his side of the love-affair is his claim in a
later scene that he needs a rest from warfare (D1ʳ;
III.iv.40–42). Rather the speech is enormously charged
with his rank. His passion is that of a king. Any great
king is supposed to love in this extravagant way; desires
are commensurate with dignity. This situation is not merely
the result of Elizabethan dramatic decorum, which does

not demand that humanity be entirely suppressed in favor of public position, that the individual yield wholly to the typical. Lyly apparently wants this. He is concerned precisely with the effect of passion on the holder of exalted rank. Alexander's speech is no more than, and no less than, a definition and description of royal desire.

This love is juxtaposed to two other abstractions, reason and power, and each of the juxtapositions is triple. First, reason. This is a love that "sense cannot conceaue"; "none can conceiue the tormentes of a king"; his sighs are not only deep but also "not to be conceiued" and his thoughts cannot be expressed. The paradox, of course, is fairly conventional: Alexander is talking quite well. But Lyly's repetition of the point drives it home as serious at least in the realm of ideas. We are four times told that love or its effects are beyond the grasp of human reason. The second aspect of this juxtaposition is that love cannot be dislodged by reason: Alexander's outburst is a reply to Hephestion's lengthy arguments against this love, and Hephestion is forced to give up "when neither reason nor counsel can be heard" (C1ʳ; II.ii.94–95). Thirdly, love cannot be induced by reason. Hephestion reminds his master that Campaspe may not return his love, a suggestion that Alexander thinks ridiculous:

ALEX. I am a conquerour, shee a captiue, I as fortunate, as she faire: my greatnes may answere her wants, and the gifts of my minde, the modestie of hers: Is it not likely then that shee should loue? Is it not reasonable?
HEPHEST. You say that in loue there is no reason, and therefore there can be no likelyhood.

(C1ʳ; II.ii.106–111)

Love not only confounds reason, it confounds power. In the first place, the situation itself is most inappropriate, as Alexander himself admits when he first confesses: "I loue *Hephestion,* I loue I loue *Campaspe,* a thing farre vnfit for a Macedonian, for a king, for *Alexander.*" The admission provides the opening for Hephestion, whose rhetorical questions, exalting Alexander as "the sonne of *Phillip,* king of Macedon. . . . that minde, whose greatnes the world coulde not containe. . . . whose hard and vnconquered heart hath made so many yeelde," drive home the disparity of the relationship. But the simple fact of the disparity is not all. Like reason, power can neither resist love nor compel it. Alexander asserts that even the gods cannot resist love (C1^r; II.ii.90), and Hephestion picks up the statement to force Alexander's admission that no one can compel it either:

HEPHEST. Suppose she loues not you. . . .
ALEX. I am a king, and wil commaund.
HEPHE. You may, to yeelde to luste by force, but to consent to loue by feare you cannot.
ALEX. Why, what is that, which *Alexander* maye not conquer as he list?
HEPHEST. Why, that which you say the Gods cannot resiste, Loue.

(C1^r; II.ii.98–105)

The power of the conqueror has received a major check. In the development of the story, of course, the check is only a possibility at this point, the state of Campaspe's feelings being unknown. In thematic development, however, the check is perfectly genuine. Indeed, the fact that Campaspe's feelings are unknown, the fact that the lovers are dramatically disengaged and that this is not a love scene, frees our attention for the thematic development. Lyly's plotlessness makes the dramatic situation less insistent, clearing the way for a fuller perception of what is happening to Alexander, of how ideas are re-grouping around him. Alexander, all-powerful both by virtue of his might as displayed in the conquest of Thebes and by virtue of his intelligence and perception as displayed in his treatment of Timoclea and the philosophers, is blocked. He who pre-eminently stood for power and for reason (the latter in its common-sense form, rather than the reasoning of "schollers arguments") has entered an area where he loses the position conferred on him by those values. He has been checked, not only on the level of fact, where he is a king, but also, by his inclusion of the gods in his admissions, on the level of aspiration, where he would be divine.[35] By the same token, Hephestion's usefulness has been cancelled out. Hephestion, associated with Alexander's power and serving him in this scene as the voice of reason, is rejected in favor of a go-between:

ALEX.   No more *Hephestion*: in this case I wil vse mine owne counsell, and in all other thine aduice, thou mayst be a good soldier, but neuer good louer. Call my page.
(Ci^r; II.ii.112–114)

In a stroke of Lyly's constructive genius, Alexander then crosses the stage to interview Diogenes, to talk with the most fiercely rational person in Athens on the subjects of power and desire. The pace of the dialogue quickens as Diogenes asserts, in various ways, the fact of his own individuality over against the fact of Alexander's. Kings he scorns as only men whose power relates to matters he

[35] The question of Alexander's yearning for divinity has been raised before. Timoclea has asserted that he "cannot subdue that which is diuine" (A1^v; I.i.45); Aristotle has rebuked Crisippus for supposing Alexander guilty of desires for divinity (B1^v; I.iii.106–109); and Hephestion has used this supposed desire of his king as an argument against his love for Campaspe (B4^v; II.ii.70).

does not care about. The opinions of Plato he would prefer to dismiss because they are not his own. He knows that desire hinders content, and that even Alexander cannot prevent death. The king admires this reductive rationalism, but its effect is to make him re-assert his own individuality: he tells his lieutenant, in an echo of their earlier exchange at the end of the philosophers scene in I.iii, *"Hephestion,* were I not *Alexander,* I would wishe to be *Diogenes"* (Cɪᵛ; II.ii.148–149). The scene comes to an end with two opposed individuals: Diogenes, despising worldly power, full of acerbic rationalism, and dismissing desire, and Alexander, powerful, reasonable, but in love.

I have called the interview with Diogenes a stroke of constructive genius because it beautifully completes the intellectual action of the scene between Alexander and Hephestion. In that scene love performs its triple damages on power and on reason. In so doing it robs Alexander of his identity; that is, it destroys the definition we have had of him hitherto. Thus torn loose from his accustomed moorings, he proposes to encroach upon the identity of Campaspe, assuming that she is malleable to his every wish. Hephestion protests, asserting Campaspe's right to her own feelings: "Suppose she loues not you." The protest is swept aside ("Call my page"), and Alexander crosses the stage. The interview with Diogenes then restores Alexander's identity: against the onslaught of Diogenes' vigorous statement of self, Alexander is reminded that he is Alexander. The interview "recreates" his "spirits" (Cɪᵛ; II.ii.118) as he had hoped it would. His flight of passion is over, his reason and his power are retained, and we will never again see him in the complete grasp of love. The problems inherent in the clash between love and power will continue to be important, but primarily in the different form in which they are seen by Apelles.

The World of Campaspe

The artist is summoned, and the world of love and beauty belongs to him.

2. *Apelles and Campaspe*

Apelles' art is lavished on love. All the paintings present in his shop or mentioned by himself or by his page are of amorous subjects. His portrait of Venus herself is twice mentioned, and his first scene with Campaspe is partly occupied with conversation provoked by his paintings of the amorous escapades of Jupiter: those involving Leda, Alcmena, Danae, Europa, and Antiopa. By the agency of these paintings, physically present on stage, the theme of love's relationship to power is continued. Campaspe objects to these divine seductions as the exploits of lust, accusing Jupiter of "a foule deceit" with Leda and "an infamous fact" with Alcmena, and giving the common tropological interpretation of the Danae story, that the lady yielded her favors for gold.[36] These myths are, of course, all parallels to her own relationship with Alexander. The virgin objects to power forcing love. The fact that we learn her views in this way, instead of from an Isabella-Angelo scene with Alexander, means that all the stress is placed on the moral position, the conviction, and none upon an event in the personal relationship. Campaspe's objections are not an element in an emotional history, but another factor in the abstract web of propriety that Lyly is weaving.

[36] C3ᵛ; III.iii.11, 14, 19. Campaspe's opinions cohere with the mythographical tradition. In Ovid, these seductions appear in Arachne's tapestry as examples of the gods' treachery (*Metamorphoses*, VI.103–114). The individual stories, of course, receive various interpretations in the Renaissance, but commentary on the group, as a group, is fairly summed up by Sandys (although he is later than the play) when he remarks that the tapestry "published the vices of great ones" (George Sandys, *Ovid's Metamorphosis Englished, Mythologiz'd and Represented in Figures* [London, 1632], p. 221).

Apelles takes a different view, not condemning the gods' amorousness but inferring from the stories the beauty and amiability of the women. This behavior is of a piece with his attitude toward Campaspe. He loves her at first sight, but his love emerges in a very different way from Alexander's. He is far less concerned than Alexander with his own feelings and position and far more concerned with the inspiration for those feelings, the beauty of Campaspe. His concern with her beauty reaches a climax in his soliloquy at the end of the third act:

> O bewtifull countenaunce, the expresse image of *Venus*, but sõwhat fresher: the only pattern of that eternitie which *Iupiter* dreaming of asleep, could not cõceiue agayne waking.
>
> (D3ʳ; III.v.40–43)

The implication that Venus, in contrast to Campaspe, is slightly stale is rather amusing (there is a lurking sexual overtone here), and much of Apelles' praise is conventionally Petrarchan (e.g. "I shall neuer drawe your eies well, because they blind mine" [C3ᵛ; III.iii.1–2]). The commonplace compliment about Venus, however, only builds up to the wonderful line about Jupiter's dream of eternity. This is a different Jupiter. The fact that his grasp upon ultimate being is only momentary indicates that we are, briefly, on the loftiest level of the Neoplatonic universe. Campaspe's face, as "the only pattern of that eternitie," has the effect on Apelles exactly proper in Neoplatonic thought: "All beauty is as it were a beame of that infinite and diuine beauty that is in God: and therefore as the diuine forme draweth vnto it true and perfect loues, so the image and similitude thereof [e.g. Campaspe's face] draweth the image of loues [e.g. Apelles' love for Campaspe, which reflects that higher form of love, that of the soul for its Creator]." [37] This fine line, with its allegorical resonance and its lengthened, deepened rhythm, stands out as an eloquent tribute to the object that inspires Apelles' love. His appreciation of Campaspe is far richer than Alexander's.

The idea of contrasting Apelles and Alexander in this way may have been suggested to Lyly by Castiglione, who handles the story in those terms in Book I of *The Courtier*: "I beleve Appelles conceived a far greater joy in behoulding the beawty of Campaspes then did Alexander, for a man maye easilye beleeve that the love of them both proceaded of that beawtye, and perhaps also for this respect Alexander determined to bestowe her upon him, that (in his minde) could knowe her more perfectlye then he did." [38] In Lyly, Alexander's overt appreciation of Campaspe's beauty is perfunctory; Apelles' is not. The nexus of relationship to Campaspe for Alexander is his own feelings; for Apelles it is her beauty, an image of ultimate being. Apelles certainly can "knowe her more perfectlye," and Alexander realizes it: in uniting the lovers, he tells Apelles, "*Alexander* is cloied with looking on that, which thou wondredst at" (F3^v; V.iv.139–140). [39]

Apelles' soliloquy is delivered in the same ignorance of Campaspe's feelings as Alexander's outburst had been. Only in Campaspe's soliloquy before her second sitting do we learn that she too has fallen in love at that first interview. The triangle has at last been completed, and the relationship between love and power has been com-

[37] Pierre de la Primaudaye, *The French Academie* (London, 1618), p. 482.

[38] Sir Thomas Hoby, tr., *The Book of The Courtier*, ed. Walter Raleigh (London, 1900), p. 97.

[39] Hunter (p. 161) calls Castiglione's point "too philosophical for Lyly's play." I think he overlooks the implications of the lines I have discussed in these two paragraphs.

plicated thereby. Now, as well as having a king in love with a captive, we have a king capable of exerting his power over a love-relationship to which he is not party. One result of the possible threat of power in this situation has already taken place: Apelles has resorted to blemishing the portrait in order to have Campaspe sit for him again.[40]

The second result is that we get a full presentation of the feelings of Campaspe. Hitherto she has merely been an object; now she becomes an active agent. She is obliged to cope with the facts of her position and her emotions. In her first soliloquy she reproaches herself for falling in love with the painter rather than the prince. She then produces a justification for such action in the form of a description of love's ways: "Affection is a fire, which kindleth aswell in the bramble as in the oak, and catcheth hold where it first lighteth, not where it may best burne" (E1^r; IV.ii.7–9). This description is supplemented in her second soliloquy by her statement, "Content is such a life, I care not for aboundance" (E2^v; IV.iv.19–20). These lines provide the first description of love itself (as opposed to its effects) in the play. Others will come from other characters, but Campaspe has taken her stand and made her choice. In the second remark she has added to the customary abstract nouns of definitional discourse a verb of emotional preference. The center of her being is discovered, and now the play must find a solution that will accommodate all the characters.

In making up her own mind, Campaspe also makes one important suggestion toward that solution. Power may distort love; therefore power will consort with love, Campaspe thinks, only when the lovers are equal in power: "In kinges there can be no loue, but to Queenes: for as

---

[40] See pp. 76–78 for a discussion of the blemished portrait and its implications.

neere must they meete in maiestie, as they doe in affection.
It is requisite to stande aloofe from kings loue, *Ioue*,[41]
and lightening" (E3ʳ; IV.iv.30–33).

3. *Alexander's Attempt to Paint*

Act III consists mostly of Apelles' scenes with Campaspe
and the activities of the pages; but its central scene (III.
iv) is a series of encounters involving all the major
characters. The three members of the love-triangle come
together for the only time in the play prior to the final
scene of resolution. Alexander and Diogenes deliver juxtaposed judgments on the begging Cynic, and the courtiers
re-appear for the first time since the opening of the play
to express their views on Alexander's stay in Athens.[42]

That stay has been long enough to become a noticeable
intermission in the conqueror's career. Perceiving something odd in Alexander's manner, Clitus and Parmenio
are worried. But Parmenio scorns Clitus' suggestion that
Alexander is in love: his strength "cannot so soone be
melted into the weake conceites of loue" (C4ᵛ; III.iv.17–
18). Rather Parmenio is inclined to attribute Alexander's
mood to a cause related to Alexander as conqueror: Aristotle's depressing announcement of the existence of many
worlds. Alexander and Hephestion, dismissing the courtiers
with a promise of imperial business, take up the same
discussion of love versus war. The king's view, surprisingly,
is very close to Parmenio's. Upon being twitted by Hephestion about his love for Campaspe, Alexander declares his
greater affection for Bucephalus "if occasion serue either
of conflicte or of conquest" (C4ᵛ; III.iv.32). Hephestion
replies that the important factor is not occasion, which

---

[41] Especially Jove the lover as presented earlier.

[42] The stage directions on A4ʳ call for their appearance in the
philosophers' scene (I.iii), but they have no lines.

appears in abundance, but will. Alexander states that he merely wants a breathing space in the midst of his labors.

This is all very odd in a man who has previously spoken of the enormous fervor of royal passion. One's immediate reaction is either that Alexander is feigning unconcern or that he is baldly rationalizing. Actually he is doing neither. He has not stopped loving Campaspe, nor is he so stupid as to deceive himself or to try to deceive Hephestion with a transparent excuse for prolonging his Athenian sojourn. What has happened is that the perspective has altered. The play has been proceeding lately on the level of the personal relationships of the lovers; now the appearance and conversation of the courtiers has pulled us back to the larger dimensions of the situation, to the dimension where Alexander is a king surrounded by a court and an army. About Alexander's psychology no valid inference can be drawn from the leap between his attitude in II.ii and his feelings here, for there is no developing psychological portrait. Alexander's love has already been stated quite strongly enough—repetition it does not need, and development Lyly does not care to give it. It is a unit that requires no expansion. It is a unit related to other issues in the play by the logical joins of a web of discrete abstractions, not by the more subtle intercolorations of an organic, psychological mixture.

The scene with the begging Cynic, which I have already discussed out of context, follows. In context, it continues and reinforces the new perspective. Alexander is behaving within the framework of his original definition. In preferring Bucephalus over Campaspe he is again the captain. In his treatment of the begging Cynic he is again the king. I hasten to add that this is not repetition. The lines of decorous relationship were easy to draw in Act I; now they are more difficult, more complex. Propriety between a captain and a conquered population is a fairly clear-cut issue. When the captain stands between his warhorse and a woman, it is a more sophisticated, delicate matter. To be a king with obedient philosophers, or even with stiff-necked philosophers such as Diogenes, is one thing: lines of proper relationship are easily drawn. To be a king with a relapsed philosopher who appeals to charity in a way that ignores public position is another. The scene with the begging Cynic fortifies our notion of kingship as Alexander's essence. He has been defined as king by his courtiers' words and in situations that he himself has brought about (the interviews with Timoclea and the philosophers). The begging Cynic provides a situation of a different kind and one for which Alexander is not responsible. In this unexpected encounter Alexander proves his essence again, and the web of propriety that Lyly is weaving gains a few more delicate filaments.

It is a brief incident, an overture for a larger rendition of the same theme in Alexander's attempt to paint. In the painting episode his function as king is again defined, but this time by a courtly rap on the knuckles from Apelles for exceeding his proper limits. Alexander approaches Apelles in his professional capacity as artist, beginning with an extravagant compliment on his "cunning" (as Apelles' skill is called throughout the play): "You may paint flowers aswell with sweete smels, as fresh colours" (D1^v; III.iv.64–65). This flight of fancy is immediately turned by Apelles into an observation on the genuine difficulties of art, portraying the inner invisibilia of the sitter: "It is no lesse harde to paint sauours then vertues, colours can neither speake nor think" (D1^v; III.iv.68–69). Alexander responds with a technical inquiry, the answer to which he immediately disagrees with. It is perhaps characteristic that in painting Alexander would "begin with the eie, as a light to all the rest" (D1^v; III.iv.72): it is his own function to be a light to all the rest, to be the guiding organ of the state. But the rules of art are not the rules of a monarchy, and there is no royal road to them. Apelles lays down the restrictions of the craft: "If you wil paint, as you are a king, your Maiesty, maye beginne wher you please, but as you wold be a painter, you must begin with the face" (D1ᵛ; III.iv.73–75). The ensuing dialogue develops the point. Speed may be remarkable but is not meritorious in art; the varied fancies of man and the diverse favors of women must be heeded; and in the work of the pencil itself there are, as the would-be sketcher Alexander concludes, "so many rules and regardes, that ones hand ones eie, ones mind muste all draw together" (D2ʳ; III.iv.108–109). Apelles finally compliments Alexander for drawing "like a king," and Alexander takes the point: "I think so: but nothing more vnlike a Paynter" (D2ʳ; III.iv.112–113).

In this scene Lyly has further developed the notions of property and propriety. Men have their specialized duties coordinate with their talents. Propriety lies not only in fulfilling them as Alexander does and the beggar does not. It also lies in eschewing the temptation to go outside of them and invade another's sphere. Submission to the temptation produces a botched job. A king's drawing is bad art, as "schollers arguments" in "kinges causes" produce bad statecraft.

4. *Scratched Faces*

So far Athens has been portrayed as a prosperous and well-ordered kingdom. The mendicancy of the Cynic and Alexander's attempt to paint have been the only improper actions dealt with. My discussion of the second movement of *Campaspe* will be complete when I have considered three other corruptions that figure in the action. These corruptions are not gross: they are treated in accordance with the prevailing lightness of tone. They are nonetheless present, one spoken of by the courtiers, one brought more forcefully into being by a direct accusation from Diogenes, and one actually performed on-stage by Apelles. The three are linked, moreover, by the fact that Lyly uses with each the image of a scratched face.

Clitus and Parmenio are a gracious pair. Yet as courtiers they are involved in more than compliments to their king; near the throne, they touch upon some of the less attractive realities and possibilities of power. In their first appearance they had indulged in some sly deprecation of each other. For example:

PARME. I but *Clytus* I perceiue you are borne in the East, and neuer laugh but at the sunne rising, which argueth though a duetie where you ought, yet no great deuotion where you might.

(A1ʳ; I.i.19–21)

This is mild raillery. In a different context, however, Parmenio's insinuation, that Clitus is more apt to support a rising power than to remain devoted to the established one, could be a grave accusation. Lyly allows their awareness of political reality to emerge more firmly at their re-appearance in III.iv: here they are worried about Alexander's mood, and yet anxious not to call down on themselves the unpleasantness that can result from interfering in the king's business:

PARME. In kinges causes I rather loue to doubte then coniecture, and thinke it better to be ignoraunt then inquisitiue: they haue long eares and stretched armes, in whose heades suspition is a proofe, and to bee accused is to be condemned.

CLYTUS Yet betweene vs there canne be no daunger to finde out the cause: for that there is no malice to with-

stand it. It may be an vnquenchable thirste of conquering maketh him vnquiet: it is not vnlikely his long ease
hath altred his humour: that hee shoulde be in loue, it
is not impossible.

PARME. In loue *Clytus*, no, no, it is as farre from his
thought, as treason in ours.

(C4ᵛ; III.iv.5–15)

Of course Alexander is no tyrant taking suspicion for
truth; there is no "daunger" or malice in the present
situation; and treason would be unthinkable for these
courtiers. Yet, if the situation is regarded publicly and
abstractly rather than in terms of personal character, there
could be tyranny, malice, and treason. The possibility of
these things is a guide for the courtiers and a further
delineation of propriety. The very reference to treason is
so far-fetched that it is all the more striking. Lyly is
deliberately carrying his picture into darker regions.

The real corruption appears in the courtiers' next and
last appearance, and it is a double one. The army, they
report, is degenerating, and Parmenio delivers a sustained
lament on the subject, enumerating the soft clothes and
habits of the soldiers turned lovers. That is one corruption;
it is doubled by the courtiers' fear of mentioning openly
the disorder they bewail. Clitus answers Parmenio's lament:

> Cease *Permenio*, least in speaking what becommeth thee
> not, thou feele what liketh thee not: trueth is neuer
> without a scratcht face, whose tongue although it cannot
> be cut out, yet must it be tied vp.

(E2ʳ; IV.iii.25–28)

Now, although the army is more Alexander's business
than Parmenio's, it *does* become a courtier to advise his
prince, and it becomes a prince to heed such counsel

whether or not it pleases him. Moreover, Clitus' expectation of martyrdom at the hands of royal wrath seems unaccountable in the light of Alexander's respect for people and for truth. Once again a point is being made for intellectual purposes—regardless of its inconsistency with the texture of the present human situation. The fact remains that the army is falling from its proper condition as a result of Alexander's dalliance, and that his dalliance is giving rise to most uncharacteristic ideas about what he might do next. The upset of order in Athens results in a dereliction from duty on the part of both the army and the courtiers. If we take "truth" as "the ideal," the powerful emblem of truth with a scratched face appears not only as Clitus' description of the dangers of untactful honesty, but also as an image of corruption itself, of that corruption of which two examples have just emerged.

Diogenes has no fears about speaking truth, and does so at length in his "flight" over Athens, his only independent undertaking in the play. On one level his rebuke of the citizens is another of Lyly's displays. Diogenes uses traditional invective against luxury, sloth, sycophancy, and hypocrisy with great energy. We all enjoy a forceful jeremiad, and Psyllus voices this reaction to his speech when he says, "It was sport ynogh for me to see these old huddles hit home" (E1ʳ; IV.i.75–76).

But Diogenes' invective has an integral function in the play, a clue to which lies in its presentation as a flight. The expectation that Diogenes will fly (the flight has been adverised in III.ii) promotes anticipation both among the citizens and in the audience. Diogenes, of course, does not fly, and the sensation-seeking citizens are enraged at being duped. Lyly's audience, whether or not it was duped, does not have to say so, and the spectators may have the pleasant experience of feeling superior to citizens who believed that the impossible would take place. At the same time their anticipations are fulfilled by Diogenes' rhetoric, which comes as a change of pace amid the courtliness of the play. The use of the word "flight" is eventually justified by a pun: Diogenes finally employs it in the sense of departure rather than aerial self-propulsion: "I will studie to flye further from you" (D4^v; IV.i.52–53).

The pun is only a literal justification, however, for literal-minded people. In its original, advertised sense, flight is important in two ways. First, the only non-combative remark that Diogenes makes in the scene is to his page:

> MANES Why maister, meane you not to flye?
> DIOG. No *Manes,* not without wings.
> (D4^v; IV.i.70–71)

The basic irony of the scene is inherent in this exchange. Diogenes is determined to fulfill his function as a man, not to attempt the functions of birds. In his sarcastic argumentativeness throughout the play, Diogenes has many lines more notable for repartee than for consistent thought, but underneath the raillery usually lurks the moral point that one should do only what belongs to what one is or professes to be. He rebukes the citizens for failing to do this, for failing to fulfill their essences and observe their limitations as men. "You build," he points out, "as though you shoulde liue for euer, and surfeit as though you should die to morow" (D4^r; IV.i.44–46). Their disordered lives lead him to the conclusion that they are *not* men: "Speak trueth of your selues, and cõfesse you are deuils. . . . Either you think there are no Gods, or I must think yee are no men" (D4^r; IV.i.33–44). We, of course, have seen nothing that supports Diogenes' accusation: the Athenian population has not previously appeared. But no earlier scene displaying Athenian vice is necessary. Support for the accusation, at least in the terms that Diogenes makes it, lies in the scene itself. Ironically, the Athenians have been brought to hear a sermon on their lack of proper manliness by their eagerness to see a man behaving unlike a man. Their receptivity to the advertisement of Diogenes' flight completely exposes them to his rebuke. A final twist of the irony lies in their response to the harangue: exhorted to behave like men, they reply by calling their accuser a dog and by promising to "cause all the boies in the streete to hisse" at him (D4ᵛ; IV.i.67). Diogenes is willing to accept the epithet—who would not be a dog if such are called men?—and he would sarcastically welcome the metamorphosis of boys into serpents as further proof of the inhuman corruption he so delights to inveigh against.

The second significance of "flight" lies in the notion of a creative act. Diogenes' harangue is a kind of creation, involving construction and display and having a rough parallel to the major example of creation in the play, the art of Apelles. In this light, Manes' reference to Daedalus has a double application. Manes, explaining to Granichus how Diogenes will fly, asserts that Diogenes "hath found *Dedalus* old waxen wings, and hath beene peecing them this moneth" (D3ᵛ; IV.i.12–13). The allusion is not merely facetious. Daedalus is the great artificer as well as the flyer, and his achievement in escaping from Crete lay as much in his construction of the wings as in his use of them. Diogenes then has an art parallel to Daedalus', a point that emerges quite strongly from the emphasis in Manes' line on the construction of the wings. Both make and then perform.[43]

---

[43] Sidney cites Daedalus as a "guide" for "the highest flying wit" in "An Apologie for Poetrie" (in *Elizabethan Critical Essays*, ed. G. Gregory Smith [Oxford, 1904], I.195). The flight of Daedalus and Icarus was moralized in the Renaissance as an example of the contrasting progresses of one who adheres to *mediocritas* or the golden

Diogenes' art is in the service of truth. Its result is the excellent possibility of his having a scratched face. The citizens' line, "Dog, dog, take a boane" (D4^v; IV.i.62) indicates the staging that any director would employ to demonstrate the outrage of the citizens and to bring the scene to a climax: they are throwing things at their accuser. The scene has presented a glaring example of the most generalized kind of corruption, marked by the dramatic realization of the emblem of truth (in this case, her temporary representative, Diogenes) having a scratched face.

The third corruption is the blemished portrait of Campaspe, another literally scratched face. The portrait is the central prop of the play, the chief example of creation, the representation (within the limits of human art) of the beauty that Apelles has exalted as a Platonic Idea, and the product of the love for her that he later swears will be eternal.[44] That such a portrait should be blemished points to a serious wrong in the whole love-situation.[45]

Ironically, Apelles mars the image of Campaspe in order to see her again. There seems no other way for the artist

---

mean and one who attempts to soar out of the range allotted to man: see, for example, Natales Comes, *Mythologiae*, VII.16 (Frankfurt, 1596), Arthur Golding, "Epistle to Leicester," ll. 173–180, prefixed to *The XV Bookes of P. Ouidius Naso, entytuled Metamorphosis*, as rep. by W. H. D. Rouse, ed., *Shakespeare's Ovid* (Carbondale, 1961), and George Sandys, p. 290. Such a moral is obviously relevant to the content of Diogenes' rebuke; since, however, the reference to Daedalus is to the wings, not to the flight itself, and does not mention Icarus, I do not think Lyly is directing our attention to that potenial dimension of the allusion. A theater audience would not have time to follow the connections without further help and emphasis from the playwright.

[44] At E2^v; IV.iv.3.

[45] Lyly has varied his presentation of the scratched-face image in a highly theatrical manner, using it in the dialogue with the courtiers, in the stage action with Diogenes, and in a prop with Apelles.

to further his love-affair, simply because he is in the social station of an artist. The soliloquy in which he calls Campaspe the pattern of eternity and which ends with his injuring the portrait, begins with a lament: "Vnfortunate *Apelles*, and therefore vnfortunate, beecause *Apelles*" (D2ᵛ; III.v.13). Because he is who he is, a painter subordinate to a king, his dilemma arises, for his emotions put him into conflict with the king. In this dilemma he concludes that "wit must worke, where authoritie is not" (D3ᵛ; III.v.56–57). He acts with craft: he turns his "cunning," the quality that has been isolated as the essence of his art, to the injury of his art. The blemish on the portrait, significant in itself, symbolizes the perversion of the art that created it and the dislocation of the man whose essential character is the practice of that art.[46]

These three corruptions do not excite great alarm in the audience. Little emotional reaction is expected; the points have been made intellectually. Nonetheless, the degeneration of the army and the allied fears of the courtiers, the imputed immorality of the citizens, and the blemish on the portrait are plain indications of disorder in the ideal

---

[46] At this point in the play, Lyly momentarily appears to create an overriding analogy in situation between Alexander and Apelles: each man's love for Campaspe works to the detriment of his professional pursuit. Although, however, such an analogy is a potential method of handling the material of the Campaspe story, Lyly does not develop it in his play. Apelles' soliloquy does not present his love for Campaspe as the sole cause for his violation of his art (as Alexander's love is the sole cause of his extended vacation from war). Rather it is the rivalry, the whole triangular situation, that prompts Apelles to blemish the portrait. Apelles' love, after all, has prompted him to paint a great work, and he is eventually united to Campaspe without any thought being given to a love-versus-art conflict. The exploitation of large analogies of situation is not Lyly's technique in this play. He comes to use such a technique in *Gallathea* and the other mythological comedies: see the more detailed discussion of the matter in Chapter III, Sections A and B.

world of the city. The portrait being the nexus of the love-triangle, its blemish is the indication of most immediate importance. A triangle of king and captive and painter whose relationships are disordered because their ranks are at odds with their personal feelings may result in the kind of wounding of the excellent that is exemplified by the blemished portrait. The dereliction of the army and the courtiers is an indication of the corruption that can take place in the general way of life represented in the play. The vices of Athens as rebuked by Diogenes extend the idea of corruption to its largest and philosophically most precise level: when men do not act in the proper manner of men, the whole estate of man is endangered. As the fourth act closes, the kingdom of Athens is awry.

E. ACT V: THE ORDERING OF THE KINGDOM

Act V takes up the tangled skein created by the incidents of the middle movement of the play and brings it to a balanced conclusion. Given Lyly's love of particulars, the conclusion is complicated, but it proceeds in a clear order of judgment: the problems raised are dealt with first on the most general level, next in relation to the opposition between love and war, and finally with the specific triangle.

The act opens with the display of the dancing, tumbling, and singing boys (Perim, Milo, and Trico) before Diogenes, who rejects their accomplishments as unworthy of men. In terms of its function and placing in the dramatic structure, the scene resembles the opening scene of Act V of *Hamlet*. In both cases a basic subject that has underlain much of the action surfaces for a full and very literal realization just prior to the concluding action of the play. In *Hamlet* the subject is death: arising repeatedly in the play, the fact of death and its physical consequences are literally rendered in the gravedigger scene. In *Campaspe* the relationship of a man's activities to his specific position in the world and to the general fact of his being a man has been an active issue in many scenes: in V.i the performing boys demonstrate courtly accomplishments that Diogenes explicitly condemns as sub-human. Perim can rule his legs but does not follow the path of learning; Milo can bend his body but not his mind; and Trico's singing is only an imitation of something done naturally and excellently by birds. The scene is a firm confrontation between the philosophic and ascetic on the one hand and the courtly and artistic on the other—between the rationalist who argues that, mind being the distinguishing characteristic of man, it is therefore the *essence* of man and the the only thing worth cultivation, and those who would find other accomplishments excellent as well. Diogenes has the most effective *lines*, pointing out the foolishness of the boys' imbalance of attainment. His position is undercut, however, by his own page Manes, who is no example of scholarly learning and whose description of what Diogenes has taught him [47] is no credit to philosophy. In theatrical performance, moreover, the trenchancy of Diogenes' criticism would be amply met by the excellence of the tumbling and dancing, which were admired Renaissance pursuits susceptible of considerable philosophic justification, and by the extraordinary beauty of the song, "What bird so sings." (We lack the music, but the lyric is a fine example of "golden" Renaissance poetry.) [48] As personal confrontation, the scene ends in stalemate. As intellectual presentation to the audience, it ends in offering a choice. You may train yourself to follow Alexander and be a courtier, or you may

[47] "To fast, lye hard, and runne away" (E4^r; V.i.49).

[48] There was, of course, a song here in the original production. That it was *this* song (whether or not Lyly himself wrote it) seems the most likely conclusion in the controversy over the songs in Lyly's plays, although the evidence does not permit a definitive conclusion. See Hunter's able review of the controversy, pp. 367–372.

be a philosopher and scrape roots. Which you regard as an evil depends on circumstances and self.

The second scene, Apelles' final soliloquy, brings the theme of the dread of Alexander's power to its height. Apelles fears that he has revealed his passion to his royal rival and that in so doing he has brought himself into the danger that he (and the courtiers in a different connection) had recognized as a potential element of the situation. But Apelles cannot resist his passion:

> O loue, I neuer beefore knewe what thou wert, and nowe haste thou made mee that I know not what my self am? Onely this I knowe, that I must endure intollerable passions, for vnknowne pleasures.
>
> (E4ᵛ; V.ii.8–11)

These lines complete the thought of his earlier portrait-blemish soliloquy. In a play involving so acutely the issue of who people are, love has wrought its greatest effect: Apelles knows not himself. It has taken him outside of the system of relationships that have defined people hitherto, the relationships based on social and intellectual orders. He defines himself as one who cannot define himself. As blemisher of his own works and as rival of Alexander, he is no longer the artist to be commissioned by kings that he should be. He is definable only in relation to the dislocating force, love. This is both a good and a bad thing. Since he is a depictor of the beauty that inspires love, and since his paintings are always of amorous subjects, he *should* have a relationship to love, but the one he has at present, doting upon a girl who belongs to the king, cancels out the rest of him.

Apelles concludes that he can only give himself up to love in the uncertain hope of unknown pleasures. Immediately upon his exit Lais appears with her two customers:

they are concerned with the definite expectation of very familiar pleasures bearing some relation to love. They are confronted with Diogenes, the person most opposed to all such pleasures. The scene is Lyly's most striking example of reversal of a theme. Not only do Lais and her friends approach love with a view opposed to that of the passionate lover whom we have just seen, but they throw the love-war controversy into a new perspective. Lais advocates just what Clitus and Parmenio had deplored, the conversion of soldiers into pleasure-seekers:

> Sweete youthes, if you knew what it were to saue your sweete bloud, you would not so foolishly go about to spend it. What delight can there be in gasshinge, to make foule scarres in faire faces, & crooked maimes in streight legges? as though men being borne goodlye by nature, would of purpose become deformed by follye, and all forsooth for a new found tearme, called valiant, a worde which breedeth more quarrelles then the sense can commendation.
>
> (F1r; V.iii.4–10)

Lais' vigorous argument, however, is not entirely convincing. Her dislike of war is founded merely upon its physical effects on attractive young men. The image of the scratched face returns, ironically reversed, to label her as part of the corrupt side of Athens. She is, moreover, afraid of Alexander, departing hastily with her friends lest they meet him. The triangle of Lais and her two boyfriends also functions as antitype to the three principal lovers: their interest is physical pleasure, what Apelles and Campaspe might have sought, the disporting of himself that Alexander might have indulged in during his rest. The scene, as I have previously noted, might have appeared earlier, where it could have prepared for Diogenes' harangue and for the courtiers' description of the army. Placed where it is, it sets up the resolution of the comedy. It demonstrates the immediate necessity of Alexander's doing something about his army of soldiers turned lovers. It also, because of the particular associations of Lais, implicitly affirms the excellence of the love of Apelles and Campaspe. Lais appears in the Renaissance emblem books as an example of voluptuous high life designed to move the reader to appreciation of contented virtue in low estates.[49] Lyly uses her in just this way: the self-indulgent courtesan contrasts with the virtuous Campaspe, who has asserted that, "Content is such a life, I care not for aboundance."

In the last scene of the play, Alexander discovers the mutual love of Apelles and Campaspe, unites them, and returns to his role as conqueror, having triumphed over his own passion. The scene must be considered from a number of angles.

Alexander acts as royal judge. Himself thoroughly restored to reason, he has resolved the problems inherent in the relationship of love to power. That relationship has arisen in two aspects: when the holder of power is himself in love, and when he is a third person standing outside of the love relationship and capable of exerting his power over it. That the first aspect has ceased to be a problem is signaled to us when Alexander declares: "I will not enforce mariage, where I cannot cōpel loue" (F3ʳ; V.iv.113–14). This line echoes Hephestion's earlier assertions of the inability of power to compel or create love, and indicates Alexander's acceptance of the truth of those assertions. The problems of the second aspect of the relationship, the threat of power against the lovers, are averted by Alexander's benevolence. Apelles' desperate and unconvincing

---

[49] Geffrey Whitney, *A Choice of Emblemes*, ed. Henry Green (London, 1866), p. 79.

denials of his love are based on that threat; but Alexander is not angry that Apelles should love the girl whom he himself loves, and he is content with remarking that Apelles should have dealt more openly with the situation: "Me thinks I might haue bin made priuie to your affection, though my counsel had not beene necessary, yet my countenance might haue bin thought requisite" (F3ʳ; V.iv.97–99). Alexander has pulled himself out of rivalry and reverted to the position of king over subjects whose marriages are of concern to him. The obvious historical context of this line is Queen Elizabeth's displeasure with courtiers who married without her permission.

Alexander not only reverts to king, he reverts to conqueror. After the united lovers depart, he gives orders for the mobilization of the army. Hephestion compliments him, under the metaphor of conquest, on the abandonment of his love for Campaspe:

HEPHE. The conquering of *Thebes* was not so honourable, as the subdueing of these thoughts.
ALEX. It were a shame *Alexander* should desire to commaund the world, if he could not commaund himselfe.
(F4ʳ; V.iv.148–151)

This understanding of Alexander's renunciation gives a formal symmetry to the play, a symmetry that has a double effect on its content. Alexander enters as conqueror; he leaves as conqueror after a victory that his loyal lieutenant considers greater. The play is thus retrospectively cast into a presentation of its central character. *Campaspe* shows Alexander going from the military conquest of a great city to the spiritual conquest of a greater man, himself. G. K. Hunter is quite right in stressing the idea of kingliness: a large part of the play may be taken as an exposition of the nature of the excellent monarch. The various incidents of the action mobilize to display his military prowess, his recognition of the abilities of his subjects, his understanding of and provision for the peacetime governance of his realm, his benevolence—in short, comprehension and performance of the duties that his position entails, even against the opposition of that royal intensity of passion that occurs as an adjunct of his high position. Thus *Campaspe* can be seen as a small but successful dramatic example of the form of moral allegory that the Renaissance delighted to find in the epics of the ancients. Sidney in the "Apologie" and Spenser in the letter to Ralegh articulated the Renaissance conception of the *Iliad*, the *Odyssey*, and the *Aeneid* as expositions of moral exemplars in the characters of Achilles (or Agamemnon), Ulysses, and Aeneas; and Ariosto, Tasso, and Spenser continued the line in Ruggiero, Rinaldo, Godfredo, and Prince Arthur. Lyly has done likewise: the virtues of a noble conqueror and benevolent prince have been shadowed under the guise of an historical fiction.

Of course, Lyly's scale is much smaller. A dramatic hero cannot rival an epic hero in either the size or the number of his exploits. The second effect of the symmetrical conclusion is to temper the significance, one might almost say the pretentiousness, of creating such a moral allegory in a Court entertainment. Like the pages' choplogic, it is a device of courteous self-deprecation. It casts the play retrospectively into the form of an interlude. A play, a mere interlude designed for the holiday recreation of Queen and Court, has been fashioned out of an interlude in Alexander's career, a brief pause for recreation in the life of a king. Alexander's real efforts lie before and after the play; as the Court prologue announces, "We calling *Alexander* from his graue, seeke onely who was his loue." The real business of being a monarch is located outside the

hours of the play, both for the central figure of the piece and for the central member of the audience.[50]

As I have been insisting throughout this chapter, however, the play is more than an exposition of kingliness. There is more than Alexander in the play, and there is more than Alexander in the final scene. The scene is cast in the form of an official inquiry with Alexander as investigator. The resolution requires the determination of the facts of the case (that Apelles and Campaspe do love each other) and an exploration of the nature of the issue (what love is). Alexander proceeds by examining the material witnesses, the lovers, and by soliciting from Hephestion and Diogenes their opinions on the nature of love. These opinions join those that Campaspe and Apelles have previously expressed in soliloquy to form an array of views that is the fullest example of Lyly's process of alternative definitions. The series is climaxed by the speech in which Alexander both unites the lovers and produces a final description of love.

In her soliloquy in IV.ii Campaspe has wondered how she came to fall in love with Apelles rather than with Alexander: she could only conclude that "Affection is a fire, which kindleth aswell in the bramble as in the oak, and catcheth hold where it first lighteth, not where it may best burne." This is a description, not an explanation, of course. She accepts love without trying to analyze it further, only deciding how to act. Fortunately for her, love coincides with propriety: she concludes about her own position that "a distaffe is fitter for thy hand then a

[50] Jocelyn Powell, in his recent article, "John Lyly and the Language of Play," *Elizabethan Theatre*, Stratford-upon-Avon Studies IX (London, 1966), pp. 147–167, has discussed the idea of recreating play in Lyly against the background of Renaissance theories of play, and linked play briefly with Lyly's habits of definitional dialogue and dramatic stasis.

scepter" and about Alexander's that "in kinges there can be no loue, but to Queenes" (E1^r; IV.ii.7–9, 12–13, and E3^r; IV.iv.30).

Apelles is in a more awkward position, for the triangular situation has put him into direct rivalry with one whom he never can and never should rival. His love has also upset his normal employment, causing him not only to blemish the portrait but also to undertaking painting things impossible for his art, "deepe and hollowe sighes, sadde and melancholye thoughtes, woundes and slaughters of conceites" (D3^r; III.v.45–47). In this dislocated position his description of love's effect is thoroughly appropriate: "O loue, I neuer beefore knewe what thou wert, and nowe haste thou made mee that I know not what my self am?" (E4^v; V.ii.8–9).

Hephestion, although pitying the lover, finds the emotion itself deceptive, divine only through superstition, and provocative of humour and eventually madness in the sufferer. Diogenes is a misogynist, and implies that women who inspire love will only end up inspiring hate. These two views of love do not causally affect the situation: Diogenes is not at all involved in the triangle, and Hephestion is connected with it only through Alexander. Technically, however, the expression of their views helps to build the final scene to its climax, and thematically it provides a greater richness of background for the practical problem. Hephestion carries the discussion of love into more metaphysical and more pathological areas than any one else, and Diogenes is the only character to touch upon the ambivalence of man's reaction to woman over a period of time. The fact that they speak at all allows the audience to see love as it may be connected to war and to philosophy through the medium of characters who are professionally and exclusively devoted to those endeavors. The solution of the main anecdote of the play is set in context by the

views of others: your reaction to this fiery passion depends, it would seem, very much upon what you are before its advent.

Alexander has the final definition of love:

ALEX. Two louing wormes, *Hephestion,* I perceiue *Alexander* cannot subdue the affections of menne, though he cōquer their countries. Loue falleth like dew aswel vpō the grasse, as vppon the high Caeder. Sparkes haue their heate, Antes their gall, Flyes their splene. Well, enioy one an other, I giue her thee frāckly *Apelles.* Thou shalt see that *Alexander* maketh but a toye of loue, and leadeth affection in fetters, vsing fācie as a foole to make him sport, or as a minstrell to make him merry. It is not the amorous glaunce of an eie can settle an idle thought in the heart, no no, it is childrens game, a life for seamesters and schollers, the one pricking in cloutes haue nothing els to thinke on, the other picking fancies out of books, haue litle els to meruaile at. Go *Apelles,* take with you your *Campaspe, Alexander* is cloied with looking on that, which thou wondredst at.

APEL. Thankes to your maiestie on bended knee, you haue honoured *Apelles.*

CAMP. Thankes with bowed hearte, you haue blessed *Campaspe.*

(F3ᵛ; V.iv.127–143)

In form Alexander's speech is euphuistic enough in the traditional sense, with its zoological references and its parallel phrases, although the glancing alliterations expand into a full sound-echo only in the picking-pricking consonance. The speech is stylistically more striking for its graceful curve, for the easy modulation of one thought into the next by means of humorous phrases of interjection and transition: "no no"; "well, enioy one an other."

Alexander's definition of love is quite full. It turns on an analysis of the facts of love ("loue falleth like dew"), an analysis that constitutes a recognition of its universal force and an assertion of the right of all creatures to experience passion. He then acts on the basis of the analysis ("I giue her thee") and expresses his own relation to the matter ("it is childrens game"). He admits the wide-ranging force of love, yet rejects its influence upon himself for as long as his function as conqueror continues. He does not deny the passion he felt earlier, but overcomes it.

Yet the personal opinion constitutes a solution to the situation. In his admission of the force of love upon all things high and low, Alexander incorporates the views of Campaspe. His conception of dew on the grass and cedars expresses the same notion as her idea of fire kindling the bramble as well as the oak. Both see love as a natural occurrence, able to happen anywhere. In his gift of her to Apelles he restores the proper order between himself and his subject. The painter is no longer the rival of the prince but the recipient of the prince's gift. Thus Apelles, while preserving the new relation to love that he has acquired during the play, regains the old identity whose loss he had bemoaned in soliloquy. The achievement of orderly relationships is marked by appropriate stage ceremony: the lovers thank their king "on bended knee," and then depart from his company, leaving him to undertake the greater tasks that are his lot.

Nothing very profound, and certainly nothing new, has been said about love. It does not even matter whether the descriptions of love be true. Although philosophical questions have been asked about love, the solution given is not philosophical but dramatic. The pattern created by the five descriptions of love clicks into place. Lyly's interest is in relations: given a number of assumed realities, what is their proper order and connection? When an arrangement has been reached that accommodates the personal emotions, abilities, and positions of the characters, the play is complete. The ruling idea of the play is not love; that is only part of the play's material. The ruling idea is propriety. That the final arrangement is based on propriety, on the overwhelming importance of fulfilling one's rank, is clear in Lyly's final twist. In the closing speech of the play, Alexander says that he will return to love only when conquest is no longer available to him as a profession: "And good *Hephestion,* when al the world is woone, and euery countrey is thine and mine, either find me out an other to subdue, or of my word I will fall in loue" (F4^r; V.iv.153–155).

F. ALLEGORY AND RETICULATION

It remains to define the nature and relationship of allegory and dramaturgy in *Campaspe.* This problem can be advantageously approached through closer analysis of Alexander's speech on love.

I have noted that the speech is moderately euphuistic in the Crollian sense. There is, however, a significant peculiarity in the element of euphuism most immediately striking both to Renaissance critics and to modern readers: the natural-history similes.[51] They are not similes. The references to sparks, ants, and flies in Alexander's speech are given the grammatical form of independent exempla.[52]

[51] Even though formal analysis in the Croll tradition has attributed less than central significance to the similes, they were and remain the most blatant idiosyncrasy of euphuism.

[52] A count of illustrations drawn from myth, antique history, and natural history in *Campaspe* reveals that there are four groups of such references that we may differentiate on the basis of grammatical form. I find ten similes of the form, "Bewtie is like the blackberry, which seemeth red, when it is not ripe" (B4^r; II.ii.48); sixteen exempla running parallel to the matter at hand, as, "Larkes that mount aloft in the ayre, build their neastes below in the earth, and women that cast

The grammatical difference points to a functional difference.

Alexander asserts that love can come to everyone, high or low. The arrival, the process, is stated in the form of a simile: love falls like dew. But in describing the state of love, he abandons simile and produces three instances of minute creatures possessing passions. We have independent *exempla*. These are, moreover, very far from the matter at hand, even for a Pliny-addict. Campaspe and Apelles are, of course, lowly when compared to Alexander the Great, and we are to some extent prepared for the parallel with ants and flies by the opening phrase of the speech, "two louing wormes." [53] But ants, flies, and sparks are very lowly indeed, and the passions attributed to them (Alexander is clearly thinking of the heat of a spark as a passion) are not even love. We are being given some very remote images.

Now in one sense the grammatical form and the remoteness of the images do not matter. It is the common pattern

---

their eies vpon kinges, may place their hearts vpon vassals" (E1^r; IV.ii.9–11); eight cases where the allusion is incorporated by means of metaphor and the preposition "with," as, "Thou maist swimme against the streame with the Crab" (D3^r; III.v.34–35) and "Wil you handle the spindle with *Hercules*. . . ?" (B4^r; II.ii.34); and three cases of direct metaphoric identification with an extended reference, as, "Affection is a fire, which kindleth as well in the bramble as in the oak, and catcheth hold where it first lighteth, not where it may best burne" (E1^r; IV.ii.7–9). In view of borderline cases, these statistics are more suggestive than precise; nonetheless, the fact remains that, as against ten similes (by nature hypotactic), there are twenty-seven cases of paratactic or identifying forms of expression. That is, the objects alluded to are placed in grammatical equality with the subject at hand nearly three times as often as they are placed in grammatical subordination.

[53] The phrase is often used of lovers in a rather superior, and sometimes genuinely scornful, manner. See the examples collected in the *NED*, s.v. worm, II.10c.

of the relationships that is important. That pattern governs the choice of the images as they work around the central idea. Ants, flies, and sparks are each possessed of an "emotional" core that exerts control over their lives; and since this is their property in nature, we can say that it must be right. These sharp images thus adumbrate the central reality, the old Empedoclean-Platonic-Neoplatonic idea of the universal occurrence and ruling power of love. It is an idea strong enough to bear the extremity of the implied comparisons.

But although the pattern is important, the images really function in the opposite direction. The images actually *create* the central idea, which is never stated abstractly independent of the exempla. The remoteness of the exempla in turn creates the force attributed to universal love. Without the independent empirical reality of flies and sparks there would be not only no illustration but also no point to illustrate. By altering his characteristic grammatical form, Lyly has caused the abstract point to arise solely from the particulars, and thus allowed them to retain their individuality while linking them in an implicit generalization. In the Plato-infected literary theory of the 1580's an abstraction is ultimately more real than its examples, but it can be seen only through particulars. Only from empirical realities, only from his perception of passion in flies and artists and captives, does Alexander draw the basis for his action.

I do not mean to exaggerate the empirical reality of these things. There is light as well as heat in sparks, industry as well as gall in ants. Alexander says of ants and sparks only as much as will allow us to draw the relevant inference, and Lyly knew, or was willing to invent, much more about them. Nonetheless, the definite existence of a number of minute creatures possessing passion yields a pattern that expands the love of Campaspe and Apelles into a matter of universal occurrence and importance. Particulars operate metaphorically and by so doing create a pattern that figures forth a universal: this is allegory.

The verbal procedure of this speech is part of the definitional process I have attempted to show as the basis of Lyly's euphuism in *Campaspe*. The limited empirical reality of the objects mentioned, and the definitional handling of their relationships, constitute the fundamental prose style. The astonishing thing about this play is that the verbal style corresponds precisely to the dramaturgy. The characters are presented with an empirical reality of the same limited order as that enjoyed by the images. They are each conceived of as having a certain status with a very limited gallery of emotions and ideas appropriate to that status. These possessions are taken as the totality of necessary facts about them, and the business of the play is to order them in proper relationships. Philosophers apt in the discussion of first causes are brought together with a king who perceives for them a useful function in the life of the kingdom; they are set to that function and warned against meddling in politics. The king desires also that the arts may flourish, but the instruction of an artist quickly induces him to forswear any personal attempt to paint. A noblewoman is conquered, but both she and her conqueror recognize that she has retained her nobility because it is spiritual in nature.

If persons fail to realize their essences, the world of *Campaspe* falls into disorder. Three disorders take place, linked by the image of the scratched face; they neatly cover the world of the play, for each of them is associated with one of the three houses on the mansion stage. On the most philosophical level, when men fail to fulfill their functions simply as men, human life in general is corrupted. Hence Diogenes' harangue—at the tub. On a national level, when a warrior-king neglects his career to dally with a lowly virgin, the army for which he is responsible degenerates, as we are told by the courtiers—at the palace. On the individual level, when the dalliance results in the disorderly situation of the king in rivalry with a painter, the painter takes to blemishing his own works—at the shop. When the king realizes the situation and, with royal magnanimity, unites the girl and the painter, the order based on status is restored, the painter kneels to utter his thanks, and the army is called back to its job.

This formulation is highly schematic, even Gothic, and it may appear to sin against literature. Lyly's works, however, particularly his earlier ones, betray him as a lover of system and elaborate pattern. Since, moreover, his plays have not been critically discussed in the detail they deserve, it is necessary to make clear their logical organization and intellectual rationale. It is not enough to say that the sources of *Campaspe* are classical anecdotes, that the characters are flat, that the production was probably gorgeous, and that the dialogue, full of poignant turns and merry taunts, must have been delightful to the Court. The characters are conceived on definite principles; they are mobilized in incidents selected to present a general idea of propriety, of the duties of men and of their places among one another. Moreover, this formulation places the central episode in correct perspective. *Campaspe* is not a narrative play about a love-affair. If we consider it as such, we must conclude it a failure because of the scantiness of treatment given the affair and the irrelevance of over half the play. The love-affair is the chief episode exemplifying an idea that operates behind the whole variety of Lyly's Athens. The individual characters and the particular ideas that appear in *Campaspe* are like nodes or cruces. The anecdotes and their juxtaposition weave lines of relationship among these nodes; they create an elaborately reticulated pattern. Each line of reticulation involves a particular kind of propriety, the kind that governs that particular situation. As a whole the reticulation creates the idea of propriety as a universal, illuminating the total spectacle presented to us. Alexander, Campaspe, and Apelles are active in a more extended episode that deals with men's relationships on a finer scale, but Timoclea, Diogenes, the philosophers, the begging Cynic, and Lais all contribute to the development of the central idea. To the entertainment they bring variety; to the intellectual structure they bring a scope and fullness of articulation equal to those of the verbal style.

III. THE GODS OF *GALLATHEA*

A. PROBLEMS

THE MIDDLE plays of John Lyly, *Gallathea, Love's Metamorphosis, Sapho and Phao,* and *Endimion,* are much like *Campaspe.* Indeed, such is their likeness, to *Campaspe* and to each other, that the student easily confuses one play with another not long after he has read through the canon. The verbal style remains much the same, and the plays lack the kind of striking action and individual characterization that rests easily in the memory. The likenesses include dramaturgy. If my analysis of *Campaspe* has been successful, I have shown how this play can be taken on its own ground rather than as an early and unsuccessful attempt to build a comedy on a romantic narrative. The four middle plays involve many of the same ideas and the same techniques. Love continues to be a major force in a various, constructed universe. Love is explored by presenting its relationships to other great abstractions: power, chastity, friendship. The dramatic action continues to consist of juxtapositions and delicate adjustments in a largely static situation.

Lyly, however, does not merely repeat a formula: the differences between *Campaspe* and its four successors are sufficient to justify classification of the latter as a second phase in situational drama. There are two major innovations. The task of this chapter is to ascertain the effect of these innovations upon the conduct and meaning of Court comedy.

The first innovation concerns content: Lyly introduces

mythological materials. In two cases a myth is a major source for a play: in *Endimion* Lyly presents a new version of the sleep of the Latmian shepherd beloved by the moon, and in *Love's Metamorphosis* he uses the Ovidian tale of Erisichthon's blasphemy against Ceres. In the other two cases, *Sapho and Phao* and *Gallathea*, the major situations are conflated from a variety of myths no one of which dominates. Olympian gods appear in three of these plays, and the central figure of the fourth (*Endimion*) is a Cynthia who is as much the classical goddess as a human queen. Other personages in these plays bear the names if not the characters of mythical figures (Eumenides and Semele in *Endimion*, Haebe and Gallathea in *Gallathea*).

Lyly's second innovation concerns technique and is less susceptible of easy description. It is essentially a simplification of dramaturgy: reducing the number of characters and the number of anecdotes in which they appear, he organizes the persons and events into stronger and more comprehensive lines of structure. *Campaspe* has twenty-nine named characters plus a crowd of Athenian citizens. *Sapho and Phao*, although first performed by the same combination of dramaturgy: reducing the number of characters and *Endimion* has twenty-three characters, *Gallathea* twenty-two, and *Love's Metamorphosis* fifteen.[1] Accompanying the reduction of cast size is a change in milieu. A wide range of characters is to be found in the imperial city of Alexander; the more limited worlds of royal courts (*Sapho and Phao, Endimion*) and pastoral retreats (*Love's Metamorphosis, Gallathea*) present societies with less internal diversity. Finally, and most important for dramaturgy, the

[1] The last three plays were performed by Paul's without the Chapel's assistance. The reduction in the number of available actors may have been the efficient cause of Lyly's new practice, but of course it does not explain the dramatic operation or the effect of the practice.

number of nodes of action is reduced. By choosing an "historical" story and a complex milieu in *Campaspe*, Lyly bound himself to a vast array of intellectual and social particulars each of which receives individual adjustment to its fellows. A great premium is placed on specialized definition, and the result is a highly complex reticulation of each part to each other part. In the four middle comedies the high degree of reticulation is replaced by a reliance upon simpler, parallel structures. Characters are grouped and actions are doubled. Sapho has six ladies in waiting, and *Love's Metamorphosis* hinges upon a triple love-affair. The characteristically English device of parodic subplot emerges in *Gallathea* and *Endimion*.

These two innovations cause a distinct change in the weight and shape of Lyly's plays. The complexity of *Campaspe* tends to keep our apprehension of it concentrated upon relationships between things rather than upon the things themselves. The characters are neat, well-defined, and possessed of a certain glamor, but they do not present themselves as figuring great metaphysical depths. For all the abstraction in the dialogue, *Campaspe* is, in contrast to the middle comedies, a very social play. Considerable attention, it is true, is focussed upon the nature of love, primarily by Alexander's collection of opinions assisted by an occasional far-ranging image, but a play so minutely concerned with so many characters does not often get further than tropology in its implications. The Olympian gods of the middle plays, however, are less neat and well-defined than Diogenes and Alexander: the long tradition behind them makes them compelling centers of energy in generating potential significances for the episodes in which they appear. The various kinds of analogous action employed in these plays develop those potential significances in more forceful and deeper-cutting ways than do the non-parallel reticulations of *Campaspe*.

This chapter and the next, then, will concentrate on the larger structural patterns and on the mythological content of the middle plays. Analysis of these two elements will require an extended interpretation of at least one play. I wish, however, to arrive at a description of the allegorical dramaturgy in the middle plays, not to spin out readings of all four of them. I shall therefore consider *Gallathea* at length in terms of structure and use of myth and, in the next chapter, apply the results of that consideration more briefly to *Love's Metamorphosis, Sapho and Phao,* and *Endimion.* I choose *Gallathea* as my primary play for reasons both positive and negative. In setting and technique, *Love's Metamorphosis* resembles *Gallathea* in almost all respects; it lacks, however, perhaps as a deliberate excision made when it was revived in 1600, the pageboys who appear in most of Lyly's comedies and who make in *Gallathea* an important contribution to atmosphere and idea. Both *Sapho and Phao* and *Endimion,* dominated as they are by virgin queens, suggest inevitably a certain amount of historical allegory. The particularization of allegorical meaning involved in such a mode of local reference would distract from the larger issues that concern us here. *Sapho and Phao,* moreover, seems to me distinctly among Lyly's poorer plays, and the number of interpretations that have been offered for the very much better *Endimion* warns us that it might be best to approach our topic with another play. The best reason for my choice, however, is the excellence of *Gallathea.* In the organization of its situations, in the articulation of its juxtaposed scenes as they focus on a single idea, *Gallathea* is the most perfectly executed and the most luminously clear of Lyly's plays. It is an exquisite work of art.

The Gods of Gallathea

B. THE PLAN OF *GALLATHEA*

Underlying all the events of *Gallathea* is a single formula: the attempted defiance of divinity.[2] Cupid, truant from his mother, causes the nymphs of Diana to fall in love and thus to chafe against the rule of chastity upheld by their patroness. After Diana has rebuked them, the nymphs reverse the defiance, capture Cupid, and set him to tasks that violate his own nature as god of love. The conflict burgeons until the two major divinities, Diana and Venus, replace their respective supporters in direct argument with each other. A third defiance involves mortals: two fathers attempt to cheat Neptune of an appointed virgin-sacrifice by disguising their eligible daughters as boys. Undeceived and unwilling to accept the local population's offer of a third virgin (who does not quite meet the requirements with respect to beauty), Neptune promises a terrible revenge. He happens upon the quarrelling goddesses, however, and works out a compromise that adjusts their problems and abolishes the virgin-sacrifice.

As in *Campaspe*, these events are not dramatically fashioned into a plot. The disguised girls (Gallathea and Phillida) meet, fall in love, and engage in artfully indirect courting, but their relationship does not develop. Their two major courting scenes cover exactly the same ground with respect to their suspicions about each other's sex. They are loved by the nymphs when the latter are shot by Cupid (the shooting takes place offstage), but they function merely as objects in that situation: they do not appear with the nymphs during the period of the nymphs' passion.

[2] All quotations from the play, except from the songs, are taken from the first and only quarto [John Lyly], *Gallathea* (London, 1592). They are acknowledged in the text by the signature numbers of this quarto, followed by the act, scene, and line numbers of R. Warwick Bond, ed., *The Complete Works of John Lyly* (Oxford, 1902), vol. II.

The usual Lylian pages turn up, oddly wandering through the forest on the banks of the Humber that provides a setting for the whole play. Their attempts to find employment are quite episodic, and a connection between them and the major characters is fortuitously arranged only in the final twenty lines of the play. Neptune makes a point of disguising himself as a shepherd, but does nothing in that costume.[3] Moreover, the virgin-sacrifice situation and the Venus-Diana situation are joined in the fifth act in a most hasty manner. Neptune's compromise depends upon Diana's resentment of the virgin-sacrifice; such resentment is natural in the goddess of chastity, but we have heard nothing of it before this act. Except for the use of the disguised girls as love-objects, the two situations have been developed independently: their relationship is purely one of analogy.

In this play, as in *Campaspe*, plotlessness is accompanied by a neglect of personal characterization. In the first scene, for example, Gallathea makes a vigorous protest against her father's plans on the ground that disguise is a dishonorable attempt to avert destiny, a protest that contrasts nicely with Phillida's acquiescence in the parallel scene. But dishonor and destiny are of no concern to Gallathea later. Lyly merely needs a strong initial statement of a theme to be developed subsequently in terms of other characters.

[3] Venus, in V.i, mentions that she has seen through this disguise; this is, however, a point of no import to the action, since this is Venus' first appearance and also the first occasion of Neptune's appearing with any other character. I do not suspect the loss of a scene in which the costume actually functioned; the play is complete without such a scene, and the disguise is thematically relevant (see my discussion in Section F). If Lyly had originally intended to make the disguise functional in the action and later changed his mind, he could easily have cancelled the soliloquy in which Neptune justifies the costume.

Thus *Gallathea,* like *Campaspe,* is non-psychological and without developing plot. The forces of Venus and Diana, opposing each other, create a peripetal structure for one situation; Lyly's limitation, in the first four acts, of Neptune's role to soliloquies prevents much development in the other situation. The play is bound to be static. The summary I have given, however, should make it clear that Lyly has altered his *conduct* of a plotless situation. There is contrast in abundance in *Campaspe,* but it is contrast of character in single situations: Apelles versus Alexander with respect to painting, Alexander versus Diogenes in their handling of the begging Cynic. Contrasts of *situation* lying nascent in the material (for example, a contrast between Apelles' love-art conflict and Alexander's love-war conflict) remain dramatically unexploited.[4] *Gallathea,* however, is built on just the latter kind of contrast, upon diverse situations employing a common formula, the attempt to defy divinity. The contrasting situations, moreover, have been developed until they become lines of analogous action each containing several episodes. The floutings of Venus and Diana are put together in a double-ended situation in which their subordinates, Cupid and the nymphs, are quite active, thus creating a definite chain of events with a forward-backward motion. The sacrifice situation has likewise several successive stages: two virgins are disguised, their fathers try to expose each other's craft, a third virgin is offered but not taken, Neptune becomes angry.

Accompanying the change in dramaturgy is the burying or transmutation of anecdotal sources. The play is a gallery

---

[4] For brief but trenchant remarks on the difference between contrast of characters in a single situation (more characteristic of modern and Greek plays) and contrasts between whole situations (the usual Elizabethan method), see the excellent discussion of dramaturgy in Bernard Beckerman, *Shakespeare at the Globe* (New York, 1962), especially pp. 59–60.

of myths: Virgil's first eclogue (the opening lines of which are imitated in the opening speeches of the play), the story of the pursuit of Galatea by Polyphemus (who, as Neptune's son, is the basis for Lyly's Agar, the sea monster who is to carry away the sacrificed virgin), the Hesione myth, the Moschian motif of Cupid as truant, the conflict between Venus and Diana, the myth of the disgrace of the goddess Hebe, and the motif of sex-transformation drawn from the Iphis-Ianthe story that is used to solve the Gallathea-Phillida situation. These mythological elements (which will be commented on in detail later) are not used as anecdotes in the manner of *Campaspe.* That is, they are not presented as self-contained, juxtaposed units in individual scenes. Rather, they lurk behind scenes, allusively present, deepening implications and adding resonance, dramaturgically subsumed into larger situations. They are threads in shot silk, rather than pearls strung in a necklace.

For the sake of easy reference, I add, on the next page, a diagram synopsis of *Gallathea,* listing the scenes in columns appropriate to the larger situations of which they are part, and listing the relevant myths opposite them.

C. THE DIVINITY OF THE PAGAN GODS

I have described the action of *Gallathea* as involving a threefold defiance of divinity that culminates in a meeting of the three major deities, Neptune, Venus, and Diana. The defiance to Neptune is a personal insult to his status: appointed homage to his godhead is denied him in the fathers' attempt to evade the virgin-sacrifice. The defiance of Diana and Venus, first by each other's supporters and then directly by each other, is a defiance of the values connected with these goddesses: chastity and love are denigrated. From the mere plan of *Gallathea,* then, two significant aspects of the gods are apparent. The first is that Neptune's divinity as such is important, his status as a

The Gods of Gallathea

power in the world. The second is that the metaphorical values of Venus and Diana are important: the goddesses are not merely angry women, but also figure forth powerful abstractions.

In my examination of specific scenes later in this chapter, I shall not argue that Lyly is dealing with two different kinds of literary figures, gods-as-divinities and gods-as-metaphors. Neptune comes to have metaphorical meaning in the play, as do Venus and Diana; Venus and Diana have divine status, as does Neptune. The problem at this point, before we can plunge into the play itself, is whether the pagan deities can have either of these things, and if so,

how. One of the central aspects of our inquiry in this
chapter is, what does the introduction of the gods do to
Court comedy? To answer this question, we must establish
an approach to the nature of the gods.

The nature of Lyly's gods has been, I believe, mistaken
in previous criticism. By this statement I do not refer to
the neglect, in older scholarly work, of the long mythographical tradition that intervened between the gods of
Homer and Virgil and the gods of the Elizabethan writers.[5] We know that the gods are not Homer's and that
they bear allegorical significances. Carrying strange marks
of their migration westward from Olympus, they turn up
as vehicles for a wide range of medieval and Renaissance
meanings. Yet two major mistakes have been made about
them. First, they can be flattened into shorthand for moral
allegory. The gods here become merely attractive ways to
costume abstractions for the stage: "For Wantonness,
[Lyly] gives us Venus; for Love, Cupid; for Chastity or
Virginity, Diana; for Cruelty or Devastation, Neptune." [6]
This is bluntly put, and the error is obvious. The literary
devices of metaphor and allegory ("continued metaphor")
have been wiped out by ignoring the vehicle for the sake
of the tenor. A somewhat more sophisticated version of the
same error uses psychological vocabulary to describe the
tenor: thus Bernard Huppé describes *Endimion* as "the

[5] It is certainly well known now that the Renaissance was more apt
to draw its classical mythology, together with the moral and allegorical
associations with which it had been bedded down, from the crabbed
pages of an agglomeration of handbooks, commentaries, and diction-
aries, than from the unadulterated lines of Greece and Rome. But recognition of the fact that in any given case Stephanus or Comes is the
source rather than Hesiod or even Ovid is really only the beginning.
Discriminations other than those of source must be made.

[6] Bond, *Complete Works*, II.255.

'psychological' love story of Endimion, the courtly lover," [7]
and reads the gods (as well as most of the other characters
in Lyly) as personifications of states of mind. This reading
does not merely assume a psychological interest that conflicts with Lyly's actual practice. The real confusion here
is placement of the meaning before the fiction that gives
rise to the meaning. Certainly, as C. S. Lewis remarked,
"the gods . . . died into allegory," but they were reborn
there, not dragged around as corpses with neat identifying
inscriptions, moral or psychological, on their shrouds.
Imaginative writers gave them life, the life that creates
the integrity of fiction. Upon that integrity rests the power
to figure forth meaning. If this is not the case, we are
reading disguised treatises, not drama however didactic.[8]

There is, however, an error so much nearer the truth
that it is more insidious. Lyly's latest critic, G. K. Hunter,
comments: "Lyly's Venus is neither the golden Aphrodite
of Homer nor the *alma Venus* of Lucretius, but the elegant
court lady, intent on love and with somewhat unusual
powers, that she had become through generations of court-
of-love and courtly poems." [9] The earlier critics had
ignored the vehicle for the sake of the tenor; Hunter

[7] Bernard F. Huppé, "Allegory of Love in Lyly's Court Comedies,"
ELH, XIV (1947), 103.

[8] The Lewis quotation comes from *The Allegory of Love* (Oxford,
1936), p. 78. The phrase "figure forth" is a useful one to indicate the
relation of sign to thing signified. Its value lies in conveying the sense
that a metaphor rather than a mere equivalency is operative. The precise operation is of course mysterious, but, since the phrase comes from
Sidney's "Apologie," it can be used in the hope (at least) that Cole-
ridgean notions of symbol and allegory will not confuse the issue. The
credit for reviving this helpful expression belongs to Rosemond Tuve,
who uses it frequently in her later works.

[9] Hunter, *John Lyly: The Humanist as Courtier* (Cambridge, Mass.,
1962), pp. 144–145.

leaves the tenor in the void, confident that we are aware of it, and then proceeds to polish the vehicle until it is very bright and shining but of considerably less weight than Lyly made it. In the first place, Venus may descend to Lyly from courtly poetry, but she has now landed in a play, which makes a difference I shall attempt to explain below. In the second place, the production of this play at Court does not necessarily mean that the personages on stage are mirror images of what could be found in the audience. Hunter's insistence, throughout his book, on the Court milieu of Lyly's works is welcome and instructive in many ways, but it damages the plays to tie them absolutely to the Court. As Hunter himself shows, the plays are among the first Elizabethan works wrought well enough to achieve independence of the task of entertaining the Court while still completely fulfilling that task.[10] Venus, Neptune, and Diana are courtly in many respects, but they are also gods, and their status as gods must be stressed. I shall attempt to justify this stress, in this section, by a look at Renaissance practice outside of Lyly, and in the rest of the chapter by examining *Gallathea* itself.

Although mythological personages abound on the pages of English Renaissance literature, the major Olympians seldom appear as genuine agents, that is, as characters caught up in the train of events, in narrative or drama that is concerned with mortals. They appear in the Court entertainments that culminate in the masques of Ben Jonson, but these works are more show, painting, and song than action, and can be safely distinguished from even the mythological drama of Lyly. The Ovidian epyllia

[10] This is the major point made in Hunter's excellent chapter, "Entertaining the Court of Elizabeth," pp. 89–158, and in his discussion of the pre-Lylian drama at the end of that chapter as contrasted to his elegant anatomy of Lyly's plays in the succeeding chapter, "The Plays," pp. 159–256.

of the period are largely concerned with mortal or semi-mortal mythological figures, but rarely with the major deities.[11] Gods appearing in Shakespeare's late plays (Diana in *Pericles*; Jupiter in *Cymbeline*; Juno, Ceres, and Iris in *The Tempest*) are carefully bracketted in dream or vision. The gods litter the pages of *The Faerie Queene*, but in similes and allusions, as figures in secluded gardens or processions, or as statues in temples. Only three times in Spenser's narrative do they act: the Venus-Diana debate in III.vi, Cymodoce's appeal to Neptune and Apollo in IV.xii, and the Mutabilitie Cantos.

The obvious explanation for this limitation in the use of the major gods lies in their extraordinarily decisive effect on action. Once a god is introduced in a human context he is apt to sweep all before him. Apollo and Neptune dispose so swiftly of the remaining barriers between Florimell and Marinell that the canto is markedly shorter than Spenser's norm. The patronage of Venus and Diana is wholly responsible for the natures of Amoret and Belphoebe. Although framed in vision, the Diana of *Pericles* is a *dea ex machina*.[12] For all their usefulness as symbols in a total literary structure, the power of the gods makes them dangerously heavy artillery in stories whose literal sense is non-divine action.[13]

[11] Exceptions occur when the poems relate the love-affairs of goddesses with mortal men: Shakespeare's *Venus and Adonis*, Drayton's *Endimion and Phoebe*, and Phineas Fletcher's *Venus and Anchises*.

[12] In view of the odious associations of *dei ex machinis*, I ought to emphasize that I am deliberately not entering into the vast significances of these events. It was clearly for these significances that Shakespeare and Spenser decided to employ the gods. My point lies in the effect on action that results from the introduction of the Olympians.

[13] The goddesses in *Venus and Adonis*, *Endimion and Phoebe*, and *Venus and Anchises* are certainly heavy artillery. Since, however, they are *female* deities in love with *male* mortals, they cannot very well exert raw power to achieve their aims. Insofar as there is conflict in

Their power, however, is an aspect of their meaning also, and this is a more complicated part of the problem. One of the reasons for using the gods at all is explained by Douglas Bush's description of mythological figures as "embodiments of power, passion, or beauty *beyond human limitations.*" [14] The power of the pagan deities may, of course, be ignored or denied. It is indeed denied from a strict Christian perspective. Arthur Golding felt compelled to point out that the pagan beliefs were not only wrong, they were also frivolous: every virtue and vice, every human activity, every brook and crag had its god. [15] But such reproofs are merely prelude to finding the gods useful. Another deflation of their power lies in the completely conventional use of them. Bond's idea of the gods as ornamentation applies to the thousands of appearances of the gods in commonplace tropological meanings and in reams of compliments to monarchs. Another conventional treatment of the gods is to turn them into a shorthand for passages of a story that are necessary only for exposition or to sketch motivation. [16] These various uses are only part of a vast diversity: the imagery of the gods is so abundant

---

Shakespeare's and Drayton's poems, it arises from the reluctance of the men: the goddesses must persuade their beloveds and much of their power is consequently cancelled. In Fletcher's poem, there is no conflict, only hesitation, between Venus and Anchises. Jove's effect on the action of this poem is true to the observations made above about the gods in *Pericles* and *The Faerie Queene*: when he blasts Anchises in Canto VI, he abruptly ends the poem.

[14] Douglas Bush, "Classical Myth in Shakespeare's Plays," in *Elizabethan and Jacobean Studies: Presented to Frank Percy Wilson*, ed. Herbert Davis and Helen Gardner (Oxford, 1959), p. 66. My italics.

[15] Arthur Golding, "The Preface. Too the Reader," in *The XV Bookes of P. Ouidius Naso, entytuled Metamorphosis*, as rep. by W. H. D. Rouse, ed., *Shakespeare's Ovid* (Carbondale, 1961), ll. 1–46.

[16] E.g., the appearance of Venus and Cupid in Thomas Preston's *Cambises*: Preston uses these gods as a rapid and convenient way to get the hero on to the next stage of his sinful career, an incestuous love.

that it forbids any easy conclusion about the depth of meaning appertaining thereto. I wish to argue, however, that Renaissance views on the gods allowed them to be used, by a writer who cared so to use them, with a full accent on their power, with their significance depending intimately upon their status as deities. In other words, I think the possibility is open that the tenor of a god-image is given great force by the fact that the vehicle is a divine power.

The exploits of mythological mortals were extensively allegorized—theoretically, they were capable of indefinite allegorization.[17] But it is the exploit, the action itself, that figures forth meaning. The stories of the immortals, of course, behave in the same way: the tale and the diction thereof control the god's meaning. At the same time, however, the major gods appear in so many stories, and come to be so famously associated with certain abstractions (as Venus with love) and with physical objects themselves potentially symbolic (as Neptune with the sea) that their literary power is much greater. Moreover, the things they manifest are things deemed to be eternal. They figure forth absolutes, permanent powers in the universe. Abraham Fraunce explains this clearly before interpreting the story of Chaos, the first in his book:

> *Before we speake, it shall not be amisse to note this generally, for the better conceauing of ensuing particularities.* Iupiter, Iuno, Neptune, Ceres, *with the rest, are therfore called Gods and goddesses, for that in the*

[17] The Renaissance mythographers conventionally call a halt "to avoid tediousness" (Sir John Harington, "Preface" to Ariosto, in G. Gregory Smith, ed., *Elizabethan Critical Essays* [Oxford, 1904], II.203, and Golding, "Epistle to Leicester" prefixed to the Ovid translation, l. 301. Cf. Natales Comes' closing sentence for nearly every chapter of the *Mythologiae*, "At de — satis, nunc de — dicamus").

superior and fierie region of the ayre noted by Iupiter,
in the inferior, represented by Iuno, *in the bowells of
the earth, figured by* Ceres, *in the deapth of the Seaes,
shadowed by* Neptune, *and so in others, there is,* τò
Θεîον, *a certaine celestiall and diuine power, so called by*
Hippocrates, *and by the ancient Poets more particularly
expressed by the sundry titles of seuerall Deities pro-
portionable thereunto.*[18]

This is an anthropological explanation, phrased to account
for the Greeks' invention of their gods. But it is also an
account of the status of the gods, and this establishment
of their status is Fraunce's prelude to allegorizing. The
essence of godhead is to τò Θεîον, celestial and divine
power.

Fraunce is indebted in this passage to the explanation
of the pagan gods given to Sophia by Philo in the second
of Leo Hebraeus' three *Dialoghi d'Amore*.[19] Leo is more
detailed and explicit:

SOPHIA. What reason have they to predicate deity of
corporeal things such as the heavenly bodies?

PHILO. On account of their immortality, splendour and
magnitude, of their great power in the Universe, and
chiefly on account of the divinity of their souls, which
are intelligences without matter or corporeity, pure and
ever actual.

[18] Abraham Fraunce, *The Third Part of the Countesse of Pem-
brokes Yuychurch. Entituled, Amintas Dale* (London, 1592), sig. B2ʳ.

[19] Fraunce cites Leo Hebraeus (Leone Ebreo) several times in the
Yuychurch. The *Dialoghi* were written in 1501–1502 and first published in Rome in 1535. One of the most popular of the Neoplatonic
love-treatises in the Renaissance, it received five Italian editions in
twenty years and was twice translated into French and once into Latin.
Fraunce's debt to Leo involves much of the organization of the *Yuychurch* and many specific allegorical interpretations.

SOPHIA. Was the title of God extended to yet other
things by the ancients?

PHILO. Yes, it was brought down to the lower world.
For the poets give the name of gods to the elements,
seas, rivers and great mountains of the lower world,
calling the element of fire Jupiter, that of air Juno,
water and the sea Neptune, earth Ceres and the depths of
the earth Pluto, the mixed fire burning within the earth
Vulcan; and so too calling many other aspects of earth
and water 'gods.'

SOPHIA. It is very strange that they should call lifeless,
insensitive, soulless bodies 'gods.'

PHILO. They called them gods for their greatness, fame,
function and the importance they have in this lower
world; and besides because they believed each of them
to be governed by a spiritual power sharing in the
divinity of intellect; or holding with Plato that each
of the elements has a formal incorporeal principle, participation in which constitutes its own nature. Such
principles he calls 'ideas,' and considers that the Idea
of fire is the true fire, as its formal essence, and that
elemental fire is fire in virtue of its partaking of the
Idea; and so with other things. Hence it is not odd to
attribute a godhead to the ideas of things. . . . They
called gods or goddesses human virtues, vices and
passions: principally because, apart from the fact that the
nobility of the first and the might of the others has in
it some godlike element, each of the virtues, vices and
passions of men in general has its own Idea. . . .

SOPHIA. Even if the virtues have Ideas on account of
their excellence, yet how can vices and evil passions have
any?

PHILO. Just as among the heavenly gods there are some
good or very good fortunes like Jupiter and Venus, from
whom many benefits ever flow, and other bad ones or

infortunes, as Saturn and Mars, from whom all evil proceeds: so too among the Platonic Ideas there are principles of good and virtue and others that are principles of evil and vices, because the Universe needs both for its preservation.[20]

To summarize Philo, certain apparently material or earthly objects or forces are called gods because there is indeed in them divinity, divinity in the form of immortality, greatness, importance to the ongoing of the universe, and power. This divinity may be philosophically crystallized in the notion of the Platonic Ideas, but that is only a suggestion; Philo does not insist on the Platonism. What is important is the metaphysical status of the gods: they figure or shadow (to use Fraunce's terms) the ruling forces of the universe *as well as* the virtues, vices, and passions that are constants in the world of man. Therefore the presence of the gods in a literary work invites us to more than moral allegory. It invites us to what Rosemond Tuve has denominated "allegory properly so called," to non-ethical statements about the nature of the universe and man's place therein, to "ideas less homiletically moral or specifically Christian than metaphysical, Platonic or timeless." [21]

The gods may figure negative absolutes, vices or demons

[20] Leone Ebreo, *The Philosophy of Love* (translators' title for *Dialoghi d'Amore*), tr. F. Friedeberg-Seeley and Jean H. Barnes (London, 1937), pp. 118–119.

[21] The last quotation is from Tuve, *Images and Themes in Five Poems by Milton* (Cambridge, Mass., 1962), p. 82; see also p. 139. The distinction between the two kinds of allegory forms a major part of the argument of the first chapter of Miss Tuve's *Allegorical Imagery: Some Medieval Books and Their Posterity* (Princeton, 1966), especially pp. 14, 27–28, 44–45. The phrase "allegory properly so called" is frequently used in that chapter, with "reading *spiritualiter*" as a synonymous expression.

or dark powers, but powers they can be in a way that
Perseus and Theseus cannot. Demogorgon is an extreme
but therefore instructive example. Once a Renaissance
writer allows that he may be a figure for something truly
existent, Demogorgon demands treatment either as a figure
for the Creator himself,[22] or as a figure for the great
Perverter, the ultimate dark power.[23] Only with the utmost
of tact can Spenser, in the episode of Agape's plea for
her sons in *The Faerie Queene*, IV.ii, reduce Demogorgon
to the status of a figure for "those dark forces that constitute the *material* source of our being." [24] That tact
consists of putting him in a context that cuts him off
from shadowing either God or the Devil: those possibilities
would be outright heresy in the story of Agape. The
reduction leaves him nonetheless a very potent power.[25]

Sixteen centuries of Christianity (preceded by a large
quantity of late pagan reductive allegorization of the gods)
made impossible for the Renaissance the Aeschylean
seriousness with which the nature of Zeus was once dra-

[22] As in Boccaccio, *Genealogie Deorum Gentilium Libri*, I. Pro-
hemium (Bari, 1951, vol. I, pp. 14–15), and in Fraunce, *Yuychurch*,
sig. B3ᵛ.

[23] As in *The Faerie Queene*, I.i.37, and in Marlowe's *Dr. Faustus*,
I.iii (ed. W. W. Greg [Oxford, 1950], B-text, I.iii.244–245).

[24] Thomas P. Roche, Jr., *The Kindly Flame: A Study of the Third
and Fourth Books of Spenser's Faerie Queene* (Princeton, 1964), pp.
19–20. My italics.

[25] Demogorgon, of course, is a very late addition to the mythology.
His name apparently arose as a scribal corruption of Plato's Demiurge;
he first appears as a god in Boccaccio. Boccaccio gives as his authority
for Demogorgon (in the passage cited in fn. 22 above) one Theodontius, about whom nothing else is known. Demogorgon's late appearance makes him a compact example for my purposes: there had not
been enough time to turn him to conventional or trivial uses. This
situation, however, does not affect the worth of my example, since I
am arguing only that the gods *could* be handled with this great respect
for their divinity, not that they are always and by all writers so handled.

matically explored. But the imagery was not yet a language of counters or a set of eighteenth-century garden statues. The Renaissance mythographers profess to be unfolding a "dark philosophy," [26] not writing "the gentleman and lady's key to polite literature." [27] A critic with any training in philosophy will perceive that they do not succeed; but a critic with any respect for literature (which includes a respect for both vehicles and tenors) will perceive that they kept available and amplified the potential resonance of some very powerful imagery. Lyly, I shall now try to show, used that resonance. His Venus is not simply a court lady, and not simply a visually pleasing way to costume an abstraction.

D. THE VIRGIN SACRIFICE

The practice of other Renaissance writers cannot, of course, prove anything about Lyly. It does, however, establish the possibility of stress upon the divinity of the pagan gods. Given that possibility, it cannot be doubted that Neptune's status as a great god is firmly developed in *Gallathea*. This section will examine the virgin-sacrifice situation in *Gallathea*, over which Neptune presides; it will also consider Lyly's handling of other myths in that situation.

In the first scene of *Gallathea*, a leisured atmosphere is established by the pastoral setting and the opening lines: imitating Virgil (from whom his name is drawn), Tyterus remarks to his daughter, "The Sunne dooth beate vppon the playne fieldes, wherefore let vs sit downe Gallathea, vnder this faire Oake" (B1ʳ; I.i.1–2). The idyllic mood is then qualified by Tyterus' account of the violent history

[26] I take the phrase from Golding's "Epistle to Leicester," l. 7, but it is commonplace.

[27] This is the title of an anonymous handbook of mythology published in London in 1776.

behind the custom of the virgin-sacrifice. The local population, in a previous era, had committed sacrilege against Neptune; the offended god had sent a devastating flood in punishment. In order to secure remission of the flood, quinquennial homage to Neptune, in the form of the less devastating but no less horrible virgin-sacrifice, had been established. The coming of the Agar, the sea-monster who fetches the virgins for Neptune, is said to make "the waters rore, the fowles flie away, and the Cattell in the field for terror, shunne the bankes" (B2ʳ; I.i.49–50). To violence is added mystery: the ultimate fate of the virgins is unknown. As Tyterus concludes this history by bringing it to bear on Gallathea, we are given the specific terms in which Neptune's deity will be pursued thematically through the play:

TYTE. I would thou hadst beene lesse faire, or more fortunate, then shouldest thou not repine that I haue disguised thee in this attyre, for thy beautie will make thee to be thought worthy of this God; to auoide therfore desteny (for wisedome ruleth the stars) I thinke it better to vse an vnlawfull meanes (your honour preserued) then intollerable greefe, both life and honor hazarded, and to preuent (if it be possible) thy constellation by my craft. Now hast thou heard the custome of this Countrey, the cause why thys Tree was dedicated vnto Neptune, and the vexing care of thy fearefull Father.

GALLA. Father, I haue beene attentiue to heare, and by your patience am ready to aunswer. Destenie may be deferred, not preuented: and therefore it were better to offer my selfe in tryumph, then to be drawne to it with dishonour.

(B2ʳ; I.i.59–71)

The connotations of Neptune—his royalty (the well-known significance of the oak under which Tyterus and Gallathea are sitting), his physical power, and his mysteriousness—are here expanded by the identification of his decree with destiny. It is spoken of as both destiny in general and Gallathea's destiny in particular (her "constellation"). The dutiful daughter has a proper attitude toward destiny; the loving father, although he is trying to evade destiny, knows very well that that is what he is doing: he himself has introduced the word.

The power thus associated with Neptune is amplified by the mythic background of the scene. A number of virgins in myth were sacrificed to sea powers: Hesione, Andromeda, the daughter of King Erechtheus of Athens. Of these unfortunate ladies, Hesione was in circumstances most resembling Gallathea's. Unlike Andromeda and Erechtheus' daughter, she was sacrificed to a monster sent by Neptune when the god had not been given his due. As D. C. Allen has observed, moreover, the details about Lyly's Agar correspond to those given about the sea-monster in Natales Comes' account of the Hesione myth. As Comes has it, Neptune and Apollo assisted Hesione's father, King Laomedon, in building the walls of Troy:

> Laomedon treated Apollo with divine honors, but Neptune, who had been helping for a long time and had received no reward, angrily sent a horrible and most dangerous sea-monster, which, vomiting sea, inundated the whole region. Consequently, Laomedon was commanded by the oracle to expose to the monster his daughter Hesione, whom he particularly loved, more than he did Aethasa or Astyoche or Medicaste, his other daughters, and many further misfortunes ensued.[28]

[28] See D. C. Allen, "Neptune's 'Agar' in Lyly's *Gallathea*," *MLN*, XLIX (1934), 451–452. In the original, Comes' passage reads as

The Gods of Gallathea

The corresponding patterns are clear enough for Lyly's situation to constitute a direct allusion to the Hesione myth, an allusion recognizable as such by his audience. In this connection, Comes' moral interpretation of the Hesione story amplifies the image of Neptune's deity:

> Moreover, the example of Laomedon's suffering these punishments for neglect of the gods and enduring many disasters forcefully urges men to the worship of the immortal deities; since he who piously and religiously reverences the gods through uprightness and integrity of life, who will render to God those things established by the wise, he alone has a gentle God in all seasons, avoids many troubles, and in all afflictions consoles himself with the awareness of righteous counsel. In truth, how can the man who neglects God, the author of all benefits and father of everything, be just, good, and

follows: "Laomedon diuinis honorib. prosecutus est Apollinem, at Neptunus vbi diu seruiuisset, nulláq; accepisset mercedem, indignatus horrendum ac infestissimū cete immisit, quod mare euomens vniuersam regionē inundauit. illa de causa & filiam Hesionen quā vnice amabat, ac multo magis quam vel Æthasam vel Astyochen vel Medicasten, quas ceteras filias habebat, ceto exponere iussus est ab oraculo Laomedon, & multa alia incōmoda inde sunt consecuta" (*Mythologiae*, II.8 [Frankfurt, 1596, p. 168]). As Bond pointed out in *Complete Works*, II.565, Lyly takes the name for his monster from the "eagre," the tidal wave on the Humber estuary. The roar of that tidal wave was heard also in several poems of the period. In Drayton's *Poly-Olbion*, the personified Humber boasts, "When my *Higre* comes, I make my either shore/Even tremble with the sound, that I afarre doe send" (XXVIII.483–484 [in *Works of Michael Drayton*, ed. J. W. Hebel, *et al.* (Oxford, 1961), vol. IV]. Drayton adds a marginal gloss on "Higre": "The roring of the waters, at the comming in of the Tyde.") In Spenser's catalogue of British kings, Humber is an invading chieftain whose death in the river gives it its name; the invasion is depicted in a flood metaphor (*F.Q.*, II.x.15, 16). The river itself is called "stormy" in the marriage of the Thames and the Medway (*F.Q.*, IV.xi.30, 38).

temperate? And if he can be none of these, how can he avoid falling into many disasters? Thus do the wise men of elder days, through this tale of Laomedon, exhort us to religion and the perpetual memory of the benefits we have received.[29]

Such moralization verges on the painfully obvious, but Comes' easy generalizations should not obscure two important points. In the first place, Comes, with total seriousness, sees the Hesione myth in a large context of man's duty and the gods' power. Gallathea's remarkably serious words on destiny and dishonor invite us to see her situation in the same context. Secondly, one of the specific details in Comes' moralization applies precisely to the situation on the banks of the Humber. Comes exhorts us to "render to God those things established by the wise" in order to escape God's wrath; Tyterus is attempting to evade the virgin-sacrifice, a rite established by an earlier generation for the appeasement of Neptune.

The conception of Neptune built by Lyly's dialogue and by his use of the Hesione story does not establish any specific allegorical meaning for the god of the type "Diana: chastity." The idea is deliberately general: Neptune is a

[29] The original reads: "Quod autem ob neglectos Deos Laomedon poenas persoluerit, multasque calamitates subierit, id etiam ad religionem Deorum immortalium homines impellit: quoniam qui pie sancteque per probitatem & integritatem vitae Deum coluerit, quiq; illa quae instituta sunt a sapientibus, Deo persoluerit, ille solus Deum placatum in omne tempus habebit, multa incomoda deuitabit, & se in omni molestia rectorū consiliorū conscientia consolabitur. Qui vero beneficiorum omniū autorem, omniumq; patrem Deum neglexerit, quo pacto vir iustus, & bonus & temperans esse poterit? aut si nihil horū poterit, quo pacto non in multas calamitates illabetur? Nos igitur ad religionem, & ad memoriam acceptorum beneficiorum sempiternam per hanc Loamedontis fabulam sapientes antiqui adhortabantur" (*Mythologiae*, II.8 [p. 175]). Allen neglects to bring Comes' interpretation to bear.

ruling force in the world, a divinity who can decree destiny
and enforce it with all the powers of the sea. He is, indeed,
the primary image of divinity in the play. He comes closest,
in the final scene, to assuming a *deus ex machina* role: he
adjudicates the conflict of Venus and Diana, who have more
particular interests to pursue. This too is a function with
a basis in the mythographical tradition: Neptune is the
peacemaker in the popular story of Vulcan's net.[30]

The brief scene in which Phillida is disguised by her
father Melebeus (I.iii) adds nothing further to the image
of Neptune. Functionally it is expository, and formally it
contributes to the symmetry that is a hallmark of the design
of *Gallathea*.[31] The succeeding scene, however, which has
nothing to do with the sacrifice story, gives us direct
dramatization of Neptune's power. A Mariner and three
boys appear, having just escaped from a shipwreck by
floating ashore on a rafter. They have been *"all sowc't
in waues,/By Neptunes slaues."* [32] The actors may have
appeared with some visual indication of their recent scrape,
a bit of seaweed or a manageable amount of dripping
water.[33] The boys are amazed at the bubbling of the sea:
clearly Neptune is not to be lightly regarded.[34]

The introduction of Neptune is completed in the sixth
scene of the play (II.ii) by the well-delayed appearance
of the god himself. He knows all about the disguises of

[30] See, for example, Fraunce, *Yuychurch*, sig. K4^v.

[31] Hunter (pp. 198–199) has given just tribute to the formal articulation of the play by likening it to a fugue.

[32] This couplet is from the song, which, since it is not included in the original quarto, I quote from *Sixe Court Comedies*, ed. Edward Blount (London, 1632), sig. P10^r. The lines occur in Bond at I.iv.85–86.

[33] They speak in a way that implies but does not require wet clothes; see B4^r (I.iv.3–4).

[34] The pageboy scenes will be treated as a group in Section F.

the girls and has just heard Cupid's plans against the nymphs of Diana. He announces his intentions in soliloquy:

> Then Neptune that hast taken sundrie shapes to obtaine loue, stick not to practise some deceipt to *shew thy deitie*, and hauing ofte͂ thrust thy self into the shape of beastes to deceiue men, be not coy to vse the shape of a Sheepehearde, to *shew thy self a God*.
>
> (C2ᵛ–C3ʳ; II.ii.17–21)

I italicize two phrases because they define Neptune's purpose: he is a jealous god and he wishes to show his godhead. I take Neptune's deity to mean his divine power and his right to have that power, his estate as a ruling force in the world. This use of the word "deity" is common in the Renaissance. Marlowe's Juno resents Ascanius because, according to prophecy, he will "wrong my deity with high disgrace." [35] Milton's God the Father plans with the Son "with what Arms/We mean to hold what anciently we claim/Of Deity or Empire." [36] The whole virgin-sacrifice situation focusses on Neptune's deity. All the hints of Neptune's status given in the previous scenes flower in his present assertion of intent. We have heard Gallathea define his decree as destiny: we have been told of his power both directly and by mythological allusion; we have seen a minor demonstration of his might in the appearance of the shipwrecked boys. Now the god promises action to the direct end of showing himself a god. He will control

---

[35] *The Tragedy of Dido Queen of Carthage*, III.ii.5 (in *The Complete Plays of Christopher Marlowe*, ed. Irving Ribner [New York, 1963]).

[36] *Paradise Lost*, V.722–724 (John Milton, *Complete Poems and Major Prose*, ed. Merritt Y. Hughes [New York, 1957]). For similar uses of the word, see "deity" in the *NED*, s.v. 1a and 1b.

the situation: "I will into these woodes and marke all, and in the end will marre all" (C3ʳ; II.ii.23–24).

Neptune "marks all" until the final scene of the play. His presence broods over the virgin-sacrifice situation, but he does nothing until the end. We must therefore direct our attention to the development of the situation itself, holding him temporarily in the background.

Adequate understanding of the initial posture of affairs requires further attention to Gallathea, particularly to the myth that lurks behind her. The story of Galatea, the nymph who tried to escape the attentions of the Cyclops Polyphemus, is a well-known myth particularly associated with pastoral settings. The first major literary treatment of it appears in Theocritus, it is recounted in Ovid, and it occurs in the Renaissance handbooks.[37] Lyly definitely has it in mind. In the first place, the appearance of a girl named Gallathea in a pastoral environment immediately directs the audience's attention to her namesake in mythology. Secondly, there is her costume. Unlike Phillida, Gallathea is dressed in her male disguise from the beginning of the play, and this disguise includes a white coat.[38]

[37] Theocritus, *Idyl* XI; Ovid, *Metamorphoses*, XIII.750–897; Boccaccio, VII.17; Fraunce, sigs. E4ʳ–F4ʳ.

[38] When Diana's nymphs are stricken with love for the disguised girls, Telusa remarks to Eurota, "I sawe Eurota howe amorouslie you glaunced your eye on the faire boy in the white coate" (D2ᵛ; III.i.42–43). It can be deduced from context that this "boy" is Gallathea, not Phillida: Ramia says later that she loves Tyterus (each of the girls is using her father's name) and Eurota responds, "So doe I, and I will haue him" (D3ᵛ; III.i.99). Which nymph is in love with which "boy" is of no significance to the action, but Telusa's remark could not be made unless Gallathea were wearing a white coat and Phillida a coat of another color. The incident shows what was probable in any case, that the productions used significant costumes. One keenly realizes how many details we do not know.

The Gods of Gallathea

Etymologically, "Gallathea" means "white" or "milky-white," and epithets of whiteness always occur in connection with the Galatea of the Theocritean myth.[39] The setting, the name, and the color-association all reinforce the correspondence of pattern between the Lylian situation and the Galatea myth. In the myth, the monstrous Polyphemus loves the nymph and resents her love for Acis. He pursues the couple and kills Acis while Galatea hides. She later turns her dead lover into a stream. With the omission of Acis, Lyly observes the same pattern: Gallathea is pursued by a monster (the Agar), and although the eventual fate of the sacrificed virgins is obscure, it is distinctly hinted to be a sexual one (see B2^r; I.i.54–55).

The introduction of the Galatea myth tempers certain dangerous possibilities in the virgin-sacrifice situation. I noted in the previous section that gods, when made agents in stories about morals, have a decisive effect upon action: being more powerful, they can sweep all before them. Now the sacrifice is a proper, if extreme, offering to the offended Neptune. It is destiny, and destiny, as Gallathea herself has said, must be fulfilled. Intellectually the audience must recognize Neptune's right, and they cannot help but recog-

---

[39] The song of the Cyclops in Theocritus begins, "O milk-white Galatea, why cast off him that loves thee? More white than is pressed milk. . ." (*Idyl* XI, tr. A. Lang, *Theocritus, Bion and Moschus* [London, 1932]; I use this translation in preference to the Loeb rendering, which, being in verse, is less accurate). Ovid's Polyphemus addresses her as, "Candidior folio nivei Galatea ligustri" (*Metamorphoses*, XIII.789 [ed. Frank Justus Miller, Cambridge, Mass., and London (Loeb Classical Library), 1916]). Fraunce follows Boccaccio in seeing Galatea as "the very froath of the Sea," and then, in his indefatigable pursuit of physical allegory, suggests that she is the "Lady of milke" and interprets the myth as shadowing various properties of that liquid (sig. F3^v). His version of Polyphemus' song also stresses the whiteness. Galatea appears in Spenser's marriage of the Thames and the Medway as "milkewhite *Galathæa*" (*F.Q.*, IV.xi.49).

nize his power to secure that right. The introduction of
the Galatea myth turns the situation so that a different
perspective is possible. The myth helps to organize the
audience's sympathy on Gallathea's side—Polyphemus is
completely wrong as well as cruel to behave the way he
does. That sympathy provides a kind of counter-force
against the god's propensity to have things all his own
way. The presence of the Agar, moreover, splits the
situation so as to make available satisfaction of both the
audience's sympathy for the virgins and their intellectual
recognition of Neptune. That is, it splits the situation so
that an eventual happy resolution is possible. The demand
for the sacrifice is Neptune's, and he announces that he
will enforce respect for his deity. But it is the Agar, not
Neptune, who corresponds to the dreadful Polyphemus
and who inspires the terror of the sacrifice. All the expressions of horror, and there are many, concern him, not
Neptune. The Polyphemian Agar is used to create the
initial strong situation; Neptune is left free to say, later
on, "Neptune should haue beene intreated, not cosened"
(F2ᵛ; IV.iii.8), and free to assume the final role of
appeaser.

After they are disguised, the girls enter the no-man's-
land of the woods and are almost completely out of touch
with the sacrifice situation thereafter. They leave the
atmosphere of violence and the problem of destiny to
engage in their paradoxical courtship. A shift in tone for
their scenes is already underway in I.iii: Phillida's objections to male disguise do not concern destiny but merely
the impropriety and difficulty of pretending to be a boy.
When Gallathea reappears (II.i) she has forgotten about
destiny and is occupied with the same immediate problem
as Phillida. Indeed, after Neptune's soliloquy in II.ii the
sacrifice situation itself is held in suspension for seven
scenes.

After this long suspension, the sacrifice situation is refreshed in our memories in a characteristically Lylian way: an Augur enters to arrange for the sacrifice, restates the issues in a long speech, and then exits to punctuate the matter.[40] After the Augur leaves, Tyterus and Melebeus quarrel, each trying to force the other to reveal the existence of his eligible daughter. This scene marks a slight advance in the action. Primarily, however, it exists to present major issues in new terms. The central theme active in the sacrifice situation has hitherto been the conflict between destiny and private desire: should one give the god his due, what he has ordered, or shall one save oneself? Now the issue is reformulated in patriotic terms. The Augur points out that failure to provide the Agar with a virgin will result in disaster for the country: "If you think it against nature to sacrifice your children," he tells the assembly, "thinke it also against sence to destroy your Countrey" (E4^r; IV.i.4–5). Tyterus pursues the same idea when he accuses Melebeus of hiding his daughter: "You haue conueyed her away, that you might cast vs all away, bereauing her the honour of her beauty, and vs the benefite, preferring a common inconuenience, before a priuate mischiefe" (E4^v–F1^r; IV.i.36–39). Thus the central issue has been modulated from a theological conflict between destiny and private desire, to a social conflict between public good and private good. Both conflicts, of course, may be subsumed under the rubric of "the general versus the particular"; they are, indeed, so handled when Neptune adjudicates all quarrels at the end of the play.

The "populus," exasperated with the quarrel of the fathers,[41] select another virgin, Haebe. While being bound

---

[40] See Chapter II, note 34, and the Tillotson article there cited, on Lyly's placement of long speeches.

[41] This quarrel shows the comic disorder that results from attempts to escape the gods' decrees. Melebeus is willing to assume the ridiculous

to the tree, Haebe delivers a speech that occupies over two-thirds of the last scene exclusively devoted to the sacrifice situation, V.ii. She laments her lot, bids a long farewell to life and to Diana, and gives a description of the Agar shocking in its directness.[42] But through her speech runs the word and the idea of destiny, and when the monster does not come, Haebe performs an astonishing—but quite believable and therefore quite moving—reversal. Addressing herself, she says:

Fortunate Haebe, howe shalt thou expresse thy ioyes? Nay vnhappie girle that art not the fairest. Had it not been better for thee to haue died with fame, then to liue with dishonour, to haue preferred the safetie of thy Countrey and rarenesse of thy beautie, before sweetnes of life, & vanity of the world? But alas, desteny would not haue it so, desteny coulde not, for it asketh the beautifullest. I would Haebe thou hadst been beautifullest.

(G2^r; V.ii.62–68) [43]

---

[42] role of a *senex amans* in order to enforce the lie that Phillida died as a child: "Did you euer see me kisse my Daughter? you are deceiued, it was my wife. And if you thought so young a peece vnfit for so old a person, and therefore imagined it to be my childe, not my spouse, you must knowe that siluer haires delight in golden lockes, and the olde fancies craue young Nurses, and frostie yeeres must bee thawed by youthfull fyers" (F1^r; IV.i.47–52). Lyly marvelously manipulates his euphuistic double and triple phrasing for absurd self-incrimination.

[42] "Come Agar thou vnsatiable Monster of Maidens blood, & douourer of beauties bowels, glut thy selfe till thou surfet, & let my life end thine. Teare these tender ioynts wyth thy greedie iawes, these yellow lockes with thy black feete, this faire face with thy foule teeth" (G1^v; V.ii.48–52). For appreciation of the range of experience Lyly can encompass with the highly artificial device of triple-phrasing, compare the second sentence in this quotation with the last sentence quoted from Melebeus' speech in fn. 41 above.

[43] To praise Lyly for characterization (when the character is not

The abortive sacrifice of Haebe occurs in the last scene but one of the play. In the final scene Neptune delivers a furious soliloquy: mortals "dallie with our deities," and a slaughter of all virgins will teach them that "destinie cannot be preuented by craft" (G2ᵛ; V.iii.12–14). Diana immediately arrives to protest, closely followed by Venus raging at Diana. At the level of divine debate the play swiftly reaches resolution. The function, then, of the Haebe scene is to complete the insult to Neptune. Not only have the likely candidates for sacrifice been hidden, but an insufficient offering has been substituted. The sentiments expressed by Haebe while bound to the tree indicate the significance of this action. Gallathea, in argument against her father's plan of disguise, had urged the honor inherent in being the willing victim of destiny (B2ʳ–B2ᵛ; I.i.68–82). The idea reappears when the fathers quarrel, each rebuking the other for attempting to elude this honor. Through her pathetic farewell to life, Haebe arrives at an acceptance of the honor, the only person to do so in the play. Her about-face when the Agar fails to arrive stresses the absoluteness of the destiny she so often mentions. Destiny cannot be gainsaid. Destiny cannot be fulfilled by those not destined, however willing they may be.

The myth that hovers in the background of the episode strengthens this significance. Haebe is named after the goddess of youth, and Lyly emphasizes the name heavily.[44] The first effect of the emphasis is to increase pathos: every

---

a wit or a flirt) may sound like special pleading on the part of one infatuated with his subject. There are very few examples of Shakespearean excellence with respect to character in Lyly's plays. But unquestionably this speech is greatly done. Moreover, given the idea of it, the excellence is achieved almost entirely with Lyly's main technical resource, mastery of rhythm.

[44] She addresses herself, as Lylian characters usually do in soliloquy, using her own name ten times.

time the name occurs it reinforces the dramatic picture of the young led to untimely death. She speaks of youth herself: "Shall it onely be lawfull amongst vs in the prime of youth, and pride of beautie, to destroy both youth and beautie: and what was honoured in fruites and flowres as a vertue, to violate in a virgine as a vice? But alas destenie alloweth no dispute" (G1ʳ; V.ii.21–24). The allusion to the patroness of youth, then, operates in the same way that the Polyphemus myth does in the first scene of the play: it intensifies our sympathies for those faced with destiny. Also in a manner parallel with the Polyphemus myth, Haebe's speech, with its horrifying description of the Agar, directs our animosities primarily at the awful instrument of destiny rather than at Neptune himself.[45] The pathos of a virgin offered to a beast, however, hardly needs greater emphasis. The allusion to the goddess Hebe functions also in another way, and serves to explain a puzzling portion of the soliloquy. Among Haebe's farewells occur these lines:

> Onely Haebe biddeth farewell to all the ioyes that she conceiued, and you hope for, that shee possessed, and you shall; fare-well the pompe of Princes Courts, whose roofes are imbosst with golde, and whose pauements are decked with faire Ladies, where the daies are spent in sweet delights, the nights in pleasant dreames, where chastitie honoreth affections, and commaundeth, yeeldeth to desire and conquereth.
>
> (G1ᵛ; V.ii.31–38)

It is rather unlikely that shepherdesses from the banks of the Humber should have such extensive acquaintance with the pomp of princes' courts. The passage appears to break

---

[45] Neptune is mentioned only by the Augur in this scene, never by Haebe herself.

the frame of the play: the boy-actress is apparently speaking straight to the Court audience. It is odd in Lyly thus to go outside the presuppositions of the story.[46] An explanation for these lines, and a deepened meaning for the whole scene, lie in the myth of Hebe. Aside from her marriage to Hercules, the story of Hebe most well-known in the Renaissance runs as follows: she was the daughter of Juno (either by Jupiter or by parthenogenesis) and cupbearer to the gods. She lost her post in disgrace when she chanced to fall while waiting at table and accidentally exposed her private parts. She was replaced by Ganymede. This sad event is read by Boccaccio, Comes, and Fraunce as a seasonal myth: Hebe is the foliage brought forth by the warm lower air (Juno); autumn leaves the trees naked and Hebe is replaced by Ganymede (i.e. Aquarius the water-bearer, a winter constellation).[47] Although a hint of this seasonal myth is present in Haebe's reference to fruits and flowers, Lyly largely ignores such implications and concentrates on one correspondence. The most important thing about Lyly's scene is that, through no fault of her own, Haebe cannot fulfill the task given her. The same had happened to the goddess: another was deemed more worthy. When Lyly's character says farewell to princes' courts, the lines are actually more appropriate for the minor goddess disgraced in the high Court of Olympus. The lines stress the parallel situation of the Hebe-archetype. Even *willing* inadequacy is still inadequate. The gods must be pleased in their own way. "Desteny would not

---

[46] I am not forgetting Lyly's references to Elizabeth and her Court, his Sapho and his Cynthia, the dreams that seem to allude to Court intrigues, and so forth. These, however, are indirect references by way of topical allegory: they do not disrupt the integrity of the fiction.

[47] Boccaccio, IX.2 (vol. II, pp. 441–442); Comes, II.5 (pp. 143–145); Fraunce, sigs. I2ᵛ–I3ᵛ.

haue it so, desteny coulde not." Neptune becomes even angrier than before at those who would "dallie with our deities."

E. DIANA VERSUS VENUS

I have spoken in no detail of the final phase of the sacrifice situation, the abolition of the rite by Neptune. First we must return to the beginning of the play and discuss the second major line of action, Cupid's involvement with the nymphs of Diana. As I mentioned before, this involvement is based upon the same formula as the sacrifice situation, the formula of the defiance of divinity. In this line of the play, however, the formula is doubled: first Diana is defied, then Venus, each by the subordinates of the other. The formula is also somewhat slower in emerging: Cupid and the nymphs expend their energies upon each other—only in the later stages do the goddesses themselves join the issue.

Cupid first appears, with an unnamed nymph of Diana, in I.ii. Cupid is also unnamed, but his costume was doubtless recognizable (within the limits of stage propriety) and by the end of the short scene the nymph has guessed his identity. Each character appears as an exemplar of his or her associated goddess: Cupid gives an oxymoronic description of love, and the nymph speaks of the joys of hunting. The Campaspean technique of dialogue by definition is pursued until the nymph formally states the opposition between the two:

I will followe Diana in the Chace, whose virgins are all chast, delighting in the bowe that wounds the swift Hart in the Forrest, not fearing the bowe that strikes the softe hart in the Chamber. This difference is betweene my Mistris Diana, and your Mother (as I gesse) Venus,

that all her Nimphes are amiable and wise in theyr
kinde, the other amorous and too kinde for their sexe;
and so farewell little god.   *Exit.*

(B3ʳ; I.ii.23–29)

Cupid then takes the same attitude that Neptune has taken:
he resolves that Diana and her nymphs "shall knowe that
Cupid is a great god" (B3ʳ; I.ii.30–31).

This confrontation, with Cupid's resolve to prove his
deity, however, is distinctly less weighty than the issues of
Neptune and destiny raised in the immediately preceding
scene.[48] The contrast between Cupid and Neptune is repeated, even more directly, in II.ii, when each of the two
gods has a soliloquy. I have already discussed Neptune's
speech,[49] but the full value of both speeches emerges only
when they are taken together. Cupid is *"in Nimphes
apparell"* (C2ᵛ; II.ii.s.d.); Neptune says he will disguise
himself as a shepherd. So far, they would appear to be doing exactly the same thing. Dramatically, however, Neptune is in the superior position: he overhears Cupid's
soliloquy (which is first) and thus can comment on it. This
he does, linking Cupid's disguise with those of Gallathea
and Phillida as opposed to his own. He doubts whether
Cupid will succeed in "ouertaking" Diana, but has perfect
confidence in his own ability to succeed in his stratagem.

Secondly, there is a difference in the disguises. Shepherd's weeds are a comedown for a god, but Neptune's disguise is distinctly less degrading than Cupid's feminine

---

[48] I cannot agree with T. W. Baldwin's statement that Cupid is
"determined to be revenged" upon the nymph (*Shakspere's Five-Act
Structure* [Urbana, 1947], p. 510). Baldwin, in his desire to see a
Terentian structure of incident in the play, is inclined to exaggerate
the quantity of action in this and other scenes. The scene does not
dramatize an insult but presents a definition. Cupid's primary impulse
to action is mischievousness, as I will discuss below.

[49] See above, pp. 119–121.

outfit. The dressing of a man as a woman is a standard motif with conventional significance in Renaissance literature.[50] It is a symbol of passionate love, the love that "turns a man into a woman." [51] Reason has resigned control of the passions, and the lover is effeminate, that is, improperly devoted to sensual gratification. Dressing such a lover in skirts symbolizes his condition: Ariosto's Ruggiero when devoted to Alcina, Sidney's Pyrochles when pursuing Philoclea, and Spenser's Artegall when enslaved by the Amazon Radigund are leading examples.[52] Mark Rose points out that the deity associated with this kind of love is the bastard Cupid, who creates the unreasonable havoc of lust.[53] Now the moral pressure at this point in Lyly's story is clearly not so great as that in the *Orlando Furioso*, the *Arcadia*, or the *Faerie Queene*: we are not presently invited to the seriousness of Musidorus' rebuke to Pyrochles or of Britomart's astonished dismay at Artegall's plight.[54] We are not, indeed, presented with a lover:

[50] The play, of course, also involves female transvestism, and the girls are worried about the propriety of their disguise, a concern to be repeated by one of Shakespeare's girl-pages, Jessica. But this offence to modesty, in a stage device so common and so readily acceptable because the actors are boys anyway, does not have the moral implications of male transvestism.

[51] Robert Burton, *The Anatomy of Melancholy*, ed. A. R. Shilleto (London, 1893), III.163.

[52] These three examples are discussed at length, and full citations provided on the significance of male transvestism, in an article to which I am much indebted, Mark Rose, "Sidney's Womanish Man," *RES*, n.s. XV (1964), 353–363.

[53] Cf. Sir John Davies' description, "That bastard Love,/Which doth usurp the world's great marshal's name," in *Orchestra*, ll. 260–261 (quoted from J. William Hebel and Hoyt H. Hudson, eds., *Poetry of the English Renaissance, 1509–1660* [New York, 1929]).

[54] *Arcadia*, in *The Prose Works of Sir Philip Sidney*, ed. Albert Feuillerat (Cambridge, Eng., 1912), I.77–79, and *The Faerie Queene*, V.vii.38–40.

we are given the bastard god himself. The disguise functions as an emblematic summary of his nature. It tells us what sort of love he sponsors.

The third determinant of our attitude to Cupid lies in the following lines of his soliloquy:

> Cupid though he be a child, is no babie. I will make their paines my pastimes, & so confound their loues in their owne sexe, that they shall dote in their desires, delight in their affections, and practise onely impossibilities. Whilst I trewant from my mother, I will vse some tyranny in these woodes, and so shall their exercise in foolish loue, be my excuse for running away.
>
> (C2ᵛ; II.ii.5–11)

Although *Gallathea* is a comedy, there is a strain of violence and horror in the story of the virgin-sacrifice. Neptune's threats and the destiny associated with him are serious. Cupid's threats and the "tyranny" he wishes to practice, on the other hand, can hardly be viewed as other than mischievous. *He* has not been seriously offended; he is out for a lark. As a clever child trying to gain attention, he naturally devises a practical joke: he is going to make a bevy of girls, professed adherents of chastity, fall in love with two boys whom he knows to be girls in disguise. His willful tone and his farcical plan are thoroughly appropriate to the concept of unreasonable love figured by his costume: he will cause "foolish loue."

As the myths of Galatea, Hesione, and Hebe shape our understanding of the virgin-sacrifice, so here also a specific myth reinforces our impression of Cupid's mischievousness. In the lines quoted above he twice mentions that he has run away from Venus. These lines constitute a reference to a classical poem that enjoyed prodigious popularity in the Renaissance, the *Eros Drapetes* (*Amor Fugitivus*) of Moschus.[55] Lyly takes the theme from Cupid's point of view (Moschus' Idyl is Venus' advertisement for the strayed godlet), but the resemblance is clear. This Cupid is separated from Venus, and the havoc he wreaks is not to be associated with her. We shall discover when Venus appears in the final scene that, angry as she is at Diana's

[55] See James Hutton, "The First Idyl of Moschus in Imitations to the Year 1800," *AJP*, XLIX (1928), 105–136; Joseph G. Fucilla, "Additions to 'The First Idyl of Moschus in Imitations to the Year 1800'," *AJP*, L (1929), 190–193, and "Materials for the History of a Popular Classical Theme," *CP*, XXVI (1931), 135–152. The Hutton article lists imitations and translations by, among others, Politian, Pontano, Giraldi Cintio, Lorenzo the Magnificent, Tasso, Marot, and Desportes. Among English writers are Turberville, Barnabe Barnes, Shirley, and Crashaw. The two most well-known English adaptations of the theme are Ben Jonson's *Lord Haddington's Masque* (*The Hue and Cry after Cupid*) and Spenser, *The Faerie Queene*, III.vi.11–38. On Spenser's use, see J. Douglas Bruce, "Spenser's *Faerie Queene*, Book III, Canto VI, St. 11ff., and Moschus' Idyl, 'Love the Runaway,' " *MLN*, XXVII (1912), 183–185, and Roche, pp. 110–111. The presence of the Moschian motif in *Gallathea* has not hitherto been noted, a surprising omission in scholarship in view of the fact that Lyly's version of it is extremely close to Spenser's. In both, the runaway Cupid is sought by Venus. In Lyly, he gets among Diana's nymphs and the resulting complications lead to a sharp quarrel between the goddesses, a quarrel eventually resolved by Neptune. In Spenser, Venus also encounters Diana; a resulting quarrel is exacerbated by Diana's outrage at Venus' suggestion that Cupid may be among the nymphs. The quarrel is resolved by the goddesses' discovery of Chrysogonee and her babies Amoret and Belphoebe. The resemblance extends to detail: Lyly's Diana carries out a threat made by Spenser's Diana, to clip Cupid's wings. Since Lyly's play was certainly finished before the publication of the first three books of Spenser's poem, but not published until after that event, no direct influence can be posited either way.

detention of her son, she rejects the lascivious love of her son for a higher kind.[56]

At the time Cupid delivers his soliloquy, Diana and her train have just met the disguised girls. The action of this strand of the play is next taken up in III.i, where three of the nymphs enter serially to soliloquize on their love-stricken state and then discover their common condition. The device of the serial entrance of the three characters, each to say the same thing, creates a brilliantly funny scene. Lyly is to use the device again for the middle scene of *Love's Metamorphosis,* in which three couples enter serially, each man passionately pleading his suit and each nymph contemptuously rejecting him. Indeed, this kind of scene becomes a staple device in English high comedy, particularly the kind in which artificiality of situation causes the play to verge on farce. Shakespeare employs the device for the recognition scene of *Love's Labor's Lost* (IV.iii), in which each of four lovers enters to read his verses and exposes the broken vows of the one entering after him. Traces of scenes so structured appear in *A Midsummer Night's Dream* and in *As You Like It,* and the device is still flourishing when the two Ernests enter to be exposed by each other's fiancée at the end of the second act of *The Importance of Being Earnest.* The effect of cumulative humiliation for the characters and cumulative

---

[56] Hunter (p. 201) has remarked, in discussing the design of *Gallathea,* that he takes "Venus to be a mere extension of Cupid." This is not the case. It is important to the design and meaning of the play that they be separate personages. The use of the Moschian motif when Cupid begins to act (*not* in his earlier appearance) effectively separates him and his actions from his mother. It is, moreover, essential to an understanding of the final scene of the play to perceive that the love of Gallathea and Phillida for each other (as opposed to the love of the nymphs for them) is spontaneous and *not* the result of Cupid's intervention. The disguised girls are already falling in love with each other before Cupid's soliloquy (C2^r–C2^v; II.i.44–66).

delight for the audience prompts analogy to knocking over a line of dominoes.[57]

Cupid has had his effect. The dominoes demonstrate his power as the history of the flood, and the Mariner's shipwreck, had demonstrated Neptune's power. The besotted nymphs immediately raise Cupid to the rank of supreme divinity:

> O deuine Loue, which art therfore called deuine, because thou ouer-reachest the wisest, conquerest the chastest, and doost all things both vnlikely and impossible, because thou art Loue.
>
> (D3ᵛ; III.i.102–105)

---

[57] The domino device not only structures the scene but also patterns particular exchanges of dialogue. Note, for example, these ridiculous parallelisms:

EUROTA How did it take you first Telusa?

TELUSA By the eyes, my wanton eyes which conceiued the picture of his face, and hangd it on the verie strings of my hart. O faire Melebeus, ô fonde Telusa, but how did it take you Eurota?

EUROTA By the eares, whose sweete words suncke so deepe into my head, that the remembrance of his wit, hath bereaued mee of my wisedome; ô eloquent Tyterus, ô credulous Eurota.

(D3ʳ; III.i.55–61)

And the closing lines of the scene clearly contain a hint for Shakespeare:

EUROTA Talke no more Telusa, your words wound. Ah would I were no woman.

RAMIA Would Tyterus were no boy.

TELUSA Would Telusa were no body. *Exeunt.*

(D3ᵛ; III.i.108–111)

This howling of Irish wolves against the moon, and the scene structure itself, are clearly a development of the techniques of euphuism. Those techniques have been modulated into strong, simpler parallelisms, which, in this case, produce more directly laughable effects in the language. Subtlety remains, but the force is greater: part of our delight in the final lines stems from the fact that Tyterus, like Rosalind, *is* no boy.

The description is perverse. In the Neoplatonic Christian universe implied by this apostrophe, divine Love is that creative, ordering, sustaining power that rules the world. The nymphs have confused divine love with a love that "ouer-reachest the wisest, conquerest the chastest," that is, turns people into fools and wantons. Sir John Davies' description of Cupid precisely expresses the power the nymphs are worshipping: "That bastard Love,/Which doth usurp the world's great marshal's name."

Three scenes later, Diana enters the conflict and quickly reverses the posture of affairs. Lyly bothers with no mechanical device to release the nymphs from their love-sick state.[58] Diana overcomes cupidinous love merely by rhetoric and the force of personality. After she has delivered several long speeches on chastity, the nymphs are as eager as she to punish Cupid. She is more powerful than Cupid. Indeed, she knows that her real enemy is not Cupid but Venus:

> And thou shalt see Cupid that I will shewe my selfe to be Diana, that is, Conqueror of thy loose & vntamed appetites. Did thy mother Venus vnder the colour of a Nimphe, sende thee hether to wounde my Nimphes? Doth she adde craft to her malice, and mistrusting her deitie, practice deceite? . . . As for thee Cupid, I will breake thy bowe, and burne thine arrowes, binde thy handes, clyp thy wings, and fetter thy feete. . . . Let Venus that great Goddesse, raunsome Cupid that little God.
>
> (E3^v; III.iv.67–80)

Cupid is reduced to the status of Moschian godlet that he had left only in the imagination of the nymphs, and set to

---

[58] In *Sapho and Phao* whatever Cupid does with his arrows must be undone with other arrows.

tasks that violate his nature (untying love-knots and re-
moving the love-stories from Diana's tapestry).
At this point in the discussion Diana's mode of speech
ought to be very familiar. She phrases the whole conflict
in terms of deity. She, like Neptune and Cupid, wishes to
demonstrate her deity, to show herself as Diana the conqueror. She wonders if Venus has resorted to craft through
mistrust of her (i.e. Venus') deity. Deity here means
power. It also means, clearly, the right to possess that
power, the ontological essence of divinity. Venus could re-
sort to underhanded means, Diana implies, only if she
doubted her own status. Diana, of course, is "the goddesse
of chastity, whose thoughts are alwaies answerable to her
vowes, whose eyes neuer glanced on desire, and whose
hart abateth the poynt of Cupids arrowes" (E3^r; III.iv.
28–31). That is, she figures virginity, Belphoebe rather
than Amoret. This self-definition, moreover, compactly
gives an added dimension to the concept of deity. The
nymphs of chastity may swerve from their vows, but the
thoughts of their goddess are always "answerable" to hers.
Diana has a thorough consistency, a singleness of essence.
She exemplifies, with a completeness unavailable even to
her own followers, the quality over which she presides.
She thus has complete right to her power, and undertakes
to dispose things accordingly. She threatens to turn Cupid's
arrows against himself and make him "inamored, not on
Psiches, but on Circes" (E4^r; III.iv.83–84). Psyche
signifies the soul, and Circe is the great Renaissance figure
for sensuality, mother of Comus and archetype of Acrasia.[59]

[59] The various medieval and Renaissance interpretations of the Cupid
and Psyche story are finely summarized in the course of D. C. Allen's
article, "On Spenser's *Muiopotmos*," *SP*, LIII (1956), 141–158; in all
of them Psyche, as her name dictates, is seen as some aspect of the
human soul. For Circe as sensuality, see Douglas Bush, *Mythology and*

Diana would divorce the Moschian Cupid from the human soul and tie him to the swine-maker with whom he belongs. But Diana is not the only power in the universe. She may, in effect, emasculate Cupid, but some of the love-knots he is set to untie cannot be loosened, for they are the knots of true love (F1ᵛ; IV.ii.34–35, 49–50). Cupid tells the nymphs that Diana herself eventually shall yield, that "she cannot conquer desteny" (F2ʳ; IV.ii.89).

Destiny has been associated with the deity of Neptune. Cupid implies that it is superior to the single and stunning power of Diana. As the play proceeds through its phases of analogous action, both the events and the issues clearly demand a confrontation of the gods who preside over each of its actions. This demand is met in the final scene when the three major deities engage in debate. I quote the debate in full:

Enter Neptune alone.

NEPTUNE   And doe men beginne to bee equall with Gods, seeking by craft to ouer-reach thẽ that by power ouer-see them? Doe they dote so much on their daughters, that they stick not to dallie with our deities, well shall the inhabitants see, that destinie cannot be preuented by craft, nor my anger be appeased by submission. I will make hauocke of Dianaes Nimphes, my Temple shall bee died with Maydens blood, and there shal be nothing more vile then to be a Virgine. To be young and fayre, shall be accounted shame & punishment, in so much as it shall be thought as dishonorable to be honest, as fortunate to be deformed.

---

the *Renaissance Tradition* (rev. ed. New York, 1963), pp. 279–280, and Merritt Hughes, "Spenser's Acrasia and the Circe of the Renaissance," *JHI*, IV (1943), 381–399, especially pp. 386–388 and the Alciati emblem reproduced opposite p. 386.

The Gods of Gallathea

Enter Diana with her Nimphes.

DIANA O Neptune, hast thou forgotten thy selfe, or wilt
thou cleane for-sake mee? Hath Diana therfore brought
danger to her Nimphes, because they be chast? shal
vertue suffer both paine and shame which alwaies deserueth praise and honor?

Enter Venus.

VENUS Prayse and honour (Neptune) nothing lesse, except it be commendable to be coy, and honorable to be
peeuish. Sweet Neptune, if Venus can do any thing, let
her try it in this one thing, that Diana may finde as
small comfort at thy hands, as Loue hath found curtesie
at hers.

This is shee that hateth sweete delights, enuieth louing
desires, masketh wanton eyes, stoppeth amorous eares,
bridleth youthfull mouthes, and vnder a name, or a
worde constancie, entertaineth all kinde of crueltie: shee
hath taken my sonne Cupid, Cupid my louely sonne,
vsing him like a prentise, whypping him like a slaue,
scorning him like a beast, therefore Neptune I intreate
thee by no other God, then the God of loue, that thou
euill intreate this Goddesse of hate.

NEPTUNE I muse not a little to see you two in this place,
at this time, and about this matter, but what say you
Diana, haue you Cupid captiue?

DIANA I say there is nothing more vaine, then to dispute
with Venus, whose vntamed affections haue bred more
brawles in heauen, then is fitte to repeate in earth, or
possible to recount in number, I haue Cupid, and will
keepe him, not to dandle in my lappe, whom I abhor
in my hart, but to laugh him to scorne, that hath made
in my virgins harts such deepe scarres.

VENUS Scarres Diana call you them that I know to be

139

bleeding woundes? alas weake deitie, it stretcheth not so farre, both to abate the sharpnesse of his Arrowes, and to heale the hurts. No, Loues woundes when they seeme greene, rankle, and hauing a smooth skinne without, fester to the death within. Therefore Neptune, if euer Venus stoode thee in steed, furthered thy fancies, or shall at all times be at thy cõmaund, let eyther Diana bring her Virgins to a continuall massacre, or release Cupid of his martyrdome.

DIANA It is knowne Venus, that your tongue is as vnrulie as your thoughts, and your thoughts as vnstaied as your eyes, Diana cannot chatter, Venus cannot chuse.

VENUS It is an honour for Diana to haue Venus meane ill, when she so speaketh well, but you shal see I come not to trifle, therefore once againe Neptune, if that be not buried, which can neuer die, fancie, or that quenched which must euer burne, affection, shew thy selfe the same Neptune that I knew thee to bee when thou wast a Sheepe-hearde, and let not Venus wordes be vaine in thyne eares, since thyne were imprinted in my hart.

NEPTUNE It were vnfitte that Goddesses shoulde striue, and it were vnreasonable that I shold not yeeld, and therefore to please both, both attend; Diana I must honor, her vertue deserueth no lesse, but Venus I must loue, I must confesse so much.

Diana, restore Cupid to Venus, and I will for euer release the sacrifice of Virgins, if therefore you loue your Nimphes as shee doth her Sonne, or preferre not a priuate grudge before a common griefe, aunswere what you will doe.

DIANA I account not the choyse harde, for had I twentie Cupids, I woulde deliuer them all to saue one Virgine, knowing loue to be a thing of all the vainest, virginitie to be a vertue of all the noblest. I yeeld, Larissa, bring

out Cupid: and now shall it be saide, that Cupid saued
those he thought to spoyle.

VENUS I agree to this willinglie: for I will be warie
howe my Sonne wander againe. But Diana cannot forbid
him to wounde.

DIANA Yes, chastitie is not within the leuell of his bowe.

VENUS But beautie is a fayre marke to hit.

NEPTUNE Well I am gladde you are agreed: and saie
that Neptune hath delt well wyth Beautie and Chastitie.

Enter Cupid.

DIANA Heere take your sonne.

VENUS Syr boy where haue you beene?

(G2ᵛ–G3ᵛ; V.iii.10–85)

This scene demonstrates how Lyly has met a problem
discussed above in theoretical terms. The direct intervention of gods in human action, we noted, requires extreme
tact in the management of the story, since the gods in their
power may carry all before them, unhindered by the human limitations that are, directly or indirectly, responsible
for most of the conflict in any narrative or drama. Lyly
has solved the problem by doing two things: he lets the
gods *do* very little until the final scene, and then he brings
them into conflict *with each other.* Until Diana's entrance
in this scene, Neptune has not appeared on stage with any
other character.[60] His importance has been kept before us
by his soliloquies and by other characters' references to
him. Only now that the shepherds have tried to foist
Haebe on him does he undertake any real action, and he is
immediately stopped by Diana's protests. Diana has been
more active, but she has functioned in a peripetal structure:

---

[60] Except in the double-soliloquy scene with Cupid, when Cupid was
unaware of his presence.

Cupid overcomes her nymphs, she overtakes Cupid, now Venus confronts her. This system of checks and balances is a form of what I have called Lyly's situationalism. Only because his play is static can he secure the services of the gods as figures of power and yet prevent them from cutting the Gordian knots of the action prematurely.[61] By holding the virgin-sacrifice situation in suspension, and by reversing the direction of the love-chastity action, he has kept the gods before us but saved their real activity until the end.

All the while, however, he has been building toward the final confrontation. Gallathea's original protest about the disguise, the quarrel of the fathers, and Haebe's acceptance of the sacrifice constitute a gradual expansion of the power of destiny. Cupid's depredations among the nymphs and their punishment of him present the conflict between love and chastity. The confrontation scene is an image for the combination of these three universals. Realism, with its demand for psychological motivation, would require that Diana display some concern with the sacrifice before a final scene that depends upon such a concern; well-made plotting would demand that Venus receive some development prior to the final debate that would make her the dramatic equivalent of her opponent Diana. But such demands presuppose that the play find its interest and its structure in psychological character. Lyly finds his interest and his structure in similar situations that throw up expanding ideas. Venus has been potentially behind the whole love-chastity situation from its beginning, explicitly signalled to us by the Moschian truancy but a likely enough figure to appear in any case simply because the situation concerns

[61] If this sentence imports into the discussion an inappropriate temporal dimension for Lyly's process of composition, it can be reversed: Lyly's peculiar use of the gods makes the play static. In any case, since the play is a completed thing, an order of causation is only a metaphor.

love. Likewise for Diana: Haebe bade farewell to her (it would be peculiar, in a more realistic play, for farewells to pass between characters who have never met), but she was potentially involved in the sacrifice from the beginning of the play. It is the coherence of ideas that counts.

The ideas are, of course, commonplace enough: love, chastity, and destiny. They can be approached, however, only through the situation by which Lyly presents them, the quarrel among the gods. The gods are here the final developments of the images Lyly has chosen to present his universals. We have seen lovers, chaste persons, and persons under the decree of destiny. We have witnessed actions involving love, chastity, and destiny. We have had discussions of these qualities in the abstract. Now, in the final appearance of the gods, we see them as simultaneously symbolizing these universals, embodying them, and giving them the force of deity. Diana has virgins under her protection, is virgin herself, and lends all the power of her position to establising virginity as an incontrovertible value in the universe. Venus protects lovers (particularly Gallathea and Phillida after the quarrel is settled), herself loves (note her expressions of affection for both Neptune and Cupid), and tries to establish love as a force over virginity. Neptune figures the power of divine will, and exerts that power in composing the quarrel of the goddesses. But for the comic grace of the scene, the sense of a cosy family spat with which Lyly keeps excessive solemnity at bay, we might identify the gods as radically Neoplatonic images of the kind described by E. H. Gombrich, forms that the Platonic ideas, conceived as entities, might take to convey themselves to the limited human mind.[62] They are thorough, whole, and undivorceable from the values that they figure.

[62] E. H. Gombrich, *"Icones Symbolicae:* The Visual Image in Neoplatonic Thought," *JWCI,* XI (1948), 180.

The scene is thus metaphorical in character. The theatrical action is the vehicle for notions of love and chastity and their relation. Venus begins by denigrating the quality that Diana figures, and then sneers at Diana herself as a "weake deitie." Diana attempts to save her devotees from the wrath of Neptune and to ensure proper "praise and honor" for the virtue she figures, and then rebukes Venus for unseemly brawling. Each begins with abstractions and then turns personal in a way that, because of their symbolic dimension, carries out metaphorically the initial abstraction. Neptune moves in the opposite direction. He is initially wrathful at the mortals who would "dallie with our deities." He turns thoughtful at the appearance and railing of the goddesses: "I muse not a little to see you two." He then settles the quarrel in a characteristically Lylian double-edged maneuver: he *appeals* to the deity of both and *establishes* the deity of both: "It were vnfitte that Goddesses shoulde striue . . . Diana I must honor . . . Venus I must loue." The progression of the quarrel is beautifully structured.

But this solution is rather mysterious on several grounds. Most notably, Neptune looks deflated. Diana preserves her virgins and Venus regains Cupid, but Neptune, originally furious, gives up the sacrifice—for what? Actually, his maneuver is the final evolution of destiny in *Gallathea*. He gives up the sacrifice, he says, to preserve the divinities of Venus and Diana. He gives it up lest he be "vnreasonable," and lest, as he admonishes Diana, a private grudge be preferred before a common grief. This last is a familiar idea. Tyterus had used it in trying to shame Melebeus into acknowledging the existence of his daughter.[63] It is not, of course, a startling anticipation of utilitarian doctrine about the greatest good for the greatest number. It is commonplace in the context of the Elizabethan world picture: the

---

[63] Quoted above, p. 124.

order of the whole is an overriding excellence in itself.[64] Neptune is giving up an accident, a custom that was the result of a particular train of historical events recounted carefully for us at the beginning of the play. He gives up this accident in order to preserve things essential to the moral and spiritual order of the world, the values of love and chastity. Neptune, as the deity of the sacrifice, has been associated from the start with destiny, that unavoidable power rightly ruling in the world. The association between destiny and the sacrifice was just: the sacrifice was due propitiation of an offended ruling power. But the realm of divine power and destiny is far larger than the particular accidental customs of legal repayment for past offences. Divine power is concerned with the order of the whole: Neptune must deal well with chastity and beauty, as he says in composing the quarrel. Essentially, the allegorical meaning of *Gallathea* is the transition from fear, deceit, and conflict to harmony under the aegis of destiny, which expands as the transition is effected. As the god has remarked in an earlier soliloquy, "Neptune should haue beene intreated, not cosened" (F2ᵛ; IV.iii.8). When he is entreated, harmony is achieved.

Also mysterious is the compromise between Venus and Diana. On the level of action all is clear: Venus retrieves Cupid (definitely a minor god when his own defender addresses him as "syr boy") and Diana's virgins are no longer threatened. But the ideas seem less clear. Chastity is not within the level of Cupid's bow, according to Diana,

---

[64] Cf. Richard Hooker on the dual character of natural law: "As in this respect [natural agents] have their law, which law directeth them in the means whereby they tend to their own perfection: so likewise another law there is, which toucheth them as they are sociable parts united into one body; a law which bindeth them each to serve unto other's good, *and all to prefer the good of the whole before whatsoever their own particular*" (*Of the Laws of Ecclesiastical Polity*, I.iii.5; in Works, ed. John Keble, rev. ed. R. W. Church and F. Paget [Oxford, 1888], I.211. My italics.)

but Venus counters by remarking that beauty is a fair target. The exchange is deeply puzzling. Lyly is apparently suggesting some impossible combination of those traditional opposites, love and chastity. But how?

I think the rest of the final scene of *Gallathea* shows how. The hinge of this last episode is the fact that it *is* impossible—for human beings. The only problem left after the gods' quarrel is the relationship between Gallathea and Phillida, much dismayed to find out each other's sex but still in love. The action of this final episode is a last demonstration of divine power. Since the problem concerns love, the demonstration is Venus', but she is careful to secure the consent of Neptune and Diana. The three gods act as one. Venus offers to turn one of the two girls into a man: "What is to Loue or the Mistrisse of loue vnpossible? Was it not Venus that did the like to Iphis and Iauthes?" ([*sic*] Hɪʳ; V.iii.142–143). The conventional allegorization of the Iphis-Ianthe story told by Ovid,[65] compactly expressed by Sandys, supports Venus' blithe attitude toward impossibilities: "*By this the Ancient declared, that men should despaire of nothing; since al-things were in the power of the Gods to giue; and giue they what was iustly implored.*" [66] The goddess has been

---

[65] *Metamorphoses*, IX.666–797. The story actually concerns Isis, not Venus. The Cretan Ligdus told his pregnant wife Telethusa that he would put to death a female child. Telethusa bore a girl, but, encouraged by advice from Isis in a dream, she deceived her husband and brought the child up as a boy under the name of Iphis. Lidgus arranged a marriage between his "son" and the beautiful Ianthe, and the couple were genuinely in love. The day before the wedding, when Iphis and Telethusa were in consternation, Isis answered their prayers for aid by changing Iphis' sex.

[66] George Sandys, *Ovid's Metamorphosis Englished, Mythologiz'd, and Represented in Figures* (London, 1632), p. 336; see also *Fabularum Ovidii Interpretatio, Ethica, Physica, et Historica, Tradita in Academia Regiomontana a Georgio Sabino* (Cambridge, 1584), sig. Aa7ʳ.

entreated (not cozened), and divine power is once again asserted. Even the fathers (again quarrelling since neither wants another son) defer to Venus, "because she is a Goddesse" (H1ʳ; V.iii.163).

This final exaltation of divine power constitutes a statement in very specific terms. Venus tests the girls' love before promising the transformation: "Is your loues vnspotted, begunne with trueth, continued wyth constancie, and not to bee altered tyll death?" (G4ᵛ; V.iii.133–135). The Venus who asks this question does not represent the same kind of love as her mischievous Moschian son. She sponsors love chaste, faithful, and eternal. She asks for a Britomart. Gallathea and Phillida fulfill the requirements. As I noted above, Cupid never had anything to do with their love for each other. At this point the homosexuality of their love, hitherto a clever hinge for the refined wit of Lyly's courtship scenes, turns to substantive benefit for his allegory. The girls are virgins; given the situation they could not possibly be anything else. Yet they are wholly in love. Thus they are devotees of *both* Diana and Venus. Their union is an image, not only of divine power, but of the great paradoxical union of formerly quarrelling goddesses. The image presents the simultaneous divinity of Venus and Diana, the harmonious coexistence of the eternal powers of love and of chastity.

F. THE PAGES AND THE PROFESSIONALS

Up to this point I have largely neglected four scenes that constitute a third line of action in *Gallathea*. These are the scenes in which the pageboys appear, and they run as follows:

I.iv. Rafe, Robin, and Dicke part from the Mariner after being shipwrecked with him.

II.iii. Rafe meets the Alchemist and his boy Peter. Peter leaves the Alchemist's service and Rafe enters it.

III.iii. Rafe leaves the Alchemist, meets the Astronomer (i.e. astrologer) and enters his service.

V.i. Rafe, having left the Astronomer, tells Robin his adventures. Robin reports on his employment with a fortune-teller. They meet Peter, who describes Dicke's job.

Boys such as Rafe, Robin, and Dicke appear in six of Lyly's eight plays. Their wit usually provides another perspective on the central situation of the play: this function has been discussed above with respect to *Campaspe*. It is the usual view that only in *Endimion* are the activities of these pages organized into a subplot parodic of the main action in the fashion we come to expect with later Elizabethan drama.[67] I take issue with this view. The activities of the boys in *Gallathea* constitute something very much like a subplot. My qualification ("very much like") is necessary because where there is little main plot there can hardly be subplot. A proper name for this dramatic entity, however, must wait until we have looked at the scenes.

The comic youngsters in *Gallathea* are connected even more tenuously to the main situations than is the case elsewhere in Lyly's plays. They are not the servants of the main characters. They have no relationship at all to the mortals, nymphs, and gods save that they wander through the same woods and, in the last twenty lines of the play, stumble into the assembled *dramatis personae* to be hired as minstrels for Gallathea's wedding. Thus they can provide no worm's eye view of high life. Their wit is directed

[67] See, for example, Hunter, p. 237.

against the three professionals, the Mariner, the Alchemist, and the Astronomer, particularly against the uncouth jargon of their trades.

Hunter sees this series of episodes as drawing on the tradition of "estates-satire," which characteristically operates by a progress through various trades and social classes, exposing their peculiar faults.[68] But as satire, Hunter notes, the episodes seem somewhat haphazard. The Alchemist and the Astronomer are quacks; the Mariner is not, and yet is presented as equally ridiculous. Thus the linguistic depravity that all three manifest in the crabbed terminology of their professions is not consistently connected with moral depravity. In any case, even if we disregard this inconsistency, it is difficult to see what estates-satire has to do with the pastoral-mythological action of the rest of the play.[69]

The difficulty here comes from our expectations. The introduction of strongly marked professionals leads us to look for something like Jonsonian comment on the various perversions of humanity wrought by improper specialization or by obsession. Actually, their professionalism and their language, although important factors, are subsidiary to a third factor common to the three: ambition. Each maintains that he can do extraordinary things; each wishes to exert power beyond the human range. Their professions are merely their means to such power. That is why the fact that two are quacks and the third is not is

[68] Hunter, p. 233.

[69] If there is no connection, Lyly's art, superbly working in integrating two quite disparate main situations, has broken down into providing mere comedy turns. Hunter (p. 233) is driven to positing a negative connection: the episodic story of the boys "in no way compromises [the] atmosphere" of the main action. Since Hunter is arguing that Lyly's great achievement lies in the unification of diverse materials, this remark sounds like desperation.

relatively unimportant. The jargon of their trades supports a common claim to power, a claim that each expresses, among other ways, in terms of ability to alter the heavens.

The first of the three, the Mariner, has barely a chance to speak of his power, so thoroughly is it undercut by his circumstances and his companions. He and the boys have just been shipwrecked and have come to land on a rafter. The boys unmercifully jeer at him and his trade because of the accident. Thus his boast involves a complication of ironies:

I can shift the Moone and the Sunne, and know by one Carde, what all you cannot do by a whole payre.[70] The Lode-stone that alwaies holdeth his nose to the North, the two and thirty poynts for the winde, the wonders I see woulde make all you blinde: you be but boyes, I feare the Sea no more then a dish of water. Why fooles it is but a liquid element.

(B4^v; I.iv.30–35)

To "shift" the sun and the moon is an obsolete nautical expression meaning to record the position of those bodies (*NED*, s.v. 13b). In the context of the boast, however, and given the rather jaundiced view we take of the Mariner through the agency of the boys' wit, the technical expression involves a pun ridiculously magnifying this worthy's view of his own powers: it sounds as if he believes he can *move* the celestial bodies. His rational understanding of the thirty-two points of the compass (a quarter of them later enumerated) has not saved him from shipwreck and dependence on a rafter. Robin has just pointed out to him, moreover, that what he refers to as a "dish of water" can "kill a man of reason, when you shall see a poore Mynow

[70] That is, a whole pack.

lie in it, that hath no vnderstanding" (B4ᵛ; I.iv.26–28).
It ill suits one to scorn the sea who has just been "*All
sowc't in waues/By* Neptunes *slaues.*" [71]

The Alchemist is more exalted and eventually more
humbled. His servant Peter describes him as "A little more
then a man, and a hayres bredth lesse then a God" (C3ᵛ;
II.iii.38–39). There is less of the Mariner's reason and
more of pretension in the Alchemist: he prefers to call his
art a mystery rather than a craft, and explains his power
thus:

> When in the depth of my skill I determine to try the
> vttermost of mine Arte, I am disswaded by the gods,
> otherwise, I durst vndertake to make the fire as it flames,
> gold, the winde as it blowes, siluer, the water as it runnes,
> lead, the earth as it standes, yron, the skye, brasse, and
> mens thoughts, firme mettles.
>
> (D1ʳ; II.iii.121–125)

Here heaven and earth are being transformed. The arro-
gance and sheer extent of the claim cancel the piety of the
initial reservation. Eventually the notion of the Alchemist's
power collapses, not only under the jargon of processes and
instruments appropriate to the art, but also under the
revelation that his only successful "multiplication" was of
the carnal sort involving those philosopher's stones that
every man has "in a priuie cupboord" (F3ᵛ; V.i.26).

The Astronomer makes no reservations at all in his claim
to divine power:

ASTRO. When I list I can sette a trap for the Sunne, catch
the Moone with lyme-twigges, and goe a batfowling for
starres. I can tell thee things past, and things to come,

[71] The song, Blount, P10ʳ, and Bond, I.iv.85–86.

& with my cunning, measure how many yards of Clowdes
are beneath the Skye. Nothing can happen which I fore-
see not, nothing shall.

RAFE I hope sir you are no more then a God.

. . .

ASTRO. I will make the Heauens as plaine to thee as the
high waie, thy cunning shall sitte cheeke by iole with the
Sunnes Chariot; then shalt thou see what a base thing it
is, to haue others thoughts creepe on the grounde, when
as thine shall be stitched to the starres.

RAFE Then I shall be translated from this mortality.

ASTRO. Thy thoughts shall be metamorphosed, and made
haile fellowes with the Gods.

(E1ᵛ–E2ʳ; III.iii.42–47, 75–82)

This burst of enthusiasm meets with a comeuppance in the
Aesopian manner: the Astronomer tumbles backward into
a pond. The whole pattern of promised impossibilities is
briefly repeated when Robin mentions that he has been
working for a fortune-teller and Dicke is reported to be
employed by a master (profession unspecified) "that will
teach him to make you both his younger brothers" (F4ᵛ;
V.i.67–68).

We do not see these last two masters. The three major
professionals, however, are presented in an ascending scale
of pretension to power. The Mariner professes to *use* the
universe for his own purposes, and therefore feels free to
sneer at the power of the sea, which is, of course, the power
of the chief divinity in the play. The Alchemist professes
to *change* the universe ("to make the fire as it flames, gold,
the winde as it blowes, siluer"), and therefore is proclaimed
by Peter as "a hayres bredth lesse then a God." The
Astronomer professes to *control* and *entrap* the universe
("catch the Moone with lyme-twigges"), and therefore
feels entitled to promise Rafe that his thoughts will be

"haile fellowes with the Gods." The connection in each case with the gods creates the close relevance of this series of episodes with the main action of *Gallathea*: the professionals are pretending, not only to power, but, quite precisely, to divine power. Each, a little more than his predecessor, would rival the deities who are active in this forest on the banks of the Humber.

Thus the satire that Hunter notes in these scenes is not ultimately satire directed at "estates" or even satire directed at foolish individuals who lack the balance and grace of the courtly gentleman.[72] It is directed at a more general human failing: prideful ambition, and the attempt to realize ambition by foolish means. The gods have their power by right; these men try to equal or master that power by inventing absurdly complicated rational systems, over-elaborate, over-measured, ridiculously subdivided. The Mariner thinks that naming thirty-two directions from which the wind may come will give him power over the wind. The Alchemist believes that painfully exact quantities in his chemical procedures will effect a metamorphosis of physical nature. The Astronomer's knowledge consists of the rational systems that schematize the things we see (he talks at length of the Zodiac and of "Iudicialls Astronomicall"); he believes that knowledge of the systems constitutes power over the things systematized. The boys' attack is directed both at the pretensions and at the uncouth jargon; since the jargon supports the pretensions, attack on it indirectly attacks the pretensions themselves. The use of the powers we have to attain the powers we can never have results only in an absurd degradation of our original resources.

But however wretched the egoism of these men, Lyly's expression of their desires is not sordid. Indeed, there is

[72] Hunter makes the latter suggestion, p. 234.

great beauty in the celestial imagery used by the professionals. The Mariner's line, "The wonders I see woulde
make all you blinde," the Alchemist's wish to turn fire to
gold and wind to silver, and the Astronomer's promise to
catch the moon with limetwigs and go a-batfowling for
stars, produce an increasing sense of glory, a glory that is
tinged with pathos. It is partially a glory particularly available in a pastoral setting. The wonders of physical nature
are close to us in pastoral: "pastoral's greatest hold upon
the imagination of its users and readers proved to be that
sense of unifying harmony between all creatures of 'Nature,' human or not." [73] But the feeling we get from these
lines also arises from the distance of the sun and the stars:
part of their glory is their remoteness, and the pathos comes
from our yearning. We cannot blame the professionals for
their desire, only for their submission to it and their belief
that they can obtain its object. Lyly has achieved an extraordinary effect, comparable to that of Nashe when he
speakes of scholars who, "Sleeping face vpwards in the
fields all night,/Dream'd strange deuices of the Sunne and
Moone." [74] It is an effect belonging particularly to the
"golden" period of Elizabethan poetry, of which Nashe's
charged line, "Brightnesse falls from the ayre," is probably the finest expression. [75] The absurdity of these dreamers is not absent from the lines I have quoted, but the
dreams themselves, the visions of power and of the great
natural phenomena of the world, are haloed with wonder.

[73] Tuve, *Images and Themes in Five Poems by Milton*, p. 124.

[74] *Summers Last Will and Testament*, ll. 1287–1288, in *The Works
of Thomas Nashe*, ed. Ronald B. McKerrow, rev. F. P. Wilson (Oxford,
1958), III.274.

[75] *Summers Last Will and Testament*, l. 1590, in *Works*, III.283.
For a sensitive discussion of these three lines from Nashe see C. L.
Barber's fine chapter on *Summers Last Will* in *Shakespeare's Festive
Comedy: A Study of Dramatic Form and its Relation to Social Custom*
(Princeton, 1959), pp. 58–86.

The scenes with the professionals thus have a double effect. Foolish ambition is mocked by the boys' wit and undone by accidents, and yet a vital glory is exposed at the heart of that ambition. This double effect, carried through the play in episodes interspersed with the main action, constitutes a thematic swelling and counterpoint that operates very much as a subplot would. Not as a subplot *does*, for this is not a plot. The continuous element is not a causal chain but a single situation presented with variations. On the level of action, the scenes are tied together by the recurrence of the boys with their skeptical and yet enterprising attitude toward the professionals. The main coherence of the episodes, however, lies in the gradual expansion of the dramatic image of pretended divinity. This is a situational play's equivalent of a subplot: it is the development and variation of a subsidiary, contrasting version of the notion central to the whole play. This is the sub-situation of pretended divinity that plays off against the real deities, and the defiance of them, in the main action.

The "playing off" is both positive and negative. It is negative because the foolishness of the pretenders sets in relief the real power of the gods. It is positive because the powers of divinity are further exalted by the wondering descriptions that the professionals give to the things they aim at. Depths open within divinity in Lyly's lyrical prose; the glory of the descriptions gives an added emotional tinge to the rest of the play.

The "playing off" is also specific as well as general. Each of these scenes is placed where it will relate to the actions of the real deities as well as contribute to the expanding image of power. I have already discussed the contribution of the Mariner scene to the initial presentation of Neptune.[76] The scene comments on men as well as on gods.

[76] See p. 119.

Tyterus and Melebeus, in disguising their daughters, are
relying upon what they call their "craft" in order to evade
Neptune. Then enters a Mariner whose great pride lies in
his craft, which he thinks gives him the right to sneer at
Neptune, the god of his craft.[77] He obviously never will
learn what the fathers ought to know about attempts to
circumvent the gods, for even after shipwreck he thinks of
the sea as a dish of water. The boys at least admit that they
have been at the mercy of Neptune's slaves.

The Alchemist appears immediately after Cupid and
Neptune have delivered their disguise soliloquies, and just
before the girls deliver a soliloquy each on *their* disguises
and how those disguises have led to and complicated their
love for each other. The Alchemist too is disguised: Peter
explains his beggarly costume to Rafe on the grounds that
"such cunning men must disguise themselues, as though
there were nothing in them, for otherwise they shall be
compelled to worke for Princes, and so be constrained to
bewray their secrets" (C4^r; II.iii.71–73). But this disguise
is really no disguise at all: Peter is trying to conceal the
real poverty of the quack. It is, as it were, a *faked* disguise
that genuinely *reveals* the status of the man while *giving
the lie* to his pretensions. In contrast, Neptune's disguise
as a shepherd is a *real* disguise that genuinely *conceals* the
status of the god while enabling him to *prove* his pretensions. The juxtaposition of the two scenes forms a perfect
dramatic horismus, a euphuistic antithesis worked out in
three terms and based on a visual motif. It says, as an
horismus should, the thing to be defined (power) is this
and is not that. Then, in a virtuoso stroke, Lyly brings in
the disguised girls to double the horismus. They are wearing real disguises in order to *escape* power; the disguises
conceal, but leave their wearers in a state of confusion with

[77] Neptune, of course, invented sailing.

regard to each other. Taken together, the three scenes constitute a dramatic image (dramatic because the vehicle of the image is the theatrical device of costume) of the relationships between divinity and man in this phase of the play. The gods may take disguise to show their power, but when mortals take disguise to assume power they are fakes and when they take it to avoid power they enter into a wood of error and confusion.

The precise terms in which the Alchemist's boast is put also have particular significance. His supposed power, as I have noted, lies in changing the world, in alteration of things as they are. Neptune and Cupid are demonstrating that the basic elements of the world cannot be changed or ignored. The nymphs will learn that love is dangerous and cannot be as lightly dismissed as the unnamed nymph who first met Cupid had thought. Mortals will learn that Neptune is not mocked.

The Astronomer scene occurs after the first paradoxical courtship passage between Gallathea and Phillida. There is perhaps a connection between these two scenes: the Astronomer pretends particularly to knowledge, and the girls are victims of a situation only half of which they understand. This correspondence, however, is rather general. Every one in *Gallathea* struggles with problems complete understanding of which is possessed only by the gods and the audience. A more particular significance lies in the direction of his boast. I noted that his claim to power is expressed in terms of ability to control and entrap the heavenly bodies. This scene occurs in the middle of Act III, the chief action of which is the domino scene (scene i) and its reversal, the capture of Cupid by Diana (scene iv). The Astronomer pretends to a power simultaneously exerted by the gods as Cupid controls the nymphs and Diana entraps Cupid.

The expansion of the image is complete. Each claim to

power has been juxtaposed to a truly divine power then being exerted. Each claim has been larger than the one before. In the boys' reunion scene two more examples of ambition are mentioned, but they merely round off the episodic chain neatly. The sub-situation has made its point. It has reached its fullest development just before Diana captures Cupid. From then on pretensions are irrelevant: the gods begin conflict among themselves.

G. ALLEGORY AND THE EXPANDING IMAGE

If the foregoing analysis of *Gallathea* be accepted, its implications can lead us to a fuller understanding of the changes in Lyly's dramaturgy since *Campaspe*. I opened this chapter by noting two major innovations in *Gallathea*: the introduction of mythology, and the simplification of dramaturgy by means of reducing cast size, restricting milieu, and organizing events into larger patterns of analogous action. The two changes are related; moreover, they signal a major alteration in the working of the allegorical mode.

The central notion of *Campaspe*—propriety—is handled in a peculiar way for allegory. We expect, in allegory, a central notion to be imaged in one or more characters or objects; we expect symbol. The meaning of a symbol, of course, can be released and controlled only in action: we cannot isolate it from the events of a work and expect it to retain significance. Nonetheless, the richness of individual elements, characters, objects, local descriptions, or emblems, provides the potential energy for allegorical meaning. The significance of Milton's Comus, for example, originates in his being the child of Circe, daughter of the Sun, and having the wealth of iconographical values residing in that figure.[78] Spenser's major characters have a

[78] This has been persuasively argued in Tuve, *Images and Themes in Five Poems by Milton*, pp. 112–161.

like energy in their names, their lineages, their physical attributes, and their costumes. This kind of energetic figure does not appear in *Campaspe*. Propriety is not directly presented in symbol or personification. It could be, if Lyly had wanted: propriety involves values presented by other Renaissance writers in personifications—one need only recall Chapman's Ceremonie and Spenser's Concord. Lyly instead chooses to present propriety entirely in actions. The adjustment and readjustment of relations between Alexander on the one hand and his courtiers, Campaspe, Apelles, Diogenes, Hephestion, the philosophers, and the begging Cynic on the other, between individual pairs of the latter characters, and among the three houses on the stage, all radiate propriety. Heeding the imperious call for action decreed by the dramatic form, Lyly shadows the ideas of the play almost wholly through events. The anecdotal nature of the action issues from the largely social conception of propriety at work: each of Alexander's relationships is different because of the varying positions of the other characters. Hence the highly reticulated form of the play. Each of the lines of reticulation presents a different form of propriety. The meaning of the play lies between the characters, not in them.

In pressing mythology into service in *Gallathea*, Lyly enlists personages of the commanding energy characteristic of Spenserian allegory. Alexander, although he is the dominating figure of *Campaspe* and the center of the additional allegory of the good king, packs little of the kind of potential significance possessed by Cupid, Neptune, Venus, and Diana. With the gods as his central figures, Lyly can rely on them for much of the meaning conveyed by the elaborate structure of fussy detail evident in *Campaspe*. *Gallathea* is still situational: it lacks a fully developed narrative plot and its scenes are juxtaposed with mathematical precision. The scenes are, however, woven into larger lines of action. In the sacrifice situation, the love-chastity situation, and the pageboy scenes, Lyly's dramaturgy has become more sinuous, more suggestive, and less intellectually rigid. The juxtaposed scenes create a series of internal echoes, parallels, and balanced contrasts that dance forward with expanded meaning and rhythm. The central movement forward is the exfoliation of the central figures of the gods. Their significance begins casually: an old tale told about Neptune, a definition and an emblematic costume for Cupid. Their values develop in the swelling analogies of the main situations, in the resonating echoes of the myths alluded to, and in the lyrical prose of the professionals. In Act III Cupid's power is most fully expanded in the nymphs' worship of him. He is then sharply deflated as the stunning force of Diana exerts itself. Neptune threatens to increase the scope of destiny's operations, and Venus arises to oppose Diana. Fully developed, the three major gods meet in open conflict. They coalesce in the harmony achieved by their agreement and emblematized in the divinely blessed marriage of the loving virgins, Gallathea and Phillida. We come to see the full range of destiny and the ultimate union of love and chastity. The new dramaturgy depends precisely upon the symbolic energy of the gods. Meaning arises as the traditional wealth of these figures flows into Lyly's action, as is the case with Spenserian allegory, not merely in the action of crisp, limited figures, as is the case with *Campaspe*. In short, allegorical dramaturgy has in *Campaspe* the multilinear power of a child's connect-the-dots design: given the dots, dramatic action reveals the proper structure that intricately ties them into a firm whole. Allegorical dramaturgy has in *Gallathea* a more organic power, the expanding power of opening blossoms: given the buds, dramatic action reveals the depths that lie within.

IV. CUPIDS, COURTS, AND
THE QUEEN

THE NATURE OF my investigation hitherto has obliged me to conduct extended readings of two plays. If one is going to assert that comedies are allegorical, one must show the allegory in operation. If one is attempting to describe different kinds of dramatic allegory, a number of plays must be explored. It is not necessary, however, to discuss all of Lyly's plays in equal detail. *Love's Metamorphosis, Sapho and Phao,* and *Endimion,* the three other plays of Lyly's middle period, manifest the sort of allegorical dramaturgy that we have found in *Gallathea,* the allegory of the expanding image. Certain variations appear in its use in *Sapho and Phao* and *Endimion.* This chapter, then, will briefly comment on the three remaining plays in the second phase of Lyly's situational drama, concentrating on their central figures.

A. *LOVE'S METAMORPHOSIS*

I start with *Love's Metamorphosis,* despite the probability that it is the last of Lyly's middle plays, because of its close resemblance to *Gallathea.*[1] Apart from its lack of

---

[1] Quotations from the play are drawn from the only quarto, Iohn Lyllie, *Loues Metamorphosis* (London, 1601). They are acknowledged in the text by the signature numbers of this quarto, followed by the act, scene, and line numbers of R. Warwick Bond, ed., *The Complete Works of John Lyly* (Oxford, 1902), vol. III. The primary mythological source is Ovid's tale of Erisichthon (*Metamorphoses,* VIII.738–878), to which a new ending has been added. The love-situation is of Lyly's own invention. As in *Gallathea,* the play's events frequently echo other myths.

pageboys, it duplicates *Gallathea* almost exactly in both design and content. Two peripetal lines of action run side by side, each focussing upon a god who is defied. The disdainful nymphs of Ceres (who is in this play the patroness of chastity) defy the power of love by rejecting three foresters; the foresters enlist the aid of Cupid, who asserts his power by metamorphosing the nymphs into a stone, a rose, and a bird respectively. Meanwhile, the farmer Erisichthon defies Ceres by cutting down her sacred tree (a nymph arborified, Daphne-like, to elude rape); Ceres sends Famine to punish him, and he is kept alive only by the self-sacrifice of his daughter Protea. Protea's display of faithful love moves Cupid to compromise with Ceres, thus bringing about general harmony.

The two situations are as widely disparate in tone as the two in *Gallathea*: the Erisichthon story repeats the strain of violence and horror of the virgin-sacrifice, while the love-stories of both plays are graceful and witty. The two situations in *Love's Metamorphosis*, however, are woven more closely together than in *Gallathea*: there are only two gods and each is defied by persons presently or eventually associated with the other.[2] Ceres and Cupid, moreover, meet not only in the final scene, but also in Act II when Ceres offers Cupid her annual homage. But Lyly is still writing the same kinds of scenes: there is a domino scene in Act III, when the three nymphs reject the three foresters, and Protea serves, just before the denouement, the same function that Haebe does in the parallel location, by accepting the laws of the presiding god.

The presiding god is Cupid. There is a measure of

[2] Protea's rescues of her father depend on metamorphoses arranged for her by Neptune, to whom she has previously surrendered her virginity. Neptune, however, remains off-stage machinery throughout the play.

equality between Cupid and Ceres: she does him homage because the earth's fruitfulness depends on love, and he returns the compliment by quoting the Terentian tag, *"Sine Cerere & Baccho friget Venus"* (E4^r; V.i.46). But the play resounds with expressions of Cupid's power. Ceres notes that he has "absolute authoritie to commaund" (C1^r; II.i.41) and that he was "neuer conquered, and therefore must bee flattered" (C1^r; II.i.43–44). He is "such a god as maketh thunder fall out of *Ioues* hand" (E3^v; V.i.12–13). This is no mischievous child out of Moschus; he has a temple of his own on stage.[3]

All of Lyly's plays but *Midas* focus on love, but in none is love more central than here. On the stage the original audience probably saw Cupid's temple flanked by two other "houses" symbolic of other approaches to love: the tree of the chaste Ceres and the rock of a very medieval Siren who, complete with comb and glass, tempts Protea's lover Petulius to lechery. Cupid occupies the commanding position here that Neptune does in *Gallathea*, and the action reflects his power by presenting an anatomy of love: the passionate devotion of the foresters, the obsession with self of the nymphs, the chaste fruitfulness of Ceres, the sensuality of the Siren, the filial devotion of Protea, and the jealousy of Petulius.[4]

[3] Paul E. Parnell appropriately describes Cupid thus: "Thoughts of a little winged boy bent on mischief are entirely out of place here. Cupid in this play is as irresistible as Venus, as irate toward transgressors as Neptune, and as all-powerful as Jove" ("Moral Allegory in Lyly's *Love's Metamorphosis*," *SP*, LII [1955], 5).

[4] Petulius is jealous of Protea because of her previous yielding to Neptune. His name reflects his instability and his temptation to wantonness. Hers refers, not to changefulness in love, but to the metamorphoses by which Neptune assists her. Both in her metamorphoses and in her connection with the sea, she is a female version of Proteus; on Proteus figures in the Renaissance, see A. Bartlett Giamatti's article in the forthcoming *festschrift* for René Wellek.

This gallery, however, is not merely a showcase of loves. It is part of the unfolding of the central image of Cupid. As destiny develops in *Gallathea* from particular cases to the force preserving the spiritual order of the world, so does love evolve in the allegorical *significatio* of *Love's Metamorphosis*. In the first line of the play, one of the foresters remarks: "I cannot see . . . why it is fain'd by the Poets, that Loue sat vpon the *Chaos* and created the world; since in the world there is so little loue" (B₁ʳ; I.i.1–3). The remark is phrased in terms of Christian Neoplatonism, and it is blasphemous. For, "seeing God hath created and framed [the world] by loue, no doubt but loue is despersed and shed throughout the whole world." [5] The lovers doubt the pervasiveness of love because their mistresses are Petrarchan mistresses and they are Petrarchan lovers: "the three ladies are really only three aspects of one person—the Petrarchan unkind mistress—alternately cruel (as Nisa), coy (as Celia), and inconstant (as Niobe). . . . The three foresters who languish under these several displeasures may also be taken to represent aspects of the Petrarchan poet-lover, his desire for absolute possession, his acceptance of merely physical pleasure, his jealousy, his humility." [6] It is the incompleteness of such love, as it is the lust of the Siren and the wavering of Petulius that Cupid corrects by installing a new notion of love. Cupid comes to represent love in the Neoplatonic sense initially doubted by the foresters: love as that which orders and preserves the world, whose power is absolute and whose realm is everywhere. Ceres is respected, but, as Cupid bluntly says, "Thou *Ceres,* doest

[5] Pierre de la Primaudaye, *The French Academie* (London, 1618), p. 482. I quote Primaudaye merely as a convenient statement, available to Lyly, of a major commonplace of cosmology.

[6] G. K. Hunter, *John Lyly: The Humanist as Courtier* (Cambridge, Mass., 1962), p. 205.

but gouerne the guts of men, I the hearts: thou seekest
to starue *Erisicthon* with thy ministred famine, whome
his daughter shall preserue by my virtue loue" (E3ᵛ;
V.i.8–10). In the final scene, Protea quotes the classical
tag, "*Omnia vincit amor*" (F1ʳ; V.ii.13), and Cupid
promises the assembled cast, "I will make such vnspotted
loue among you, that there shall bee no suspition nor
iarre, no vnkindnesse nor iealousie" (F4ᵛ; V.iv.160–161).
With his last speech Cupid includes heaven as well as
earth in the ordering power of love: "I will soare vp into
heauen, to settle the loues of the gods, that in earth haue
dispos'd the affections of men" (G1ʳ; V.iv.168–170).

B. *SAPHO AND PHAO*

Sapho and Phao was written between *Campaspe* and
Gallathea, and shreds of the old dramatic method appear
alongside intimations of the new.[7] The old concern for
complex social hierarchy operates strongly in the first part
of the play with its scenes of Sapho's attendants, the quips
of the pageboys, and the dialogues of the courtier Trachinus
with the scholar Pandion. This concern also forms an
important strand of the major situation: propriety decrees
that Sapho should not love the ferryman Phao and that
Phao should restrict his love for the queen to worship
from afar. Indeed, the theme of propriety causes the play
to end in much the same way as *Campaspe*: the characters
variously depart in their proper directions rather than
harmoniously assembling as in *Gallathea* and *Love's Meta-*

---

[7] Quotations from the play are drawn from the first quarto [John
Lyly], *Sapho and Phao* (London, 1584). They are acknowledged in
the text by the signature numbers of this quarto, followed by the act,
scene, and line numbers of Bond's *Complete Works*, vol. II. The
ultimate, but rather remote, sources in mythology for the story are
Sappho's letter in Ovid, *Heroides*, XV, and Aelian's account of Phao in
Varia Historia, XII.18.

morphosis. The careers of both title characters resemble that of Alexander in their circularity: Sapho withdraws from love and remains the ideal monarch, and Phao sets out on his travels.

On the other hand, neither Sapho nor Phao is quite as unchanged as Alexander by the events of the play. Whereas Alexander leaves Athens as he had arrived, Phao retains his love for the queen and Sapho has displaced Venus as the patroness of Cupid. These changes result from Lyly's use of his new dramaturgy in the major situation of the play. *Sapho and Phao* anticipates the peripetal Venus-Diana situation of *Gallathea*: the major conflict is between Sapho (figuring chastity) and Venus (figuring love). This conflict rocks back and forth under the influence of Cupid's ubiquitous arrows, plunging into internal conflict as Sapho suffers the throes of desire. The conflict is climaxed by an event causing permanent change: Sapho adopts Cupid and discredits Venus. The event is analogous to the resolution of the divine quarrel in *Gallathea,* both in its function in solving the impasse and in its meaning in uniting love with chastity.

The image of Sapho expands through the play. Early scenes resound with her praise. Her artfully delayed entrance is prepared for by Trachinus' description:

> Sapho faire by nature, by birth royall, learned by education, by gouernment politike, rich by peace: insomuch as it is hard to iudge, whether she be more bewtifull or wise, vertuous or fortunate.
>
> (A4ʳ–A4ᵛ; I.ii.7–10)

Sapho has thus all the graces of person and position, all desirable human qualities whether worldly (beauty and fortune) or spiritual (wisdom and virtue). She is "natures miracle" and "without comparison" (A4ᵛ, B1ʳ; I.ii.38,

51–52). Thus it is a distinct shock to find her tossing agonizedly in her bed when stricken with desire for Phao. The indignities she suffers in Act III, however, are amply repaid in Act V, where the image of Sapho expands to eclipse the powers and usurp the function of Venus. She adopts Cupid by bribing him with sweetmeats—such trivial defense has the god against a Sapho. The adoption serves not only to abolish Sapho's personal difficulties but also to ensure the better direction of love in the whole world:

> But if I gette Cupid from thee [Venus], I my selfe will be the Queene of loue. I will direct these arowes with better aime, and conquer mine own affections with greater modesty.
>
> (F3ᵛ–F4ʳ; V.ii.25–27)

Venus sneers at her—"you the Goddesse of Loue?" (F4ᵛ; V.ii.70)—but can only exit with a fanfaronnade of threats startlingly like those of Malvolio and the defeated villainesses of Restoration drama: "I will be euen with you both, & that shortlye" (G1ʳ; V.ii.93). At this point a mythological analogue to the play provides its greatest resonance for Lyly. The whole story of Sapho runs parallel to that of Dido as told in the first and fourth books of the *Aeneid*. Both concern the passion of a Mediterranean queen for a handsome stranger come up from the sea with the power of Venus behind him, and both contain an incident in which the queen dandles Cupid on her lap. The analogy stresses the differences between Dido and Sapho. In Virgil, Dido is completely the victim of Venus, and Cupid is Venus' agent; in Lyly, when Sapho dandles Cupid, she causes him to sever his connection with Venus and is thus able to triumph over the goddess. The wrath of Venus testifies to the solidity of Sapho's new position: the queen has been apotheosized as the new goddess of both love and chastity. As in *Gallathea*, the resolution produces two dramatic images of love and chastity joined, one divine and one human. The divine image is Cupid on Sapho's lap; the human one is Phao in the last scene standing stage center, between Sapho's city and the cave of the Sybil who has given him such quantities of Ovidian advice, hopelessly in love with the queen and forever bound from consummating his love.

Sapho and Phao is not a wholly satisfactory play. Its aesthetic defects arise primarily from the transitional nature of its dramaturgy. It has neither the complex architecture of *Campaspe* nor the beautiful modulation and slow unfolding of *Gallathea*; rather it has an attempt at the former through III.ii and an attempt at the latter for the rest of the play. The delicate adjustment of relationships at the court is left almost entirely behind as the figure of Sapho begins to unfold. Another difficulty lies in the pull of historical allegory. The overwhelming praise given Sapho clearly makes her a figure for that phoenix of the age, Queen Elizabeth. Although we may be able to sit lightly enough with such allusions as to reject any stray thoughts of the Virgin Queen while Sapho is tossing in her bed, the allusion almost decrees that Sapho's triumph at the end of the play be total and thus that Venus be wholly discredited. As a result we are left with Sapho's adoption of Cupid as a resolution of the issues of the play, and it is a less satisfactory resolution, dramatically and symbolically, than that of *Gallathea*. Dramatically it is less interesting than the quarrel and compromise of Neptune, Venus, and Diana, and symbolically the union of love and chastity that it figures is weighted, by virtue of Cupid's triviality, far too heavily on the side of chastity. Finally, there are lumps of apparently undigested material in the play. The long discussion of dreams in IV.iii is probably a matter of topical allegory to which we have lost the

key, and it is therefore unfair to judge it; but there are
also the enormous speeches of the Sybil in II.i and II.iv.
The Sybil's position in the design of the play is clear—
she is the purveyor of Ovidian advice, self-contradictory
and rather dishonorable, about the conduct of venereal
affairs—but the point could have been made with greater
economy.[8]

C. *ENDIMION*

With the approach provided by our discussion of Lyly's
previous comedies, it may now be possible to enter that
mysterious play that has perplexed so many critics of
Lyly, *Endimion*.[9] So many readings of its allegory have
been offered, meeting with such general dissatisfaction, that
one is hesitant to tread. I hope not to add merely one
more discordant voice to the confusion, and I do not intend
to "explain" the entire play. I propose only to look at
some implications of its action and language, in the hope
of suggesting that its allegorical mode is consistent with,
although more elaborate than, that of the other mythological comedies. Whatever its ultimate significance in the
misty realms of topical allegory, courtly love, Christian
traditions, Neoplatonism and the like, I shall try to keep
in mind the fact that *Endimion* is a play. In the critical
discussions of its allegorical shadows, it has often been
forgotten that on stage action and language must work
together to a common goal.

There are two good reasons for the perplexity *Endimion*
causes. First, there is the range of the play. It opens with

[8] Hunter (pp. 174–177) has made a valiant and sensible but in-
conclusive attempt to deal with the dreams and with one of the Sybil's
speeches.

[9] Quotations are drawn from the first and only quarto [John Lyly],
Endimion, The Man in the Moone (London, 1591). They are acknowledged in the text by the signature numbers of this quarto, followed
by the act, scene, and line numbers of Bond's *Complete Works*, vol. III.

a discussion as to whether the object of the hero's love is sublunary, translunary, or the Moon herself. This astronomical scope recurs in the opposition between Moon and Earth manifest in Cynthia and Tellus. The astronomical scope is matched by geographical and temporal scope: philosophers come from afar, Eumenides goes on a long journey, and the time span of the play is simultaneously forty years and a few days. A similar intellectual range emerges: a host of abstract topics, love, friendship, constancy, anger, truth, justice, and time, crop up for discussion. Secondly, all these matters are dramatized with a cast that is mathematically elaborated to a bewildering degree. Endimion loves Cynthia; his friend Eumenides loves Semele; his former love Tellus is wooed by Corsites; Tellus hires a witch, Dipsas, who is courted by the comic Sir Tophas but eventually claimed by her estranged husband Geron, whereupon Sir Tophas transfers his affections to Dipsas' maid Bagoa. There are three pages for the three leading male characters, three maids, two watchmen, two lords, two philosophers. This pairing and opposing, with its constant hints of reflection and distortion at various angles, causes one to feel one has entered a roomful of mirrors—or the middle books of *The Faerie Queene*.[10]

Yet we have met this mathematical technique before. These are, albeit more elaborately developed, the doublings and parallels characteristic of Lyly's middle comedies. They are, moreover, accompanied by the same static quality we have seen in other plays. There are so many arrangements of characters for Lyly to establish that there is little time for anything in the way of a plot to happen. The central situation, indeed, is almost completely static.

[10] J. A. Bryant, Jr., has stressed the mathematical elaboration of the cast as the key to Lyly's handling of the Endymion myth and to his method of composition in general, in his provocative article, "The Nature of the Allegory in Lyly's *Endymion*," *Renaissance Papers*, Southeastern Renaissance Conference (1956), pp. 4-11.

For two acts Endimion soliloquizes on his love. Only
when he is asleep in Act III does Cynthia first enter. We
have arrived at Act V before the hero and heroine meet
each other on stage and awake. The secondary love-affair,
between Eumenides and Semele, is likewise on ice except
for Eumenides' soliloquies. Sir Tophas talks a great deal
about war and love but does nothing (which is characteristic
of the *miles gloriosus*) and is not exposed in failing to
do something (which is not characteristic of the *miles
gloriosus*). The only real action in the play is Tellus'
plot against Endimion and Eumenides' effort to rescue
him.

Instead of action there is the expanding image of Cynthia
and her court. The expansion, however, is not so simple
as in *Gallathea* and *Love's Metamorphosis*. In those plays
single ideas are firmly in control, and Lyly's compositional
procedure seems fairly abstract. We know from the beginning that Neptune figures destiny; the expansion process
reveals what destiny really means. Cynthia, however, is
far more mysterious. No "subject" for the play is given
in the way that Gallathea's father conveniently gives us
the term destiny, to be picked up by others, or, for that
matter, in the way that Spenser gives us a book-title ("The
Legend of —") as a door to his allegory. The central
figure of Cynthia develops, and the hints thrown off echo
and reflect across the mirrors of the *dramatis personae*
with a multitude of implications that seem irresolvable
into any schematized system of allegory.

It would be helpful to give three examples of the kind
of implications that develop. First, there is a fully worked
out example of the Renaissance fad of physical allegory
in the opening scenes of the play.[11] Endimion identifies

[11] To the modern reader physical allegory is apt to appear tedious
in the extreme. It is very popular with the mythographers (Comes,
Fraunce, Bacon), in whom it has an air of explaining myths away,
of rationalizing fantastic stories on (ill-defined) anthropological

Cynthia literally with the Moon, speaking in I.i of her waxing and waning and her control of the tides. Then her rival Tellus ("Earth") appears with an attendant Floscula ("Little Flower"). Tellus describes herself as being literally the Earth: "Is not my beauty diuine, whose body is decked with faire flowers, and vaines are Vines, yeelding sweet liquor to the dullest sprits, whose eares are Corne, to bring strength, and whose heares are grasse, to bring abundance?" (B2ᵛ; I.ii.19–23). Since these associations are so strongly enforced, we are prepared to notice extensions of the idea. The earthiness of all other women in contrast to Cynthia reappears in the presentation of the two pagegirls. Scintilla and Favilla, when egged into dispute by the pageboys, are associated first with fire and then with water:

SCINT. *Fauilla* though she be but a sparke, yet is shee fyre.

FAVIL. And you *Scintilla* bee not much more then a sparke, though you would be esteemed a flame.

(C4ᵛ; II.ii.19–21)

The quarrel ends in tears, whereupon the pageboys remark:

SAM. A strange sight to see water come out of fire.

DARES It is their propertie, to carrie in their eyes, fire, and water, teares and torches.

(D1ʳ; II.ii.52–54)

---

premises. Certain modern habits of thought may concur with this demythologizing, but it is difficult to know what to make of physical allegory when encountered in a thoroughly sophisticated imaginative writer. As Rosemond Tuve has noted, the rise of natural science has weakened physical allegory almost beyond recovery. Given knowledge of Renaissance backgrounds, good Renaissance moral allegory appears to us timeless, but studies of physical allegory have difficulty ridding us of the impression that it is merely quaint. See Tuve, *Allegorical Imagery: Some Medieval Books and Their Posterity* (Princeton, 1966), pp. 224–225 and note.

All this is very neat. Cynthia and Tellus clearly offer to Endimion higher and lower kinds of love, rapt adoration of a goddess or pursuit of ordinary earthly beauty. One wonders, however, why the physical allegory is so extensively and carefully worked out, for it is dropped after Act II. Cynthia, of course, continues to be semi-divine, but Tellus has no particular powers associated with her chthonic self-description: she has to hire a sorceress to do her dirty work for her.

There is also Court allegory in *Endimion*. I do not mean a dramatic transcript of a particular intrigue: the topical readings that have been advanced for *Endimion* are largely unconvincing and based on ill-considered assumptions.[12] But Cynthia is a compliment to Queen Elizabeth, and the adoration of Endimion betokens the proper worship of the ideal courtier for his monarch. In this context recurs the Gallathean theme of divine power as opposed to pretensions thereto. Cynthia's power is life-giving:

FLOSCULA [to Tellus] But knowe you not fayre Ladie, that *Cynthia* gouerneth all things? Your grapes woulde be but drie huskes, your Corne but chaffe, and all your vertues vaine, were it not *Cynthia* that preserueth the one in the bud, and nourisheth the other in the blade, and by her influence both comforteth all things, and by her authoritie commaundeth all creatures.[13]

(B2ᵛ; I.ii.27–32)

---

[12] See my Introduction, pp. 6–7, and Hunter, pp. 186–191.

[13] Cynthia's fructifying influences may strike the reader as odd; normally we associate such powers with the sun rather than the moon. Cornelius Agrippa, however, has the following passage explaining the powers of the moon: it is "the wife of all the Stars, is the most fruitful of the Stars, and receiving the beams and influences of all the other planets and Stars as a conception, bringing them forth to the inferior

The authority here attributed to Cynthia later becomes her hallmark. Endimion, constructing a comparison between Cynthia and Tellus, notes that the latter has beauty, wisdom, honor, and fortune, but that Cynthia also possesses that right to and fulfillment of authority, "Maiestie" (D3^r; II.iii.16). With Cynthia thus exalted, it is unsurprising to hear direct echoes of *Gallathea*. The witch Dipsas boasts in exactly the manner of the Alchemist and the Astronomer:

> I can darken the Sunne by my skil, and remooue the Moone out of her course; I can restore youth to the aged, and make hils without bottoms.
>
> (C2^r; I.iv.20–22)

The boast is more warranted than those of the professionals in *Gallathea*, but it serves the same function in the play, to set off the real power of the dominant figure: Cynthia overcomes Endimion's enchanted sleep with a kiss. The handling of the theme, however, is more complex here

---

world as being next to it self; for all the Stars have influence on it being the last receiver, which afterwards communicateth the influences of all the superiors to these inferiors, and pours them forth on the Earth; and it more manifestly disposeth these inferiors, then the others, and its motion is more sensible by the familiarity and propinquity which it hath with us; and as a medium betwixt both, superiors and inferiors, communicateth them to them all; Therefore her motion is to be observed before the others, as the parent of all conceptions" (Henry Cornelius Agrippa, *Three Books of Occult Philosophy*, tr. J. F. [London, 1651], II.xxxii [p. 284]). The passage suggests an intellectual connection between Cynthia as Moon and Cynthia as Elizabeth: the function here attributed to the Moon is like that of the Queen in being God's representative on earth. We can be fairly certain that Lyly knew this work of Agrippa's: he refers, in the Court prologue to *Campaspe*, to the "daunsing of *Agrippa* his shadowes," the ghosts discussed in the *Occult Philosophy*.

than in *Gallathea*. In the earlier play it is a straightforward matter of gods and pretenders. But Cynthia is a human queen as well as a goddess; consequently the situations she must deal with also involve court etiquette (her rebuke to the sharp-tongued Semele) and politics (the dangers to her sovereignty mysteriously shadowed in Endimion's dream of the old man's book).

In order to demonstrate the bewildering refraction at work, my third example is much more complex. It concerns an expanding image that operates in at least three different ways. I suggest that *Endimion*, particularly in Act V, makes extensive use of the Christian allegory of the Four Daughters of God.

The allegory of the Four Daughters of God figures the dialectic of divine mercy.[14] It derives from Psalm 85:10: "Mercy and truth are met together; righteousness [or justice] and peace have kissed each other." [15] Both St. Bernard of Clairvaux and Hugo of St. Victor developed the imagery of this verse into a full allegorical debate. In St. Bernard's version, the more influential, the Four Virtues debate the fate of man after the Fall. Truth and Justice demand man's death in fulfillment of their natures. Mercy requests forgiveness in fulfillment of hers. Peace protests the dispute. God proposes that a guiltless being, dying for love of man, could overcome Death and free the dead. Mercy, searching Heaven, and Truth, Earth, can find no qualified volunteer; in the offer of Christ, the dilemma is solved and the virtues are reconciled. The allegory is extensively used in medieval and Renaissance

[14] I rely upon the account of this allegory amply set forth in Hope Traver, *The Four Daughters of God* (Philadelphia, 1907), and in Samuel Chew, *The Virtues Reconciled* (Toronto, 1947). Chew adds more Renaissance examples and brings the visual arts into his account.

[15] In the Vulgate it is Psalm 84:11: "Misericordia et veritas obviaverunt sibi; justitia et pax osculatae sunt."

literary and visual art, although modifications occur as other virtues join the dispute, as the cast is reduced to Mercy and Justice, and as the occasion of the debate is altered. In drama, the debate occurs in the Coventry mystery of the Salutation and Conception, taking place immediately before Gabriel is sent to Mary. It recurs in the spectacular morality *The Castle of Perseverance,* being held over the soul of the dead Humanum Genus, and is secularized for propaganda purposes in the Marian play *Respublica.* Shreds of the debate lie under the secular surface of the trial scene of *The Merchant of Venice* [16] and possibly in the intellectual structure of *Measure for Measure.*[17] Milton apparently planned to employ such a debate in the original dramatic version of his epic; in *Paradise Lost* itself the Father and the Son engage in a dialogue that resolves "the strife/Of Mercy and Justice in thy [the Father's] face discern'd." [18]

Now in *Endimion,* the hero, upon awakening in V.i, recounts a dream that has been presented in dumb show at the end of Act II. In the dream, Endimion is approached by three ladies. One, carrying a knife and a looking glass, is about to harm him; the second, with malice in her face,

[16] See the excellent interpretation of the trial scene in Nevill Coghill, "The Basis of Shakespearean Comedy," *Essays and Studies,* III (1950), 1–28.

[17] See the suggestions made by Roy W. Battenhouse, *"Measure for Measure* and Christian Doctrine of the Atonement," *PMLA,* LXI (1946), 1034.

[18] *Paradise Lost,* III.406–407 (John Milton, *Complete Poems and Major Prose,* ed. Merritt Y. Hughes [New York, 1957]). In the Trinity College MS, Milton's "second draft" notes for a tragedy on the *Paradise Lost* theme include Justice, Mercy, and Wisdom among the *dramatis personae.* The "third draft" notes for Act I specify that these three personifications will be "debating what should become of man if he fall" (*The Works of John Milton,* Columbia Edition [New York, 1938], XVIII.228–229).

encourages the first; the third sorrowfully laments, but dares not stop the proceedings. Finally, after the first lady has long considered, "Mercie ouercame anger, and there appeared in her heauenly face such a diuine Maiestie, mingled with a sweete mildenes, that I was rauished with the sight" (H2ᵛ; V.i.96–98). Bernard Huppé cautiously suggests that the dream-ladies appear to be related to the Four Daughters of God.[19] J. A. Bryant strenuously endorses the suggestion, using it for an interpretation of Cynthia's actions in the final scene.[20]

Bryant's interpretation, that in the last scene Cynthia manifests Mercy, Justice and Truth, is unquestionably correct. His development of the notion, however, is limited, and I here present an expansion of his idea. Mercy is the most evident quality in the final scene. Cynthia pardons Endimion's presumption in loving her and gives him her favor:

> *Endimion*, this honorable respect of thine, shalbe chris-
> tned loue in thee, & my reward for it fauor. Perseuer
> *Endimion* in louing me, & I account more strength in
> a true hart, then in a walled Cittie. I haue laboured to
> win all, and studie to keepe such as I haue wonne.
>
> (K1ʳ; V.iii.179–183)

Clearly the speech has reference to more than one courtier's relationship to Cynthia. The generalization in the last sentence shadows divine mercy as the means by which all souls are striven for. Cynthia also shows mercy to those whose sin is far greater than Endimion's. Tellus and Dipsas, threatened with justice at the beginning of the scene, are forgiven when Endimion is shown to have

[19] Bernard F. Huppé, "Allegory of Love in Lyly's Court Comedies," *ELH*, XIV (1947), 105n.
[20] Bryant, pp. 7–8.

suffered no permanent injury from their treatment. However, the threat of justice is a dramatic actuality for a time ("As for you *Dipsas,* I will send you into the Deserte amongst wilde beastes" [I3ʳ; V.iii.66–67]), and is eventually generalized into a statement of position about the alternative to mercy:

> Those that neither my fauour can mooue to continue constant, nor my offered benefits gette to bee faithfull, the Gods shal eyther reduce to *trueth,* or reuenge their trecheries with *iustice.*
>
> (Kiʳ; V.iii.183–186. My italics.)

So Cynthia manifests three of the Four Daughters: active Mercy, contingent upon love and repentance, and potential Justice and Truth for the obdurate. Bryant does not explicitly mention Cynthia in the role of the Fourth Daughter, Peace, nor does the word "peace" occur in the scene. I do not think that it is stretching the interpretation, however, to point out that Cynthia is notably a peacemaker. Her court has been a wrangling one (more so than Lyly's other royal courts). Cynthia brings it to peace, especially by arranging, with some difficulty, a whole series of satisfactory marriages.

The union in Cynthia of the practice of Mercy, the respect for Truth and Justice, and the bringing of Peace, serves two ends for Lyly. It provides a dramatic formula for the conclusion of the play, a scheme for forgiveness. It is the same formula, secularized, that the author of *The Castle of Perseverance* had achieved by moving the allegory of the Four Daughters from its original location after the Fall and its location in the Coventry mystery before the Annunciation to the time of judgment on the human soul. By this move, the author of *The Castle* had transformed the allegory from an explanation of the sacrifice of Christ to an account of the means of forgiveness for individual human beings.[21] Keeping this dramatic function, Lyly transfers it from an eschatological context to a secular, courtly context. Thus he shadows the manner in which the ideal monarch should deal with erring subjects. This leads us to the second end of the allegory here: Lyly shadows the Four Daughters in the words and actions of one queen. The Four Daughters are, of course, attributes of God, as Milton saw when he put "the strife of Mercy and Justice" in the very face of the Father. To unite the Four is a property of God. To unite the Four in Cynthia is to make her the ideal monarch in spirit as well as in practice. Lyly's figure of Cynthia suggests that the ideal kingdom will mirror God's kingdom when the monarch mirrors God in quality as well as in function, a mirroring possible only because Lyly has been continually attributing to Cynthia an indefinable semi-divinity.

All this is prepared for by Endimion's dream. Without the physical appearance of the three ladies debating over Endimion in the dumbshow, refreshed in our minds by Endimion's elaborate description of the dream, we would not have the context to perceive the allegory working out at the end of the play. As Bryant points out, the "function of these ladies is *unmistakably* that of the Four Daughters, and their presence here . . . leads one to anticipate precisely the solution that follows." [22] Both by visual and verbal means a context is established for our understanding. It is a superb example of thoroughly theatrical preparation for allegory.

[21] I take the point from Robert Grams Hunter, *Shakespeare and the Comedy of Forgiveness* (New York and London, 1965), pp. 17–19.

[22] Bryant, pp. 7–8. We are also led to anticipate the values of major importance in the final scene by a line in the conversation that opens it: Zontes tells his fellow philosopher Panelion that he expects Cynthia to "heare of [the case of Tellus] in iustice, and then iudge of it in mercy" (I2ʳ; V.iii.10–11).

This, then, is one way in which the allegory of the Four Daughters operates in *Endimion*. One could leave the matter here. But such is the self-mirroring quality of the play, with hints picking up and reflecting across scenes, that one can perceive at least two other ways in which the allegory works.

First, the three dream-ladies do not resemble the Four Daughters in function alone. Each of the ladies is identifiable with a particular Daughter. Bryant attempts no such identification; Huppé labels them as True Love, Justice, and Mercy.[23] Huppé is certainly right about the latter two. The second lady has "a sterne countenance" (H2ᵛ; V.i.86) and urges the first on, and the third, "with visage sad and constant onelie in sorrow" (H2ᵛ; V.i.88) laments the proposed violence. But Huppé's identification of the first lady as True Love depends on the assumption that Endimion has somehow lapsed from love, that True Love has some reason to threaten him. This assumption is connected to Huppé's interpretation of Endimion's sleep as a failure in love, a dissipation of the concentration of love by a turning to wordly ambition.[24] There is no warrant for either of these readings in the literal story of Endimion. His love for Cynthia has been unabated and wholehearted (until the sleep, which is hardly his fault), and Cynthia never makes any criticism of him.[25] Endimion's behavior has been questionable only at one point: his love for Cynthia replaces a love for Tellus, and he is forced into equivocation when Tellus jealously accosts him in II.i. His only moral failure is a mild violation of Truth. This fact immediately

---

[23] Huppé, p. 105.

[24] Huppé, pp. 104–105.

[25] Inconstancy to Cynthia has been the key to historical readings of the play, but any interpretation based on a lapse in Endimion's devotion contradicts the fiction. If Oxford or any such lies behind Endimion, he has been thoroughly whitewashed.

suggests the identification of the threatening but inde-
cisive first dream-lady. She is Truth, who in the allegory
of the Four Daughters is an advocate for punishment
supported by Justice and opposed by Mercy. The iconography of the dream supports the interpretation: the first
lady carries a mirror. Mirrors are fairly common properties
for medieval personifications, held variously by Pride,
Lechery, and Wisdom. Truth also carries a mirror on
occasion, because she knows herself.[26] Truth is the only
possible candidate.

But this reading of the three dream-ladies as Truth,
Justice, and Mercy is complicated by a peculiar result of
the use of the religious allegory in a secular fiction. Since
the dumbshow occurs immediately after Endimion is put
to sleep, we are tempted to see the three ladies as echoing
the characters involved in that action as well as figuring
abstractions. The first lady suggests Tellus, who both loves
and hates Endimion and does do him harm; the second
Dipsas, who helps Tellus against Endimion; the third
either Bagoa, who has just remarked that she regrets the
enforced sleep but dares not prevent it, or Floscula, who
has expressed similar feelings in I.ii.

This temptation leads to my final suggestion concerning
the use of the Four Daughters in *Endimion*. The linkage
suggested by the dumbshow between the Four Daughters
and individual ladies of Cynthia's court appears to be carried out in the final scene of the play. To be specific, the
dumbshow suggests, via the second dream-lady, that Dipsas and Justice are related. In the final scene Dipsas pleads
for Justice—on herself:

[26] See, for example, Cesare Ripa, *Iconologia* (Rome, 1603), p. 501,
and the caryatid of Truth in the Chapel of Henry VII, Westminster
Abbey, photographed in *Royal Commission on Historical Monuments
(England)*. *An Inventory of the Historical Monuments in London*,
Vol. I (London, 1924), Plate 120.

Madam, thinges past may be repented, not recalled:
there is nothing so wicked that I haue not doone, nor
any thing so wished for as death. Yet among al the
things that I committed, there is nothing so much tor-
menteth my rented and ransackt thoughts, as that in the
prime of my husbands youth, I diuorced him by my
deuillish Arte, for which, if to die might be amendes, I
would not liue till to morrowe. If to liue and still be
more miserable would better content him, I would wish
of all creatures to be oldest and vgliest.

(I2ᵛ–I3ʳ; V.iii.39–47)

Dipsas offers no extenuating explanations and pleads for no
mercy. She wants pure Justice, something that will make
"amendes"—preferably death, which was Justice's remedy
for the Fall.

The dumbshow suggests, via the first dream-lady, that
Tellus and Truth are related. This connection is certainly
borne out in the last scene. Much of the scene consists of
Tellus' long confession, and repeatedly Lyly stresses the
truth of the confession:

TELLUS   Truth shall be mine answere.

CYNTHIA   *Endimion* is it true?

END.   In all things Madame. *Tellus* doth not speak false.

TELLUS   Thus Madam in all trueth, haue I vttered. . . .

CYNTHIA   Hath *Tellus* tolde troth?

END.   Madame in all things, but in that shee saide I loued
her, and swore to honour her.

(I3ʳ, I4ᵛ; V.iii.55, 134–136, 151–152, 156–158)

Tellus clearly does not figure Truth throughout the play.
She is a vengeful and mischievous woman. Yet Truth is
connected with her position. Endimion has equivocated
with her, and she is partially justified in her attitude to

him. He has offended against Truth to her: hence the connection between Tellus and Truth in the first dream-lady of the dumbshow. But in the dumbshow the first dream-lady had eventually forborne from harming Endimion, as Tellus should have forborne. In the final scene she tells truth and in so doing comes to understand and accept Endimion's change of loves. Then the ringing echoes of the word "truth" fitly surround her, and she has become the ornament that she should be in Cynthia's court.[27]

The roles of Dipsas and Tellus in connection with Justice and Truth are apparent in the language of the final scene. Neither Floscula nor Bagoa, whom I have tentatively linked with the Mercy figure in the dream, has a sufficiently important role in the final scene to carry such a value there. Rather the value of Mercy is borne entirely by Cynthia. Cynthia figures, I have suggested, all Four Daughters, but Mercy is the most prominent of them in her actions. Everything she does is merciful, and it would be impossible for Lyly to set up another Mercy figure next to her. The assignment of this value to the dominant figure is decorous: in the allegory of the Four Daughters, the Virtues are reconciled, but Mercy is triumphant.

The pattern thus created leaves the role of Peace still to be filled. I think that careful examination of one puzzling character in *Endimion* reveals completion of the pattern. Semele is a prominent character in the play by virtue of

[27] There may be a connection between Tellus as Truth and Tellus in the physical allegory as Earth. Psalm 85, in the verse after the description of the meeting of the Four Daughters, goes on to say, "Truth shall spring out of the earth." This verse may also explain Truth's costume of "sad green" in *The Castle of Perseverence*, a costume that has puzzled Chew (p. 45) and for which Richard Southern gives no explanation in his brilliant reconstruction of the staging of *The Castle* in *The Medieval Theatre in the Round* (London, 1957).

Eumenides' devotion to her. Actually, hers is a very small role, but it is heavily marked by one quality: acidity of tongue. Appearing first in III.i, she makes a single rude remark, which instantly gains Cynthia's rebuke. Reappearing in IV.iii, she is sentenced to a year's silence for contemptuous speech (although she has spoken only one more line), and she is later said to laugh spitefully. She maintains silence through V.i and V.iii until Cynthia gives her to Eumenides. Then she protests, and is won over by the persuasion of Cynthia and the promises of Eumenides: "I am content your Highnesse shall command, for now only do I thinke *Eumenides* faithfull" (K2ʳ; V.iii.233–234). For so small a role to be so firmly distinguished by one characteristic, and that an unpleasant one at odds with Eumenides' devotion and provoking very peremptory behavior from Cynthia, is peculiar. There would seem to be a point in this procedure. I suggest that we see in Semele wrangling first ordered into peace (necessarily a false peace) and then cheerfully embracing Peace. The progression of Semele's relationship to Peace resembles that of Tellus' relationship to Truth: first there is an identification that is tentative and heavily qualified, suggesting the gap between the person and the ideal; then, in the final scene, there is action in thorough accordance with the ideal. Semele's last line begins, "I am content. . . ." [28]

To sum up my third example of allegory in *Endimion*, then, the Four Daughters of God would seem to appear variously throughout the play. They are unmistakably and most theatrically suggested to us by the dumbshow; then one of the Four Virtues appears to be achieved by

[28] The significance of Eumenides' name is obvious ("the benevolent one, the well-wisher," possibly with an atrocious etymological pun, since he does make a wish at an enchanted well). I have been unable to discover any reason why Semele should be named after the mother of Dionysus.

each of four ladies of the court, while all Four are collectively attributed to Cynthia. The fifth act of *Endimion* thus climaxes Lyly's portrayal of royal courts. By using high Christian allegory he has suggested the divine perfections of the ideal monarch and the ideal court under her sway. I do not insist on all the details of my interpretation: I may have made mistakes or adhered too rigidly to a pattern. The central notion, that the values of Mercy, Truth, Justice, and Peace are present in an expanding structure in *Endimion* seems to me unquestionable. In the shimmering unfolding of the play, however, the critic may be tempted into over-ingenuity or into bemusement with certain details.

It is precisely the shimmering that I wish to emphasize. Cynthia as the Moon, Cynthia as the ideal queen, Cynthia as Mercy: all these figures are there, and no explicit relationship among them draws them into a structure of common meaning save the fact that a single character suggests all three overtones. *Endimion* is pre-eminently the Lylian play in which the fable, the situation, the literal sense is primary. The other plays present a clear dominance of idea: they smell a bit of the lamp or bear the impress of the geometer's rule. *Endimion* certainly *sends* one to the midnight oil, for its tantalizing suggestions of arcane areas of thought bid us gently to heed Boccaccio's advice about sitting up nights in order to understand literature; and it certainly has mathematical elaborations in its construction; but the stamp of these things is not the clear signpost of an idea dominating the play. All of Lyly's plays require complete respect for the literal sense. This one promises more depths beyond that sense than any other, and gives the least firm roads for travelling there.

G. K. Hunter concludes his section on *Endimion* by remarking that "the mind of the sovereign has retreated to an altitude out of descriptive range," to "a state of aloofness where she ceases to have much effect on the conduct of the play." [29] It is a shrewd observation. No longer does the sovereign suffer and love before us as Sapho and Alexander do. But the fact that Cynthia does not greatly affect the conduct of the play should not obscure the fact that she greatly affects the impression that the play makes on us. Aloof as she is, she is its center. Ultimately the mystery of the play is appropriately the mystery of the queen. She is a figure ordinary mortals *cannot* comprehend. Endimion himself sets the keynote, and we follow him, since his long soliloquies in Acts I and II and his onstage sleeping body in Acts III and IV make him our point of view. Cynthia is not to be understood, but to be wondered at and contemplated. One might call the play, with its radiating central image, its mathematical elaboration, its receding depths, its near motionlessness and queer timelessness, more a contemplation than a comedy.

[29] Hunter, p. 193.

V. TRANSITION TO NARRATIVE

A. ALLEGORY AND THE ANAGOGIC DENOUEMENT

SITUATIONAL drama was a short-lived phenomenon. It held the Court stage, and only the Court stage, for less than a decade. Even in that short period, not all of the extant mythological Court plays are wholly situational in form. The anonymous *Rare Triumphs of Love and Fortune* and Peele's *Arraignment of Paris*, both dating probably within a year of Lyly's *Campaspe*, exhibit individual blends of situationalism and narrative. In the mythological Court plays of the 1590's the movement toward narrative is intensified. *Midas* and *The Woman in the Moon*, probably Lyly's last two Court plays, display shreds of situational technique, but are essentially narrative plays; the movement is climaxed by the anonymous *Maid's Metamorphosis*, which puts its gods into a full-blown romantic plot. It is the task of this chapter to trace what happens to allegorical dramaturgy in this transition from situational to narrative plays.

Before we can deal with these plays, however, it is necessary to establish just what is lost when the situationalism of the 1580's is discarded for developed plots. The nature of this loss is apparent, I think, when we consider the inherent problems of presenting allegory on a stage.

Performed drama has an enormous advantage over all other forms of literature because it has at its disposal a greater variety of materials with which to create artistic effects. The poet, the novelist, and the essayist normally have only two tools: words and the possibilities of different arrangements of words on the page (paragraphs, meters, stanzas). The playwright, besides having dialogue and pauses, has other resources: actors, physical properties, blocking, music, and lights. With these resources the playwright can finely shape the audience's experience. The actor who helps a scene even when he has no lines, the music that reinforces an action or sustains an emotion, the lighting or stage arrangement that focusses upon an object pregnant with symbolism, greatly aid the playwright in making his points. Unfortunately, the actors, music, and lighting of the Court plays are irrecoverable; I have tried to make use of the information we have concerning their physical setting and properties. The playwright, however, has a major disadvantage that does not beset the poet. He has little time. He can easily make a great immediate impact, but he will have difficulty when he wants to make an audience think, to observe deeper patterns and perceive complicated developments. A reader may experience a poem with his own time, his own intermissions, his own re-readings of parts of the text. An allegorical poet may thus be as lengthy and as difficult as he pleases. He knows that the allegorical reader has the leisure to ponder over a thicket of iconography or to look back to the previous appearance of a character. But a theater audience cannot pause and will not sit long: a produced play is an experience rigidly controlled in both pace and length. Hence it has been frequently said that allegory is suited to the study and very ill-suited to the stage.

Various factors may mitigate the difficulties for the allegorical playwright. A literate, intellectual, coterie audience, familiar with certain traditions, will respond to the implications of allegorical drama more quickly and be able to follow more attentively than a general audience. The Court audience, knowing Sidney, Castiglione, and

Euphues, allowed Lyly to do things he could not have done at Newington Butts. A familiarity with other courtly works, and with the symbolism of the frequent shows at Court, readied the audience for Lyly.[1]

The problem of audience preparedness, however, is external. The difficulty of time, of being sure that your audience understands you before you go on to the next event, is inherent in allegorical drama. The problem is solved in the medieval drama by straightforwardness. Vices and Virtues are clearly labelled and their actions are in a general way predictable. The work is radically allegorical and known to be so. The action may proceed its lively way and no problem of "how to take this" ought to arise. With the more allusive, more "literary," allegory of Lyly, the problem of time must receive another solution. That solution is the static quality of the plays.

The situationalism of Lyly's comedies frees the audience for allegorical perception because of the peculiar kind of absorption it invites. The problem of time is really a problem of absorption. An unfolding narrative plot tends to engross the spectator. Suspense has always been the most successful device for entertaining hundreds or thousands of disparate persons who have been, at their own cost, packed into a place where they have less comfort and liberty than they like. It is, I think, the absorbing power of a story acted

---

[1] Ben Jonson, in the preface to his *Masque of Queenes,* explains how he counts on the quickness of his audience: "A *Writer* should alwayes trust somewhat to the capacity of the *Spectator,* especially at these *Spectacles;* Where Men, beside inquiring eyes, are vnderstood to bring quick eares, and not those sluggish ones of Porters, and Mechanicks, that must be bor'd through, at euery act, wth Narrations" (*Complete Works,* ed. C. H. Herford, Percy and Evelyn Simpson [Oxford, 1925–1952], VII.287). It is not even necessary to sneer, as Jonson does, at the understanding of the lower classes to maintain this argument. The real issue is not quickness of intelligence (however that may be socially distributed) but literary preparedness.

out by real people that scholars worry about when they speak of the unsuitedness of allegory to the stage. If the playwright can substitute an interest in the implications of the present situation for an interest in what is going to happen next, he may slow down his story and abolish plot altogether.[2] A Lyly audience is not caught up in the consecutive links of a linear plot; it can therefore attend to the gradual expansion of the central images of *Gallathea* or the elaborate pattern built up by the anecdotes of *Campaspe*. On a stage ever the same because of the fixed houses, the seen actors and properties move back and forth creating an unseen reality.

When the drama goes narrative, it loses the "breathing space" for allegory provided by the situational form. No longer do we have a central reality slowly turning like a prism for us to inspect its various facets. Instead, we are urged to advance along a line of related experiences, and infused with an emotional excitement contingent upon following that line. Different methods must thus be adopted for the projection of allegorical implications. In the surviving Court plays, one of two choices is made. Either some very firm, obvious, and explicit definitions are adopted at the beginning of the play, or allegorical meaning becomes intermittent, concentrated in one or two intensely significant moments usually occurring in the final scenes.

The Rare Triumphs of Love and Fortune illustrates the first procedure.[3] In this play, a prince objects to his sister's love for an apparent commoner, and the quarrel leads to a duel resulting in the commoner's exile. In the desert the commoner meets an old hermit-magician who turns out to

---

[2] This is what Antonioni and Fellini have done in films, although they usually stress psychology and mood rather than symbolism.

[3] *The Rare Triumphs of Love and Fortune*, ed. W. W. Greg, Malone Society Reprints (Oxford, 1931).

be his father, a nobleman unjustly deprived of his estates by the previous king. An eventful plot involving intrigues, magic, disguises, madness, mutilation, and repentance leads to the happy ending. This romantic story, however, has a frame occupying all of the first act and half of the last: a contention among the gods as to whether Venus or Fortune is the greater power. The human story is a test to determine divine pre-eminence, and at the end of each act there is a "triumph" of the goddess who has temporary control over events. Jupiter eventually decrees a compromise: the lovers are both united and fortunate at the close. The play is certainly allegorical: the pattern of earthly events shadows the heavenly pattern of disputatious gods. The gods' powers, moreover, are not only exemplified in the human story, but debated, displayed in heavenly shows, and reflected in decorous devices such as Jupiter's use of rime royal. The play, however, is not very profoundly allegorical. The relation between heaven and earth is a matter of simple equations swiftly made at the beginning of the play and strictly maintained through the action without any deepening of implication. The gods are nearer to flat abstractions than to the expanding metaphors of Lyly's comedies. The same simplicity is observable in Robert Wilson's *The Cobbler's Prophecy*.[4] This play is a semi-morality of rather confused action centering upon a Vice called Contempt. It abounds in social satire and possibly specific political allegory; the text has been tampered with and at times is rather difficult to follow.[5] As in *The Rare Triumphs of Love and Fortune*, the action is introduced by the gods: Wilson feels it necessary to explain who the gods are, and

[4] A. C. Wood, ed., *The Cobler's Prophecy*, Malone Society Reprints (Oxford, 1914).

[5] See Irene Mann, "A Political Cancel in *The Coblers Prophesie*," *The Library*, fourth series, XXIII (1942), 94–100.

the explanations are of the equational type, Venus is "lust." [6]

Neither *Love and Fortune* nor *The Cobbler's Prophecy* is a particularly good or a particularly interesting play. Except for the possible relationship between *Love and Fortune* and Shakespeare's *Cymbeline*, neither is an important play in the history of Elizabethan drama.[7] The method of deriving allegorical implications by imposition of a frame on a narrative does not lead, in these two cases at least, to richness of meaning. The case is otherwise with the second means of projecting allegorical meaning in a narrative drama, the technique of intermittent allegory that concentrates particularly in the final scenes. This means is employed in *Midas, The Woman in the Moon, The Arraignment of Paris,* and *The Maid's Metamorphosis.* Each of these plays ends with what might be called an anagogic denouement. We follow a narrative until we experience a moment of vision, of direct sight into the heart of the universe. In these moments of vision, three things happen. First, there is usually a change of place into some more potent environment. Second, language heightens poetically and the action becomes formal ritual. Third, and most important, there is either a direct intervention of the divine or a radically altered relationship between divine and human levels. A theophany occurs, and the ruling forces of the universe are presented to us, somewhat in the manner of the core cantos of Spenser's books. It must be emphasized that we are *led* to this final vision: the events of the narrative produce it, and in one case create it wholly. The moment of vision, the theophany, crowns the

[6] sig. A3^{v}.

[7] J. M. Nosworthy, in the Introduction to the New Arden edition of *Cymbeline* (London, 1955), argues for the influence of *Love and Fortune* upon Shakespeare's play. He is right about the influence on plot, but I think that Shakespeare's handling of significance in *Cymbeline* is more strongly influenced by the plays I am about to discuss.

end. It may be present *potentially* at earlier moments of the play, but the characters, and therefore the audience, are not ready for it until the end. It does not exfoliate throughout the play, a fact that sufficiently distinguishes the allegorical operation of these plays from that of the situational plays. Neither is it imposed *ex definitione* upon the narrative, a fact that sufficiently distinguishes these plays from *The Rare Triumphs of Love and Fortune*.[8]

These statements will be supported by brief analysis of the four plays mentioned. I shall make some general remarks on the dramaturgy and structure of the plays, but shall concentrate primarily on the moments of final vision.

Of all Lyly's plays, *Midas* adheres most closely to its mythological sources.[9] The stories of the golden touch and

[8] I am aware of the fact that I am stretching the meaning of the word "anagogic" here. Strictly speaking, anagogy is that kind of allegory which yields ideas of the "last things," of apocalypse and the kingdoms of heaven and hell; it teaches *quo tendas*, as the medieval mnemonic has it. The gods shown forth at the ends of these plays figure vital forces that underlie the world, but we will not join them permanently in a new kingdom as Christians will join the heavenly kingdom in triumph over death. Likewise, the divine interventions in these comedies are minor events in comparison with the end of the world (as any other event would be). I need a word, however, to distinguish these theophanies, which suddenly reveal to us ultimate orders and energies, from the allegorical operation of the gods in Lyly's middle plays. In the discussion of allegory, a certain flexibility is necessary in the use of terms, as the medievals well knew.

[9] Quotations are drawn from the only quarto [John Lyly], *Midas* (London, 1592). They are acknowledged in the text with the signature numbers of this quarto and the act, scene, and line numbers of R. Warwick Bond, ed., *The Complete Works of John Lyly* (Oxford, 1902), vol. III. The best discussion known to me of the whole of *Midas* occurs in Stephen S. Hilliard's unpublished doctoral dissertation, "Dramatic Allegory in the Mythological Plays of John Lyly and his Contemporaries" (Princeton University, 1967). Hilliard's convincing interpretation of the play as "a comic anatomy of tyranny," with ample support from the mythographers and from sixteenth-century discussions of kingship, is presently being prepared for publication.

the ass's ears are dramatized with few changes from Ovid's *Metamorphoses*, XI.85–193. There is a narrower range of characters than is Lyly's custom, fewer swirls of subordinate activity, and no developed love interest. A subplot concerns the conflict between pageboys and Midas' barber, but otherwise the play concentrates on the two main stories. Interest in the supporting characters arises almost entirely from their direct comments on Midas. Lyly's decision to dramatize both Midas stories committed him, of course, to serial treatment in place of his usual structure of simultaneity and juxtaposition. *Midas* is therefore a narrative play concentrating on the title character with a constancy displayed by no previous Lylian comedy.

It is not, however, a very good narrative play. Lyly can arrange no genuine plot-link between the two main stories: there is a lull of interest between Midas' trip to the Pactolus, which washes off the golden touch, and his happenstance encounter with the music contest between Apollo and Pan. Consequently, the plot appears broken-backed. Moreover, the concentration on the title character, wrought by the omission of subsituations, is not justified by any developed interest in characterizing Midas. Indeed, the king is rather tiresome as he repents the golden touch at enormous length, and then goes on, with a "head more fat than wyse," [10] to make another disastrous choice. I find *Midas* Lyly's only dull play.[11]

[10] Arthur Golding, *The XV Bookes of P. Ouidius Naso, entytuled Metamorphosis*, as rep. by W. H. D. Rouse, ed., *Shakespeare's Ovid* (Carbondale, 1961), XI.166.

[11] In a recent article, "A Theory of the Literary Genesis of Lyly's *Midas*," *RES*, n.s. XVII (1966), 133–140, Michael R. Best concurs with my low view of the technical facility of *Midas*. By close examination of the prologue and of inconsistencies in the narrative, Best arrives at an interesting theory of revision in the play. Lyly, he suggests, originally wrote two plays on Midas, one on each of the two Midas stories. At least the second of the two contained scenes commenting on

Unsatisfactory as the dramatic structure of the play may be, however, *Midas* has sound intellectual unity. The king lacks knowledge of the good, and both of his mistakes are poor choices of divinely offered goods.

First Bacchus offers Midas whatever he wants. Midas' ministers suggest three possibilities: empire (to be obtained by war against neighboring kingdoms), love, and gold. Midas chooses gold since, as he argues, it will also give him success in love and war. None of the three possibilities is virtuous, at least as Midas and his ministers think of them. The princess Sophronia, whose name indicates her status as a spokeswoman for wisdom, explicitly condemns all three: "Let Phrygia be an example of chastitie, not luste; liberalitie, not couetousnes; valor, not tyrannie" (B3^v; II.i.104–105). All three entail sinful disruption. Midas' wars are "vnlawfull" and his loves "vnnaturall" (B3^r; II.i.88–90); [12] his desire for gold is, of course, starving him. Midas endorses his daughter's criticism when he repents of the golden touch, saying that gold and war have ruined him, Phrygia, and other nations. In his second repentance at the end of the play, he echoes Sophronia's criticism of his loves.

---

the Marprelate controversy. In response to the Privy Council's attempt to stamp out the controversy, Lyly suppressed his anti-Martin scenes and, in order to make a comedy of proper length, hastily joined the remains of his two plays together. I find it somewhat difficult to follow Best in the initial assumption of Lyly's writing two plays on the same character: it seems a risky procedure if one is trying to impress the Queen with an ability to entertain variously, and two-part Elizabethan dramas otherwise occur only in history plays, special circumstances of popularity such as *Tamburlaine*, and the anomalous *Promos and Cassandra* (which was apparently never acted). In any case, the genesis of the play does not affect my criticism. However Lyly arrived at the text we have now, he evidently thought it a produceable and publishable work.

[12] The respect in which Midas' loves are unnatural is never made clear.

Midas' mistake in the music contest may look uncon-
nected with his choice of the golden touch. It seems merely
an aesthetic error. One wonders, moreover, since the choice
is between two gods, what Pan would have done to Midas
had Midas preferred Apollo's music. But the language in
which Lyly presents the music contest pulls it into close
intellectual relation with the golden touch and reveals that
Midas has a more serious flaw than poor artistic judgment.

Lyly begins the music-contest scene with the two gods
in debate. Pan claims equality with Apollo since both are
deities. Usual Ovidian commentary makes this a false claim:
"Pan *presents illiterate rusticity*; Apollo *a mind imbued
with the divine endowments of art and nature.*" [13] Actually,
Ovidian commentary need not be resorted to; Lyly makes
the point abundantly clear. Apollo retorts to Pan's claim
of equality by saying that his opponent is "excluded from
heauen" (D4ʳ; IV.i.24). Pan is only an earthly god, not a
celestial one. Apollo, moreover, is the pre-eminent celestial
deity, and his music, the talent about to be judged, is the
instrument of that pre-eminence. He introduces himself as
the god responsible for celestial harmony: "*Pan* wilt thou
contend with *Apollo*, who tunes the heauens, and makes
them all hang by harmony?" (D3ᵛ; IV.i.1-2). Supporting
Apollo's claim is the nymphs' judgment in favor of his
music, and the fact that he (having a harp) can play and
sing simultaneously whereas Pan (with his pipes) must
apologize for performing serially. Since these values are
attached to Apollo, Midas' mistake in judging the contest
is not merely an aesthetic error. He does not recognize
Apollo's position as creator and sustainer of the universal
order. His misjudgment is thus a generalized version of
his previous, more particular desires, all of which involved
significant disruptions of natural order. As Midas pursued

[13] George Sandys, *Ovid's Metamorphosis Englished, Mythologiz'd,
and Represented in Figures* (London, 1632), p. 390.

destructive war, unnatural love, and transforming gold, so
he insults and rejects the founder of universal harmony.
The two Midas stories are thus intellectually bound together.

The full revelation of the significance of Midas' second
misjudgment is reserved until the final scene. This scene is
an anagogic vision. Ovid's version of the story ends with
Midas still possessed of the ass's ears and the traitorous
reeds telling all. Lyly adds a new episode: Midas goes to
Delphi, repents, and is released by the god. The scene at
Delphi receives great emphasis, not only because of its
climactic position, but also because the earlier repentance
(for the golden touch) has been down-played: true, Midas
expressed his sorrow then at length, but Bacchus merely
sent a message instead of appearing himself. Here we have
a theophany of Apollo. There is a scene change to the more
potent environment of Delphi, the geographical heart of
Apollo's power.[14] Action becomes ritualized as Midas goes
through a formal repentance. Language heightens as first
the oracle and then the god himself respond to Midas in
verse. Above all, the power of the god is shown forth. One
by one we are reminded of his aspects by the terms in
which he is invoked. He is the slayer of Python,[15] he is

[14] In view of the lasting tradition that Delphi is the navel of the
earth, it is a perfect example of what Mircea Eliade has called a
"symbol of the center," a place in which a universal power originates
and to which a hero is drawn to receive a vision of his destiny. See
Eliade, *Cosmos and History: The Myth of the Eternal Return*, tr.
Willard R. Trask (New York, 1959), pp. 12–17, and *The Sacred
and the Profane*, tr. Willard R. Trask (New York, 1959), pp. 73–76.
See also Angus Fletcher, *Allegory: The Theory of a Symbolic Mode*
(Ithaca, 1964), pp. 210–219, 348–352, for discussion of "symbols of
the center," especially Spenser's houses, as they fit into the structure
of non-dramatic allegorical narrative.

[15] One of Midas' scornful ministers suggests that Apollo is not at
home, that he is away "taking measure of a serpents skinne" (G2^v;

the god of medicine and music,[16] he is through his oracle the source of wisdom,[17] he is the god of the sun.[18] His mercy is shown in his forgiveness of Midas. The presentation of his power is climaxed by the song that ends the play:

> *Sing to* Apollo, *God of Day,*
> *Whose golden beames with morning play,*
> *And make her eyes so brightly shine,*
> *Aurora's face is call'd Diuine.*
> *Sing to* Phoebus *and that Throne*
> *Of Diamonds which he sits vpon;*
> Io *Paeans let vs sing,*
> *To Physickes, and to Poesies King.*
> *Crowne all his Altars with bright fire,*
> *Laurels bind about his Lire,*
> *A* Daphnean *Coronet for his Head,*
> *The Muses dance about his Bed,*
> *When on his rauishing Lute he playes,*
> *Strew his temple round with Bayes,*
> Io *Paeans let vs sing,*
> *To the glittering* Delian King.[19]

V.iii.13–14). The line alludes to Apollo's slaying of Python, which was allegorized, as far back as Fulgentius and straight through the Middle Ages, as the triumph of truth over the falsehood of the world, or wisdom over false belief. See Fabius Fulgentius, "Mitologiarum," in *Opera,* ed. Rudolph Helm (Lipsiae, 1898), p. 28; Fausto Ghisalberti, "Arnolfo d'Orleans un cultore di Ovidio nel Secolo XII," *Memorie del R. instituto Lombardo di scienze e lettere,* XXIV (1932), 202; and Fausto Ghisalberti, "Giovanni del Virgilio espositore delle 'Metamorfosi,'" *Il Giornale Dantesco,* XXXIV (1931), 45.

[16] G3r; V.iii.23.

[17] Apollo gives Midas twelve lines of advice on ruling, G4r; V.iii.81–92.

[18] G4r; V.iii.100.

[19] Hunter's masterly review of the issues surrounding the authorship

Apollo is hailed here as patron of music, leader of the
Muses, and god of medicine: that is, he figures the order
and preservation of the universe. He is also hailed as god
of the sun, and splendidly so, with all the glittering light
imagery of the song: he figures the source of light and
life, the energy of the universe.[20] He is a figure for all

of the songs in Lyly's plays concludes that it is most likely, although
not finally provable, that the songs printed in Blount's *Sixe Court
Comedies* were the songs used in the original productions (G. K.
Hunter, *John Lyly: The Humanist as Courtier* [Cambridge, 1962],
pp. 367–372). Even with a slight doubt lingering over the authenticity
of the songs, however, one violates, I think, no canons of scholarly
caution in using this song as evidence in interpreting the play. In the
first place, the final lines of the dialogue call for a song in praise of
Apollo. In the second place, everything said about Apollo in the song
has been said somewhere in the scene that it ends. No fresh associations
are added. What the song does add is the *emphasis* on light, and the
upsurge of intensity inevitable in any song that concludes a prose
dialogue. The song is the tightest expression of the idea of Apollo
that pervades the scene. I have quoted it from Edward Blount, ed.,
Sixe Court Comedies (London, 1632), sig. Z2ᵛ–Z3ʳ. In Bond it occurs
at V.iii.129–144.

[20] Relevant to Apollo as the sun are the associations attached to
that heavenly body by Stephan Batman: "The Sunne is the fourth
[of the planets] in place, as it were a king in the middest of his
throne: for vnder him is *Luna, Mercurius* and *Venus*: and aboue him
in position & place, he hath as many, that is to wit, *Mars, Iupiter,
Saturne,* by the which placing is expressed the most mightie ordinaunce
of God, to the benefite of Nature. . . .

"By his mouing ordinate, and by his course not distourbed [the sun
is not subject to the apparent retrogressions of the other planets], he
ordayneth and disposeth, and perfecteth all thing in this world. . . .
Also *Marcianus* sayth the same in this manner: The Sunne is the
Well of inwit, and minde, and of reason: head and well of lyght,
king of kinde, inwit of the world, shiner of heauen, moderatour of
the firmament" (Stephan Batman, *Batman vppon Bartholeme, his Booke
De Proprietatibus Rerum* [London, 1582], VIII.28. The text is in
black-letter; my italics correspond to Roman type).

creative and preservative powers: he is the heart of the cosmos.[21]

Thus *Midas,* for all its dramaturgical flaws, has a clear structure and a clear mode of meaning. We follow a narrative. It has various ethical implications (the debates about love, war, and gold) and a fleeting political allusion.[22] But, absorbing these implications, we follow a literal narrative until it climaxes in a blaze of anagogy. The climax puts Midas' career into ultimate and divine perspective, and the career leads us to a vision of the ultimate and divine.

Lyly's last comedy, *The Woman in the Moon,* also concludes with an anagogic display.[23] It reaches this display, however, by a very different route, and the object revealed is not a god whose power and glory are eternal, but a woman being turned into a goddess. The object of the final

[21] Jean Seznec (*The Survival of the Pagan Gods,* tr. Barbara F. Sessions [New York, 1953], pp. 140-147) has discussed the tradition that gives Apollo this role. I should add that it is not necessarily the case, as Seznec asserts in this passage, that "every trace of Christianity has disappeared" from the cosmos of which Apollo is soul. Christianity need not be present in the vehicles of metaphors, nor need we suppose an unorthodox paganism on Lyly's part for not wrenching the myth into direct reference to Christianity. As a matter of fact, Christine de Pisan, in *Othéa,* Fable 26, had used the story of Midas' misjudgment of Apollo as an analogue to Pontius Pilate's failure to recognize Christ: the connection fails to survive in tradition, according to Rosemond Tuve, because of the stronger pull of the gold association with Midas. See Tuve, *Allegorical Imagery: Some Medieval Books and Their Posterity* (Princeton, 1964), pp. 300-301.

[22] It has long been noticed that Midas' plans to establish, by means of a fleet later destroyed, sovereignty over islands whose monarch is a wonder of the world ($C2^r$-$C2^v$; III.i.31-60), make him an analogue of Philip II.

[23] Quotations are drawn from the only quarto, Iohn Lyllie, *The Woman in the Moone* (London, 1597). They are acknowledged in the text with the signature numbers of that quarto and with the act, scene, and line numbers of Bond's *Complete Works,* Vol. III.

vision is thus created wholly by the action of the play, and the regular Olympians assume subordinate roles in the dramaturgy. Moreover, the dramaturgy itself is a peculiar combination of situationalism and narrative.

Like *Midas,* the play focusses on a single figure. Pandora, created by the goddess Nature at the request of four Utopian shepherds, is dowered with the excellencies of the various Olympians. Resenting this new paragon, the gods, in the form of the seven planetary deities, take ascendency over her from the middle of Act I to the middle of Act V. Her resulting behavior so exasperates the shepherds that they finally refuse to have anything to do with her, whereupon Nature offers her a seat with one of the gods. Pandora chooses the sphere of the moon, for "change is my felicity,/And ficklenesse *Pandoraes* proper forme" (G2^r; V.i.301–302).

Situationalism is apparent in the first half of the play. Under the influence of Saturn, Jupiter, and Mars (Lyly works downward in the Ptolemaic universe), Pandora is melancholy, imperious, and warlike in turn. The acts that Pandora performs in these moods bear only the most tenuous relation to each other. Indeed, in the Jupiter episode the play goes off on a real tangent: the shepherds are skimped and the scene consists largely of Jupiter's own courtship of Pandora, with a jealous interruption from Juno. The play thus operates like a revolving display case: see what deeds you can expect of this and that divinely inspired frame of mind. When Sol (who has here all the characteristics of Apollo) takes charge, Pandora falls in love with one of the shepherds. The episodic quality then disappears, to be replaced by causally linked action. Under the influence of Venus, Pandora converts her love for one shepherd into lust for all four. Although Mercury (causing deceit and eloquence) and Luna (also called Cynthia, causing fickleness and madness) get their innings, their influences coincide with the pyramiding of a series of farcical intrigues already well in motion. The influence of the gods is less felt than the natural progress of a comic plot. Pandora's final choice of Cynthia's sphere is the logical issue of these events. What could be a more fitting home for a woman whose character has changed so often?

Hunter has well described this process of display turning into narrative, but his remark that *The Woman in the Moon* "should be put beside *Gallathea* and *Love's Metamorphosis* in terms of construction" is misleading. Hunter supports this classification on the ground that all three plays "disperse . . . interest through a series of symmetrically arranged episodes, which show in their interrelation the different phases of the world depicted," rather than concentrating on "an intrigue round a central dilemma." [24] On the contrary, an intrigue is precisely what *The Woman in the Moon* develops. The intrigue, moreover, becomes the major source of dramatic interest. The gods begin to turn into counters. Conventional ideas on the influence of planetary deities have been somewhat stretched to provide the almost invariably malign effect of their ascendency,[25] and, as the plot gathers momentum, they are gradually reduced to mere decoration. We are absorbed in the nature and effects of this all-gifted woman, this Pandora who is herself her box.[26] The play drives toward her final transformation into the woman in the moon.

The final transformation is the moment of allegorical

[24] Hunter, p. 212.

[25] See Johnstone Parr, "Astrology Motivates a Comedy," in *Tamburlaine's Malady and Other Essays on Astrology in Elizabethan Drama* (University, Ala., 1953), pp. 38–49.

[26] Dora and Erwin Panofsky, in their elegant history of the motif, *Pandora's Box: The Changing Aspects of a Mythical Symbol* (New York, 1956, rev. ed. 1962), do not mention Lyly's version of the Pandora myth.

from what she has done in the play. Her apotheosis isolates a pattern of action. No image expands here; the shape of the narrative itself figures forth a meaning that is directly presented in the final scene.

The kind of narrative structure that Lyly develops in his last two Court comedies had been earlier adumbrated in Peele's *The Arraignment of Paris*.[30] This is unsurprising, since the climactic moment of vision forms an excellent vehicle for compliment to the Queen.

Peele's play fits into the category of "drama" in an uneasy way. As Hunter has pointed out, Lyly's great achievement in unifying his materials stands out when contrasted to contemporary Court plays, such as *The Arraignment*, which frequently break down into a series of shows.[31] Peele postpones the development of narrative until late in the play, occupying the early acts with what Hunter has well called "scenes from the Classical idylls." [32] The primary organization of *The Arraignment* is purely formal. Act III presents two pastoral love-affairs that are inversions of each other: Oenone lamenting the desertion of Paris and Colin Clout dying because of Thestylis' rejection. Acts II and IV present the contention of Juno, Pallas, and Venus, climaxing respectively in Paris' judgment upon the goddesses and the gods' judgment upon Paris. Act V presents the final award of the apple and the homage of the goddesses and the Fates to Elizabeth; it mirrors Act I, in which woodland deities present gifts and homage to Juno, Pallas, and Venus. The construction is perfectly symmetrical.

Given the symmetry, one might look for Lylian situa-

[30] Quotations are taken from the first and only quarto (1584) as reprinted by Harold H. Child and W. W. Greg, eds., *The Arraignment of Paris*, Malone Society Reprints (Oxford, 1910).

[31] Hunter, p. 154.

[32] Hunter, p. 155.

vision. There is in this case no change of place, although one is spoken of in the translation-to-come of Pandora to the lunar sphere. An element of formal ritual enters as each of the seven gods begs Pandora to choose his or her sphere, and as Pandora methodically rejects all but Cynthia. And there is a new relation between divine and human levels. The transformation of Pandora is more than an Ovidian metamorphosis convenient for ending the play. Pandora becomes a goddess. Since her future influence on all other women is declared to be the cause of feminine instability and newfangledness, the whole comedy turns retrospectively into an etiological fable.

This climactic transformation closely resembles a passage of superb effect in *The Faerie Queene*: the transformation of Malbecco into Gealousie.[27] Malbecco is so consumed with possessiveness, both of his gold and his wife, that, losing both and unable to relieve his feelings because of his fear of Paridell and Braggadocchio, he turns himself before our eyes into an abstraction. This transformation is not moral allegory—although it contains a moral implication frightening enough—but direct presentation of an essence. As Rosemond Tuve has said, "From being a human so filled with the humor of jealousy that he represents it, like the persons of *Every Man In His Humour*, he becomes . . . the very quality itself in its universal aspect." [28] Likewise Pandora, having changed continually, and having had her character in the Luna episode consist of fickleness, becomes herself the deity of change, holding sway over changeful mortals.

But Pandora's career differs from Malbecco's in an important respect. Malbecco starts as a human being, displaying jealousy as a natural reaction to Paridell's ex-

[27] Book III, Canto x, especially stanzas 56–60.

[28] *Allegorical Imagery*, p. 106.

tended visit, to the threats on his wealth, to the rape of Hellenore. The transformation itself is of course deeply mysterious, but it involves shifting the basic quality of the man's soul, the central emotion of his life, to a new level of being. The final metamorphosis of Pandora does not so isolate an emotional entity; it isolates an action, changing. A deed she has repeatedly performed, rather than an emotion that has repeatedly taken her soul, becomes an essence.

The distinction is important. In it, I think, lie the answers to two questions about the dramaturgy of *The Woman in the Moon*: why does Lyly develop a narrative plot here instead of his usual situational structure? and what difference in effect lies between the handling of Pandora in a narrative plot and the gradually expanding images of *Gallathea* and the other middle plays?

Pandora, when created, is nearly a blank. She has, of course, various physical attributes (e.g. beauty) and various mental and emotional capabilities (a mixture of the gods' attributes as bestowed upon her by Nature). But all she really *is* at the beginning is "an vnderstanding soule,/To know the difference twixt good and bad" (A3^r; I.i.89–90). That is, she possesses basic human moral capacity. But she has no personality until the planets get to work. The peculiar dramaturgy of the play, the series of displays building into narrative, is necessary for the task of taking Pandora from her initial blankness to a *justified* final character. Since that final character is based on an idiosyncratic action rather than an idiosyncratic emotion, her actions must, for justification of the final character, hang together in some pattern of natural transition or cause-effect relation. And they do. The first part of the play, the display case involving Saturn, Jupiter, and Mars, is artfully arranged so that the emotions of the display (though not the events themselves) naturally slide one into the next. Saturnian disdain leads sensibly to Jovial imperiousness and thence to Martial

pugnaciousness. A real break occurs when Sol causes [...]dora's faithful love for one of the shepherds,[29] bu[...] Venereal phase is again a matter of natural transitio[...] under Venus' influence Pandora merely expands her [...] for one shepherd into promiscuous physical desire f[...] four. Finally events burgeon into genuine cause[...] plotting: the presences of Mercury and Luna merely [...] the deceitful eloquence and fickleness that Pandora [...] cope with the difficulties she has created in her V[...] phase (making assignations with all four shepher[...] the progression from display scenes to narrative [...] change coming to be Pandora's most characteristic [...] The peculiar dramaturgy has the effect of justify[...] conclusion of the play. Apparently random actio[...] into necessary action and thus creates Pandora's ess[...]

Moreover, this process, although quite allego[...] different from the expansion of the images of the [...] the middle comedies. True, Pandora eventually [...] ruling power in the universe, and, true, she achie[...] status by means of an apotheosis like Sapho's: she [...] the goddess of the moon and Cynthia resigns that [...] as Venus is forced to resign her function at th[...] *Sapho and Phao*. But Pandora's final meaning [...] arise out of any wealth of associations and pote[...] gorical energy in the initial figure. Lyly jettison[...] the Pandora myth and creates a new significance [...] for her. The final significance of Pandora aris[...]

[29] Sol, as I have said, is identified with Apollo here, [...] briefly turns poet and prophet in this scene. That she shoul[...] may not seem the most immediately predictable result o[...] influence, but it is reasonable in connection with Apollo'[...] with order and harmony. Apollo announces that she wi[...] and kinde" (C1^v; III.i.4), and she is also, for the only tim[...] sensible and peaceful. Batman's passage on the sun, quote[...] 20, provides a useful gloss on the scene.

tionalism. And indeed, Peele presents the contention among the three goddesses as in part a debate between three ways of life: the pursuit of riches and empire (Juno), of wisdom and chivalry (Pallas), and of love (Venus).[33] A variety of points are made on the values of these ways of life, and part of Paris' oration to the gods in Act IV appeals specifically to the shepherd's perspective on such values. Peele, however, is no intellectual euphuist: he does not build an elaborate structure, scene by scene, under the aegis of these ideas. The relationship of the Oenone and Colin scenes to the rest of the play remains intellectually vague, and the appeal of many scenes lies purely in poetry and song. Moreover, a narrative pattern does slowly emerge. Juno and Pallas contest Paris' award to Venus, a trial is ordered, the gods assemble, Paris is indicted for favoritism, defends himself and is acquitted, and the gods, after fruitless debate, turn over to Diana the problem of bestowing the apple upon the fairest. This narrative leads to the anagogic moment of the award to Elizabeth.

The award to Elizabeth displays the characteristics of anagogic vision that we have previously noted. It involves a change of place: the fiction of the pastoral setting is abandoned as we turn to the potent environment of Elizabeth's Court (Diana *"deliuereth the ball of golde to the Queenes owne hands"* [E4ᵛ]).[34] Action turns to formal ritual as Diana awards the apple and the three Fates "lay downe their properties at the Queenes feete" (E4ʳ). Language is heightened as Diana's formal praise of the Queen

[33] The judgment of Paris had been early moralized as a presentation of the possibilities open to men of wealth, wisdom, and love, or the active, contemplative, and voluptuous lives, or some variant thereof. These interpretations are compactly summarized by Hallet Smith, *Elizabethan Poetry* (Cambridge, Mass., 1952), pp. 4–7.

[34] To an Elizabethan, Elizabeth's Court is certainly a "symbol of the center."

is succeeded by the Fates' Latin song. Finally, a new relation between the human and the divine is made when Elizabeth is hailed as a goddess. Honor belongs to her "more then may belong,/By natures lawe to any earthly wight" (E4^r). She becomes the three Fates in one as Clotho, Lachesis, and Atropos surrender to her the distaff, spindle, and shears. She solves the problem of the judgment of Paris by embodying the well-nigh impossible union of the three goddesses (adding, for good measure, the virtue of the fourth as well):

> In state Queene *Iunos* peere, for power in armes,
> And vertues of the minde *Mineruaes* mate:
> As fayre and louely as the queene of loue:
> As chast as *Dian* in her chast desires.

$$(E3^r-E3^v)$$

The narrative has come to its climax in a vision of the goddess on earth who possesses all the values that have been active in the play.

The plays discussed so far in this chapter illustrate different degrees of narrative development. *The Arraignment of Paris* derives a narrative out of a series of shows; *The Rare Triumphs of Love and Fortune* frames its narrative with a debate; the narrative of *Midas* has a conspicuous lull in mid-play; and *The Woman in the Moon* presents a combination of situationalism and narrative highly decorous to its subject. In our last play of anagogic vision, *The Maid's Metamorphosis*, narrative has completely taken over from situationalism.[35]

---

[35] Quotations are drawn from the only quarto (1600) as reprinted by J. S. Farmer, *The Maydes Metamorphosis*, Tudor Facsimile Series (London, 1912). Bond does not regard the play as Lyly's, but reprints the text in volume III of *The Complete Works*; I include his act, scene, and line numbers in my references.

Transition to Narrative

The maid of the title is Eurymine, a girl of obscure birth beloved by Prince Ascanio. Ascanio's father, the Duke, disliking the misalliance, has Eurymine taken out by two courtiers to be murdered. The courtiers pity her, however, and deceive the Duke with the heart of a beast, while Eurymine establishes herself in pastoral comfort with shepherds and foresters. Apollo, struck with desire for her, descends to woo her. Anxious to preserve her virginity, Eurymine tricks Apollo into changing her sex, thus effectively terminating Apollo's suit. Meanwhile, Ascanio seeks his beloved, aided by a dream sent through the kindness of Juno and by the cryptic prophecies of an old hermit, Aramanthus. The joy of the lovers' eventual meeting is marred by Eurymine's continued masculinity. Finally both the Duke and Apollo relent. Eurymine is re-metamorphosed and the lovers are married in a garden sacred to Apollo and the Muses. Aramanthus is discovered to be a deposed prince and Eurymine his daughter Atlanta.

All this is straightforward romantic plotting. Many scenes, notably those in which Eurymine is saved from murder and in which she is wooed by Apollo, have a vigorous dramatic impact quite foreign to situational drama. The pastoral atmosphere is heavily influenced by Ovidian tradition: Apollo's description of the death of Hyacinth and the scene of Ascanio's dream (Juno, via Iris, orders the dream from Morpheus) borrow material straight from Golding's translation of the *Metamorphoses*.[36] Although

[36] Juno describes the Cave of Morpheus thus:

> Where fennish fogges, and vapours do abound:
> There *Morpheus* doth dwell within the ground,
> No crowing Cocke, nor waking bell doth call,
> Nor watchfull dogge disturbeth sleepe at all.
> No sound is heard in compasse of the hill,
> But euery thing is quiet, whisht, and still.

no direct borrowings from *The Faerie Queene* can be demonstrated, the story and occasionally the verse have a distinct ring of Spenser.[37]

The Maid's Metamorphosis is perfectly satisfying—and utterly charming—as a romantic comedy. Allegorical implications are not vital to our enjoyment of the play. But they do greatly enrich that enjoyment. These allegorical implications are clustered around the figure of Apollo. As in *Midas*, the god appears twice, once when his significance is suggested and again, climactically, when it blazes forth to end the play.

> Amid this Caue, vpon the ground doth lie,
> A hollow plancher, all of Ebonie
> Couer'd with blacke, whereon the drowsie God,
> Drowned in sleepe, continually doth nod.
>
> (C1ᵛ; II.i.118–127)

Golding's translation runs thus:

> A foggye mist with dimnesse mixt streames vpwarde from the ground,
> And glimmering twylyght evermore within the same is found.
> No watchfull bird with barbed bill and combed crowne dooth call
> The morning foorth with crowing out. There is no noyse at all
> Of waking dogge, nor gagling goose more waker than the hound,
> Too hinder sleepe.
>   . . .
> Amid the Cave, of *Ebonye* a bedsted standeth hye,
> And on the same a bed of downe with keeverings blacke dooth lye:
> In which the drowzye God of sleepe his lither limbes dooth rest.
>
> (Golding, XI.691–696, 709–711)

The retelling of the Hyacinth story exhibits similar verbal resemblances, notably the fact that Golding's alteration of Apollo's discus to a "sledge" (X.186) is repeated in *The Maid's Metamorphosis* (D2ʳ; III.i.62).

[37] Two attempts have been made, with less than full success, to demonstrate direct imitation of passages in *The Faerie Queene*: W. W. Greg, *Pastoral Poetry and Pastoral Drama* (London, 1906), p. 341n., and S. R. Golding, "The Authorship of *The Maid's Metamorphosis*," *RES*, II (1926), 270–279.

Apollo first enters with three Muses or Graces.[38] These Muses explicitly supply us with all the proper associations for the god: they speak of his music and of his slaughter of Python. But he is changed: "How differ you from that *Appollo* now" (D1^v; III.i.29). He no longer uses the lyre or the bow. He explains his melancholy as grief for Hyacinth, but, when the Muses depart, he remarks that this is a "forg'de excuse" (D2^v; III.i.88): his condition really arises from desire for Eurymine. In short, the passage with the Muses reveals that Apollo is at present none of the things he should be: he no longer partakes in divine harmony, he is no longer truth triumphing over falsehood, and he is no longer wit honorably attracted to beauty.[39] When the Muses themselves exeunt, Apollo is

[38] The anonymous author conflates these two groups of ladies. They are called Charites, the usual name for the Graces, in the stage directions of III.i. One of them, however, is addressed as "Eurania" (D2^r; III.i.75). When Aramanthus describes the sacred garden, he remarks that there "The Graces sit, listening the melodye" (G1^r; V.i.109). When we arrive there, however, we meet the stage direction, *"Enter three or foure Muses"* (G2^r; V.ii.s.d.), and the ladies are addressed as "sacred sisters of faire *Hellion*" (i.e. Helicon, G2^v; V.ii.33) and as "sacred Muses of *Pernassus* hill" (G3^r; V.ii.70). The author, who uses "Apollo" for stage directions in III.i and "Phoebus" for stage directions in V.ii, seems to regard "Graces" and "Muses" as equally interchangeable. The Muses, however, are uppermost in associations provided. In the first place, although the Graces occasionally attend Apollo in the Middle Ages and the Renaissance, the Muses are more often found in that position. In the second place, only in Aramanthus' speech are the ladies present called Graces in the dialogue as opposed to the stage directions; all other dialogue references are to Muses, and even Aramanthus' speech puts them in a musical context. The original theatrical audience would, I think, have concluded that the ladies were Muses, and so I shall call them.

[39] The cancelling of Apollo's participation in divine harmony by his abandonment of the lyre is too obvious to need comment. His abandonment of the Python-slaying bow refers to the usual allegorization of that story discussed above in fn. 15. The case of Hyacinth presents a

left a very undivine god. Thus introduced, he propositions
Eurymine, who perceives the implications of his request:
she tells him flatly, "You worke dishonour to your deitie"
(D3ᵛ; III.i.178, repeated almost verbatim at D4ʳ; III.i.-
187).

But Apollo relents, reforms, and emerges at the end of
the play as the god he should be. The final moment of
vision is carefully prepared. Aramanthus suggests, in the
finest passage of poetry in the play, that the only way to
secure Eurymine's retransformation is to request the Muses'
intercession with Apollo:

> Then in these verdant fields al richly dide,
> With natures gifts, and *Floras* painted pride:
> There is a goodly spring whose christal streames
> Beset with myrtles, keepe backe *Phoebus* beames:
> There in rich seates all wrought of Iuory,
> The Graces sit, listening the melodye:
> The warbling Birds doo from their prettie billes
> Vnite in concord, as the brooke distilles.
> Whose gentle murmure with his buzzing noates,
> Is as a base vnto their hollow throates.
> Garlands beside they weare vpon their browes,
> Made of all sorts of flowers earth allowes:

---

moral problem for the commentators: the homosexual affairs of the
Greek gods, at least considered as a group, are usually condemned as
unnatural loves (see Golding's blanket comment on Book X of the
Metamorphoses in the "Epistle to Leicester" prefixed to his translation,
ll. 213–223, and Sandys' expression of the necessity to "vindicate"
Jupiter "by the allegory" in the case of Ganymede [which appears in
Ovid just before the Hyacinth myth], p. 358). *The Maid's Metamorphosis*, however, clearly does not deal with a homosexual Apollo
(else Eurymine's sex change would present little obstacle), and the
specific interpretations of the Hyacinth story are *in bono*. See the
allegorizations collected by Sandys (p. 359), stressing Apollo as wit
and Hyacinth as the beauty of the young unfolding mind.

From whence such fragrant sweet perfumes arise,
As you would sweare that place is Paradise.
To them let vs repaire with humble hart,
And meekly shew the manner of your smart:
So gratious are they in *Apollos* eies,
As their intreatie quickly may suffice.
(G1r; V.i.104–121)

This lyrical speech, reminiscent of Spenser,[40] effects the scene change for the moment of vision. We move to the more potent environment of the Muses' garden near the palace of Apollo. Aramanthus' suggestion that the garden resembles Paradise is reinforced by a later speech: Eurymine declares that she stands amazed "as in another world of greater blis" (G4r; V.ii.129).[41] The heightening of language that is obvious in the quoted passage continues and becomes part of a formal ritual as Ascanio and the Muses beg Apollo for Eurymine's retransformation. Apollo himself is specifically exalted as the sun god:

Illustrate bewtie, Christall heauens eye,
Once more we do entreat thy clemencie:
That as thou art the power of vs all,
Thou would'st redeeme *Eurymine* from thrall.
(G2v; V.ii.25–28)

The phrase "the power of vs all" is ambiguous. Since a Muse is speaking, the "power of vs all" may be the power of music. If, however, the "vs all" refers to all assembled on stage, Muses and mortals, Apollo becomes the central

[40] See especially the description of the music in Acrasia's bower, *Faerie Queene*, II.xii.70–71.

[41] That the garden is Paradise, even if only in simile, makes it, like Delphi in *Midas* and Elizabeth's Court in *The Arraignment*, a "symbol of the center."

power of the universe. In any case, as the sun god in this speech, as the god of harmony in Aramanthus' speech, in all his aspects as stressed by various epithets throughout the final scene, he is that bright Apollo at the core of the world's ongoing that we found at the end of *Midas*. As in *Midas* also, he shows clemency. As he had not been in his earlier appearance in this play, he is the agent of truth, for he reveals Eurymine's parentage and true name. Finally, in the last spoken lines of the play, he resumes his function as maker of harmony, thereby blessing the marriage of Eurymine and Ascanio:

PHOE.   Meane space, vpon his Harpe will *Phoebus* play,
    So both of them may boast another day
    And make report, that when their wedding chaunc'te,
    Phoebus gaue musicke, and the Muses daunc'te.
                                    (G4^v; V.ii.165–168)

Shot through with the glory of Apollo, this is one of the gayest endings in Elizabethan comedy.

The narrative Court comedies end, then, with the presentation of divinity. *Midas* and *The Maid's Metamorphosis* present a known god, Apollo. *The Arraignment of Paris* and *The Woman in the Moon* deify mortal women, Elizabeth and Pandora. But the question naturally arises: in what way precisely do these final scenes end the plays? What effect do the anagogical visions have on the narratives that precede them?

There hangs over each of these denouements the suggestion of a *deus ex machina*. Apollo frees Midas and Eurymine from their afflictions; the invocation of Elizabeth solves the problem of the golden apple; the deification of Pandora concludes what could be an endless train of character changes. The gods solve the final problems of the plot, which is what *dei ex machinis* are supposed to do.

The term has disreputable associations: whether in the Greek form of a god flown in by a crane or in the modern form of the relative who unexpectedly bequeathes the hero a fortune, a *deus ex machina* suggests a fortuitous and therefore illegitimate means to cut the Gordian knot of the plot predicament. A consideration of the legitimacy of the device in these plays can, I think, lead us to a conclusion about the use of allegory in them.

It is unfortunate that the *deus ex machina* should have an odious reputation. The history of the device through Western drama should be studied. The term is persistently associated with Euripides, whose fondness for unravelling the most inextricable situations (see, notoriously, the *Orestes*) by bringing in a god is well known. The odious associations of the term, however, are unfair. William Arrowsmith has brilliantly shown how integral to the intellectual structure of his plays Euripides' gods are.[42] The criticism of fortuitous denouements directed at Euripides results from the use of a purely realistic criterion of artistic judgment. A realistic criterion is similarly unhelpful for understanding Elizabethan plays.

Even on a realistic level, however, the final appearance of the gods in our comedies is justified by preparation. Apollo's involvement in the earlier stages of the stories of Midas and Eurymine adequately prepares us for his final intervention. He has inflicted the disabilities from which they suffer, and he intervenes at the end because he is asked to, not because he opportunely lands on the roof. The final metamorphosis of Pandora is not, in Dr. Johnson's smooth criticism of Pope's Lodona, a ready and puerile expedient, but an hypostatization of what she has

[42] William Arrowsmith, "A Greek Theater of Ideas," in *Ideas in the Drama*, Selected Papers from the English Institute, ed. John Gassner (New York and London, 1964), pp. 1–41.

been throughout the play.[43] The stories of these plays continually skirt and occasionally involve divine power: it is far less of a surprise than it is even in Euripides that a god should end the play.

Dramatic preparation, however, is only one side of the issue. There are also considerations of genre. All these plays are pastoral, at least in part, and the world of pastoral has always mingled deities and mortals. The divine and the human tend to exist there with less rigid separation than elsewhere. We really experience no sense of ontological confusion, no sense of violation of the human level by intrusion of the divine. The pastoral landscape, at least in its more idyllic portrayals, is instinct with the divine in any case. The appeal of pastoral lies not only in its simplicity, but in the sense that its simplicity is closer to ultimate, non-material reality. Even after the decay of the pastoral convention in the eighteenth century, that sense of closeness to the gods lingers in nature poetry, as is obvious in Wordsworth. It is therefore significant, I think, that mythological Court drama should make its transition from the highly artificial situational plays to narrative plays of greater human impact and natural human appeal under the aegis of pastoral.

On the other hand, it cannot be denied that we are led to a new level of experience in the final scenes of these plays. Each of them insists on the divinity of the god

[43] It is less easy to argue that the entry of Elizabeth into *The Arraignment of Paris* is prepared for. Peele tries to slide her in as *"the Nymphe Eliza a figure of the Queene"* (E3^r), thus presenting her as another member of the pastoral world in which we have been for four acts. All sense, however, of Eliza being a "figure" vanishes when the actors begin to play directly to her and with her. For the rest of the audience, however, Elizabeth was probably within the ambit of the play from the beginning. They came to see her as well as the play, and the kind of compliment Peele arranges was common in Court entertainments.

shown forth. And yet the plays, by being narrative, by presenting a natural sequence of action instead of an obviously constructed series of scenes that does not pretend to imitate the careers of men, call for human interest and identification more than do the middle comedies of Lyly. The final scenes may not *violate* the framework of our expectations, but a blaze of anagogy can hardly be understood as existing *on the same level* as a narrative. There is a difference between them, a difference that necessitates the scene-changes, the ritualized action, and the heightened language that take us from narrative to final display. The divine atmosphere and its accompanying significations, which are suffused throughout the action of an early Lyly play, are here compressed into a moment of climax that contrasts with what has gone before. If we do *not* feel that we have been taken to a new level of experience, then there is no point in using the gods at all: Apollo becomes merely a convenient neighbor who happens to have more power than any one else, a *deus ex machina* of the most vulgar kind.

It is for this change in the level of experience that the playwrights devise their final scenes. Each of these scenes gives us a larger perspective on the action that has preceded it. A human narrative is fascinating in its own right, but the human mind always wants to follow its implications more deeply. A king makes two silly mistakes when offered choices, and he is consequently visited with humiliating, wholly appropriate afflictions. How does this mundane (if fantastic) story fit into the order of the universe? What has Midas really done? Is it simply a cautionary tale (hardly necessary, since we shall not encounter such choices)? The display of Apollo answers these questions. Although Midas' misjudgment looks trivial, it is a direct offence to those mysterious forces at the heart of the world's thriving. The display enlightens the human story.

Furthermore, and this is equally important, the human story leads us to the display. The trivial filaments of human life can, if followed, take us to the strong strands that bind the world together. So it is with *The Maid's Metamorphosis*: the display deepens the implications of the marriage that it graces (and the marriage at which it was possibly performed). The apotheosis of Pandora has something to say about the formation of human character. *The Arraignment of Paris* can be read with some serious concern about the nature of the true beauty that deserves the great prize.

Thus allegory is put to a new use in Court drama. We have seen in Lyly's middle comedies the slow exploration of universals working throughout a play. Great images arise, are inspected, reshaped, and reinspected as they evolve toward an integrating denouement. In the narrative Court plays allegory is differently employed. We follow a story and are concerned with its characters on the literal level. Allegorical potential is established for later use, but its thrust is reserved for the end. Then it suddenly widens the scope of the play so that we see, through the literal narrative, a new vision of the world.

B. ICASTIC ART

Recognition of John Lyly's art, as G. K. Hunter has pointed out, has been impeded by the scholarly desire to treat him as a forerunner of greater men, thus eclipsing his intrinsic qualities.[44] Such treatment is peculiarly damaging to some aspects of his art, for in at least one way he is not a forerunner at all. He is answering a plea. Sir Philip Sidney had requested, in some distress, that "the whole tract of a Comedy shoulde be full of delight." [45]

[44] Hunter, p. 1.

[45] Sir Philip Sidney, "An Apologie for Poetrie," *Elizabethan Critical Essays*, ed. G. Gregory Smith (Oxford, 1904), I.199. Subsequent quota-

It has been several times observed that Lyly's plays are the first to fulfill Sidney's request. They fulfill it perfectly, for delight is, I think, the appropriate word to describe appreciative response to Lyly. Indeed, Lyly specifically requests this reaction. Sidney had distinguished between delight (which "hath a ioy in it, either permanent or present") and laughter (which "hath onely a scornful tickling" [p. 199]). Lyly constructs precisely this distinction in the Blackfriars prologue to *Sapho and Phao*.[46]

The exigencies of exposition in this book have perhaps obscured the delightfulness of the Court comedies from time to time. My eagerness to expound the serious ideas figured in these plays has occasionally pushed into the background the prevailing comic mode. There is, of course, no real opposition between serious ideas and comic form, particularly in a didactic age—there is merely the verbal confusion forced upon us by the fact that we ask the word "serious" to do double duty as meaning both "significant" and "non-comic." There are significant ideas explored in these comic fables. The significant ideas, moreover, are intended to contribute to our pleasure. Delight is an appropriate response to allegory. In a salutary article, Judith

tions from the "Apologie" will be acknowledged in the text by Smith's page number.

[46] "Our intēt was at this time to moue inward delight, not outward lightnesse, and to breede, (if it might bee) soft smiling, not loude laughing: knowing it to the wise to be as great pleasure to heare counsell mixed with witte, as to the foolish to haue sporte mingled with rudenesse" ([John Lyly], *Sapho and Phao* [London, 1584], sig. A2^r). This connection between Lyly and Sidney has been touched on by E. C. Pettet, *Shakespeare and the Romance Tradition* (London and New York, 1949), p. 36, and by William G. McCollom, "From Dissonance to Harmony: The Evolution of Early English Comedy," *Theatre Annual*, XXI (1964), 90. I do not mean to assert that Lyly had read a manuscript of Sidney's essay. Indeed, it seems the case that he had not: see the review of Hunter's book by Jean Robertson in *SQ*, XV (Winter, 1964), 104–106.

Dundas has reminded us that, to an Elizabethan, Spenserian allegory is as much a form of wit as Donnean paradox.[47] Of course, the Elizabethan meanings of wit are various. As Dundas reviews them, wit may be the rational soul (as opposed to the sensitive and the vegetative), reason (as opposed to passion), the selector among the materials thrown up by fancy when literary invention is operating (what came to be called "judgment"), and the whole faculty of invention, both imaginative and selective. In any case, the exercise of intellectual faculties implied by all four definitions was something demanded by Elizabethan critics of literary invention. George Gascoigne lays it down that "the Inuention haue in it also *aliquid salis* . . . some depth of deuise." [48] Sidney echoes the demand: an audience should not believe a poet's tale but "vse the narration but as an imaginatiue groundplot of a profitable inuention" (p. 185). The real "skil of the Artificer standeth in that *Idea* or fore-conceite of the work" (p. 157). Sidney is very far from forgetting the primacy of the literal level in our experience of the work ("with a tale forsooth he commeth vnto you . . ."), but the finer delight of literature lies in how the invention reaches beyond the tale.

The Court playwrights, indeed, appear to offer a perfect example of allegory as wit. Operating in the form of comedy, sharper and more limited than Spenser's epic narrative, they produce swifter and more allusive, though inevitably less fully explored, allegorical implications. Entertaining with colorful show, rapidly shifting scenes, classical glamor, and the flashing dexterities of Lyly's prose, they also entertain with delicate evocations of profound ideas.

[47] Judith Dundas, "Allegory as a Form of Wit," *Studies in the Renaissance,* XI (1964), 223–233.

[48] George Gascoigne, "Certayne Notes of Instruction," in Smith, I.47–48.

Sidney's essay, moreover, offers the terms in which a description of the allegorical mode of meaning of Court comedy may be made. Lyly's art is certainly controlled by a "fore-conceite": the elaborate juxtapositions of scenes and characters in *Campaspe* and *Gallathea* can be understood only as efforts to figure forth ideas. The Court playwrights, with the very considerable help of classical mythology, are "lifted vp with the vigor of [their] owne inuention" and "growe in effect another nature, in making things either better then Nature bringeth forth, or, quite a newe, formes such as neuer were in Nature" (p. 156). If ever "golden world" were created in drama, it is in Lyly's pastorals. The ideas of the playwright are delivered "in such excellencie as hee hath imagined them. Which deliuering forth also is not wholie imaginatiue, as we are wont to say by them that build Castles in the ayre," but substantially creative, bestowing new images of reality on the world (p. 157). The theophanies of Apollo, the union of Gallathea and Phillida, Apelles' final kneeling to Alexander, yield "to the powers of the minde an image of that whereof the Philosopher bestoweth but a woordish description: which dooth neyther strike, pierce, nor possesse the sight of the soule so much as that other dooth" (p. 164). In short, the art of Lyly and his fellows is icastic, "figuring foorth good things," rather than phantastic, "which doth, contrariwise, infect the fancie with vnworthy obiects" (p. 186). Sidney introduces these useful terms casually, but the distinction between them underlies the whole argument of the "Apologie," notably the passages that I have been quoting. Sidney's defense is built on the icastic capabilities of poetry, its power to shadow universals, as opposed to phantasy, mere representation of sense experience. The Court playwrights exploit that power.

Sidney tends to think of the icastic power of poetry in a moral dimension. Concerned with moving men to virtuous action, he speaks of Xenophon's influence in making many Cyruses and of "fayning notable images of vertues, vices, or what els" (p. 160).[49] The art of the Court playwrights is of course also moral. The concern with propriety in *Campaspe* makes it a play primarily to be understood in the tropological sense, and the discussions in the later plays of chastity and love, riches and empire, friendship and constancy, naturally appeal to our moral sense. On the whole, however, morality is not stressed in the Court comedies. The golden world in which these plays take place is largely free of intense moral pressure. With the single exception of Alexander, Lyly has no heroes. He does not attempt, as Sidney does in the *Arcadia*, to turn pastoral into a vehicle for the exploration of heroic action. Even in *Campaspe*, the scene in which moral issues are most pregnantly generalized is quite open-ended: when the rationalism of Diogenes confronts the courtly accomplishments of the singing, dancing, and tumbling boys, Lyly does not urge us to choose one side or the other. The scene is a presentation of things that exist, of things between which we must choose at some point in our lives— but it is not in itself a choice or an argument leading toward one. Now the terms "icastic" and "phantastic" originally come from Plato's *Sophist*, and they are used there, not in a moral, but in an ontological dimension: the true artist figures forth the Platonic Ideas through icastic images, while the sophistic artist merely reproduces unreal

[49] This moral drive, as well as the fact that few other comedies were available to him, causes Sidney to discuss, in his most particular comments on comedy, the Roman tradition and its exploitation of domestic virtues and vices in stock characters: "We get as it were an experience, what is to be looked for of a nigardly *Demea*, of a crafty *Dauus*, of a flattering *Gnato*, of a vaine glorious *Thraso*" (p. 177).

appearances.[50] Lyly, in his own light way, is closer here
to Plato than to Sidney. The universals exhibited and
explored in his plays invite our attention to themselves
as things that simply *are* in the super-sensuous world.
The ruling forces figured by the gods may call for our
obedience, but the Court playwrights are more concerned
to make us *see* them than to make us go out and act in
accordance with them. In *Gallathea* Lyly shows us what
love and chastity *are*, and that they are ultimately one,
joined in the agreement of Venus and Diana, in the union
of Gallathea and Phillida. *Midas*, although more moral
in tone than the other late plays, ends with its final stress,
not on human action, but on divine being.

In all my emphasis upon the eternal essences figured by
this icastic art, we must not forget that, first and last, it
is drama that we are dealing with. These essences are
figured in a moving, temporal art. In the course of the
1580's and 1590's, moreover, the temporal aspects of the
Court drama are developed. The nearly motionless and
timeless situational plays give way to swiftly moving,
developed plots. In the narrative plays icastic art comes
into the realm of an art far more mimetic than that of
Lyly's early and middle plays. Although the stories are
still mythological, human life and human character come
more firmly into focus. In the later plays, the icastic
images of the gods are used for punctuation and expansion
of significance, but not for the primary dramatic substance.

I would suggest that this pattern of development is a
paradigm of the key phase in the history of Elizabethan
drama. Somehow, out of mysteries and moralities came a
drama that, although secular and superb in its exploration
of secular humanity, retained the power forcefully to
figure meanings on the universal, quasi-religious level.

[50] *Sophist*, 234–236, 265–268.

Douglas Bush has suggested that the allegorical tradition provided the Elizabethan drama with a form of dynamic unhampered by the demands of realistic verisimilitude. Far more than the rediscovery of Aristotle and his theory of ideal imitation, the centuries of allegorical drama gave the Elizabethan playwrights a mode of vision that permitted them to suggest and explore the superhuman in terms of the human.[51] The development of Elizabethan drama is so rapid and so various that it is extremely difficult to trace this gift of dynamic from the medieval allegorical tradition to the Shakespearean age, extremely difficult to watch the transition actually taking place. The very specialized phenomenon of the Court comedies, however, provides one example of this great literary process. Lyly starts, in *Campaspe*, with an exploration of moral ideas upon the groundplot of classical anecdote. Developing a more sinuous dramaturgy, he passes to a more strictly allegorical exploration of universals embodied in classical gods. He and his fellow playwrights then go on to enrich with the gods narrative plays that are rendered more naturalistically, to use the gods as dramatic images pointing toward the ultimate orders and energies of the world in which the story occurs. The popular Elizabethan drama, as I have pointed out, usually avoids the gods. Other images are used for the expansion of significance, although Shakespeare himself came to use the gods at the end of his career. But Lyly and his fellows, availing themselves of this ancient imagery, invented and developed techniques that enabled them to shadow eternal meanings in that most earth-bound of literary forms, the drama.

[51] Douglas Bush, public lecture at Princeton University, March, 1965.

APPENDIX

OR THE sake of easy reference, I have here assembled what is known or reasonably conjectured about the dates, locations, and auspices of the first productions given the Court comedies. The authorities relied upon are E. K. Chambers, *The Elizabethan Stage* (Oxford, 1923), Chapters XXIII and XIV, and H. N. Hillebrand, *The Child Actors: A Chapter in Elizabethan Stage History* (Urbana, 1926; in *University of Illinois Studies in Language and Literature*, vol. XI), pp. 132–143, 285–294. Chambers and Hillebrand agree on most points. Although subsequent investigators have raised the problems with which they deal, no new facts have come to light and none of their conclusions has been significantly questioned.

THE CENTRAL GROUP

Campaspe, by John Lyly. Performed at Court, by the combined companies of Paul's and the Chapel Royal, on 1 January 1583/4. Three quartos in 1584, one in 1591.

Sapho and Phao, by John Lyly. Performed at Court, by the combined companies of Paul's and the Chapel Royal, on 3 March 1583/4. One quarto each in 1584 and 1591.

Gallathea, by John Lyly. Performed at Court, by Paul's on New Year's Day, probably that of 1587/8, although the Stationers' Register entry is 1 April 1585. Quarto, 1592.

Endimion, by John Lyly. Performed at Court, by Paul's, on 2 February, probably that of 1587/8. Quarto, 1591.

Love's Metamorphosis, by John Lyly. Described on the title-page as "A Wittie and Courtly Pastorall." Performed by Paul's, probably in the period 1588–1590, and revived by the Chapel in 1600. Quarto, 1601.

PLAYS DISCUSSED IN THE FINAL CHAPTER

The Arraignment of Paris, by George Peele. Performed at Court, by the Chapel, in the period 1581–1584. Quarto, 1584.

The Rare Triumphs of Love and Fortune. Anonymous. Performed at Court, by the Earl of Derby's Men, on 30 December 1582. Quarto, 1589.

The Cobbler's Prophecy, by Robert Wilson. The allusion to an audience who "sit and see" and the stage direction for Ceres to *"Cast Comfets"* argue private production. Probably performed in the 1580's. Quarto, 1594.

Midas, by John Lyly. Performed at Court, by Paul's, on 6 January, almost certainly that of 1589/90. Quarto, 1592.

The Woman in the Moon, by John Lyly. Performed at Court, apparently by an adult company, in the period 1591–1595. Quarto, 1597.

The Maid's Metamorphosis. Anonymous (once attributed to Lyly, apparently through confusion of the title with *Love's Metamorphosis.* The most thorough discussion of the authorship is S. R. Golding, "The Authorship of *The Maid's Metamorphosis,*" *RES,* II [1926], 270–279). Performed by the revived Paul's company in 1600; possibly commissioned as entertainment for the marriage of Anne Russell to Lord Herbert on 16 June 1600, a wedding attended by the Queen. Quarto, 1600.

INDEX

Index

Index

Index

Index

Index

Sybilla, 18, 19, 23, 167–168
"symbol of the center," 197n, 207n, 213n

Tellus, 17n, 170, 172–174, 177, 180–184
Theocritus, 121–122
Theodontius, 113n
Tillotson, Geoffrey, 57n, 124n
Timoclea, 30, 34, 49–53, 61, 69, 94
Traver, Hope, 175n
Tuve Rosemond, 5–6, 7n, 105n, 112, 154, 158, 172, 200n, 203

Venezky, Alice, 52n
Venus, 63, 64, 109, 111, 163; in *Arraignment of Paris*, 16n, 206–208; in *Cobbler's Prophecy*, 192; in *Gallathea*, 99–106, 114, 119, 126, 129, 132–134, 136–147, 159–160, 223; in *Love and Fortune*, 191; in *Sapho and Phao*, 14, 23, 166–168, 205; in *Woman in the Moon*, 201, 205
Venus and Adonis, 107–108n
Venus and Anchises, 107–108n
Virgil, 10n, 16–17, 84, 102–104, 114, 167
Vitruvius, 17
Vulcan, 111, 119; in *Sapho and Phao*, 19, 23–24

Westminster Abbey, 181n
Whitney, Geffrey, 82n
Wilson, Robert, *see Cobbler's Prophecy*
Wordsworth, 216

vision. There is in this case no change of place, although one is spoken of in the translation-to-come of Pandora to the lunar sphere. An element of formal ritual enters as each of the seven gods begs Pandora to choose his or her sphere, and as Pandora methodically rejects all but Cynthia. And there is a new relation between divine and human levels. The transformation of Pandora is more than an Ovidian metamorphosis convenient for ending the play. Pandora becomes a goddess. Since her future influence on all other women is declared to be the cause of feminine instability and newfangledness, the whole comedy turns retrospectively into an etiological fable.

This climactic transformation closely resembles a passage of superb effect in *The Faerie Queene*: the transformation of Malbecco into Gealousie.[27] Malbecco is so consumed with possessiveness, both of his gold and his wife, that, losing both and unable to relieve his feelings because of his fear of Paridell and Braggadocchio, he turns himself before our eyes into an abstraction. This transformation is not moral allegory—although it contains a moral implication frightening enough—but direct presentation of an essence. As Rosemond Tuve has said, "From being a human so filled with the humor of jealousy that he represents it, like the persons of *Every Man In His Humour*, he becomes . . . the very quality itself in its universal aspect." [28] Likewise Pandora, having changed continually, and having had her character in the Luna episode consist of fickleness, becomes herself the deity of change, holding sway over changeful mortals.

But Pandora's career differs from Malbecco's in an important respect. Malbecco starts as a human being, displaying jealousy as a natural reaction to Paridell's ex-

[27] Book III, Canto x, especially stanzas 56–60.
[28] *Allegorical Imagery*, p. 106.

tended visit, to the threats on his wealth, to the rape of Hellenore. The transformation itself is of course deeply mysterious, but it involves shifting the basic quality of the man's soul, the central emotion of his life, to a new level of being. The final metamorphosis of Pandora does not so isolate an emotional entity; it isolates an action, changing. A deed she has repeatedly performed, rather than an emotion that has repeatedly taken her soul, becomes an essence.

The distinction is important. In it, I think, lie the answers to two questions about the dramaturgy of *The Woman in the Moon*: why does Lyly develop a narrative plot here instead of his usual situational structure? and what difference in effect lies between the handling of Pandora in a narrative plot and the gradually expanding images of *Gallathea* and the other middle plays?

Pandora, when created, is nearly a blank. She has, of course, various physical attributes (e.g. beauty) and various mental and emotional capabilities (a mixture of the gods' attributes as bestowed upon her by Nature). But all she really *is* at the beginning is "an vnderstanding soule,/To know the difference twixt good and bad" (A3^r; I.i.89–90). That is, she possesses basic human moral capacity. But she has no personality until the planets get to work. The peculiar dramaturgy of the play, the series of displays building into narrative, is necessary for the task of taking Pandora from her initial blankness to a *justified* final character. Since that final character is based on an idiosyncratic action rather than an idiosyncratic emotion, her actions must, for justification of the final character, hang together in some pattern of natural transition or cause-effect relation. And they do. The first part of the play, the display case involving Saturn, Jupiter, and Mars, is artfully arranged so that the emotions of the display (though not the events themselves) naturally slide one into the next. Saturnian disdain leads sensibly to Jovial imperiousness and thence to Martial pugnaciousness. A real break occurs when Sol causes Pandora's faithful love for one of the shepherds,[29] but the Venereal phase is again a matter of natural transition, for under Venus' influence Pandora merely expands her love for one shepherd into promiscuous physical desire for all four. Finally events burgeon into genuine cause-effect plotting: the presences of Mercury and Luna merely stress the deceitful eloquence and fickleness that Pandora uses to cope with the difficulties she has created in her Venereal phase (making assignations with all four shepherds). In the progression from display scenes to narrative we see change coming to be Pandora's most characteristic action. The peculiar dramaturgy has the effect of justifying the conclusion of the play. Apparently random action slides into necessary action and thus creates Pandora's essence.

Moreover, this process, although quite allegorical, is different from the expansion of the images of the gods in the middle comedies. True, Pandora eventually figures a ruling power in the universe, and, true, she achieves that status by means of an apotheosis like Sapho's: she becomes the goddess of the moon and Cynthia resigns that function as Venus is forced to resign her function at the end of *Sapho and Phao*. But Pandora's final meaning does not arise out of any wealth of associations and potential allegorical energy in the initial figure. Lyly jettisons most of the Pandora myth and creates a new significance altogether for her. The final significance of Pandora arises entirely

[29] Sol, as I have said, is identified with Apollo here, and **Pandora** briefly turns poet and prophet in this scene. That she should fall in love may not seem the most immediately predictable result of Apollonian influence, but it is reasonable in connection with Apollo's associations with order and harmony. Apollo announces that she will be "gentle and kinde" (C1^v; III.i.4), and she is also, for the only time in the play, sensible and peaceful. Batman's passage on the sun, quoted above at fn. 20, provides a useful gloss on the scene.

from what she has done in the play. Her apotheosis isolates a pattern of action. No image expands here; the shape of the narrative itself figures forth a meaning that is directly presented in the final scene.

The kind of narrative structure that Lyly develops in his last two Court comedies had been earlier adumbrated in Peele's *The Arraignment of Paris*.[30] This is unsurprising, since the climactic moment of vision forms an excellent vehicle for compliment to the Queen.

Peele's play fits into the category of "drama" in an uneasy way. As Hunter has pointed out, Lyly's great achievement in unifying his materials stands out when contrasted to contemporary Court plays, such as *The Arraignment*, which frequently break down into a series of shows.[31] Peele postpones the development of narrative until late in the play, occupying the early acts with what Hunter has well called "scenes from the Classical idylls." [32] The primary organization of *The Arraignment* is purely formal. Act III presents two pastoral love-affairs that are inversions of each other: Oenone lamenting the desertion of Paris and Colin Clout dying because of Thestylis' rejection. Acts II and IV present the contention of Juno, Pallas, and Venus, climaxing respectively in Paris' judgment upon the goddesses and the gods' judgment upon Paris. Act V presents the final award of the apple and the homage of the goddesses and the Fates to Elizabeth; it mirrors Act I, in which woodland deities present gifts and homage to Juno, Pallas, and Venus. The construction is perfectly symmetrical.

Given the symmetry, one might look for Lylian situa-

---

[30] Quotations are taken from the first and only quarto (1584) as reprinted by Harold H. Child and W. W. Greg, eds., *The Arraignment of Paris*, Malone Society Reprints (Oxford, 1910).

[31] Hunter, p. 154.

[32] Hunter, p. 155.